THE SILVER SPADE

THE SILVER SPADE

THE CONRAD HILTON STORY

by Whitney Bolton

WITH A FOREWORD BY CONRAD HILTON

FARRAR, STRAUS AND YOUNG · *NEW YORK*

For

FRED JOYCE
who enthused

and

NANCY COLEMAN BOLTON
who encouraged

and

my twin daughters
CHARLA and GRANIA
who kept quiet so patiently.

AUTHOR'S NOTE

THERE are living men whose lives are easily measured and almost totally predictable. This defined status in no way drains the color from or reduces the excitement of their lives. It only makes things easy for a biographer, who has no more racking task than to pick up the story of such a personality at birth and move the story methodically through to whatever current eminence has been attained in our world.

No such assembly-line documentation is possible in writing the definitive biography of Conrad Nicholson Hilton. A biographer finds himself daily becoming more convinced that there is nothing of a definitive nature to be done about this astonishing, vivid man.

Any man who in less than a quarter of a century can convert 35¢ in cash and $500,000 in debts into a corporation owning world-wide hotels with a cash value of more than $200,000,000 and a real estate and tax value of more than $300,000,000 is catnip to a biographer. By his own deeds, this kind of man becomes a creature of vast and irresistible fascination. The ever present problem with such a man is that a book about himself is but a single prism in a gigantic, restless kaleidescope.

And within a lone day after the book has been published, he may accomplish a feat which pales all of the preceeding and recorded feats.

This has happened with the Hilton who, until a few days ago, was an accomplished biographical fact. His life story was on the presses, destined to go between covers on August 28th and to reach bookstores for distribution on September 10th. The bookkeeping on his enterprises was in ruled columns. He controlled almost 20,000 sleeping rooms the world over. His hotels were added up and totaled. There was no reason why the presses shouldn't run.

Except that Hilton, once more, was making history.

On August 3, as calmly as most men buy a new necktie, Hilton announced acquisition of the entire Statler Hotel chain, consisting of eight operating hotels and two in construction. The consideration was $76,000,000. Made public at the same time, but separate from the Statler deal, was the purchase of the almost legendary Shamrock Hotel, in Houston, Texas, which involved $18,000,000 . . . $11,000,000 for the hotel and its real estate and $7,000,000 for an additional 500 acres of land.

These purchases, thrown together added 10,000 sleeping rooms to Hilton's already gigantic holdings. They also put him almost exactly fifty percent ahead of his nearest competitor in the number of hotels and rooms in single corporate control.

If anything is ever final about Hilton it is this: he is indisputably the world's greatest hotelier. And to have created all of this from a forlorn dime and an abject quarter, which jingled thinly in his pocket while creditors clamored for the half a million dollars he owed them, is by itself and without any other life factor a great human story. It is a story of a man who refused the easy solace of bankruptcy, who paid back every nickel of his debts dollar for dollar and emerged from that torment whole in honor and mind and ambition.

This brings to date, as of August 4, 1954, the defined biography of Hilton.

Hopefully it will remain exact . . . but there are those 500 acres in Houston. That may be the lid over oil—which will be another Hilton story all over again.

IT must be easier to write a book about an individual than to write a thousand words about one's self, else no biographies ever would be written. I have approved the biography which is this book. It now becomes my lot to write a foreword, and the request is that it be a statement of my personal philosophy.

It is impossible for a man to live fully without a program for his life. Since my earliest recollection, as this book will establish, I have been fortunate in the possession of enthusiasm. With enthusiasm as a base and prayer as a buttress, I have liked my life. The probabilities are that this kind of equipment leads directly to a full and happy life. Give a man ambition to spur him, faith to guide him and health to sustain him and he must arrive at some kind of success. The equipment is all there.

We are favored as Americans. We are born to a rich and vivid heritage. As in no other country in our world the combinations for full living exist and are nurtured. We are born to splendid freedom, vast opportunity, an uninhibited choice of faith and the complete, rewarding benefits of a gracious land in which liberty of the individual is jealously guarded and openly given. All of us trace our ancestry to other countries. My own forebears were Norwegian and German. But here in this last human stronghold of liberty I am an American. I say it with pride and I say it with gratitude.

We encourage enterprise, give fullness to courage and respect every individual's rights. It is a magnificent privilege to have this freedom of action.

Our America asks no more of the individual than that he love his country and live uprightly. The price of life under the tremendous benefits of liberty is simple: faith, loyalty, honesty.

With those virtues the individual can go anywhere and become anything in this country.

I believe in God. I believe that the way to God and His love is through prayer.

I believe in my country. I believe that its destinies are great and noble.

I believe in truth. I believe that the man who willfully tells a lie is a man willfully crippling himself.

Most certainly I believe in courage and enthusiasm, for without them the individual is hampering his own most desired wishes.

This country has been good to me. I was modestly born in the smallest of communities, a cluster of humanity set back from the paths of trade and world notice. I had ambition. In the beginning it centered in my community. As I grew, my ambitions expanded until they encompassed dreams of attainment within the borders of our largest state. Then they became national in character, and now, I am applying my equipment for life to an international concept which already is bearing fruit and taking tangible proportion.

I say plainly and directly that without the liberties we enjoy in this country, none of these things would have come to pass, no matter how ardent my enthusiasms nor how bold my courage. Enthusiasm several times carried me not only to the brink of disaster but indeed into disaster itself. My position was bleak and inextricable, or so it seemed. But I found that a reputation for truth and my own faith saved me. Men gave me aid and support from directions that were least expected.

Ability is an obvious need in life, but it must be vitalized by enthusiasm. To have enthusiasm is to have eagerness. If you are eager enough you will find that our measured day is too short to accomplish all that one wants. Enthusiasm is inexhaustible. A man can possess it when his physical being is tired and drawn. Used rightly it moves man constantly forward into realms he otherwise would not have dared to enter. There

viii

are a dozen words for it: zest, eagerness, flavor, drive, ambition and many more. But they come together in the simple word: will. One wills to accomplish both for himself and for the world he lives in. The will to accomplish only for one's self amounts to a kind of greed. But when this will to do takes into account other men and other lives, then it is a formidable and confident virtue.

One may attain success in a spiritual sense without much material evidence of it, and, on the other hand, material success can be managed with ethical means and substantial decency.

I confess that I delight in truthful men. I have an inbuilt abhorrence for dishonesty. I cannot conceive of enjoying for a moment a single dollar arrived at by deceit or greed. I confess that I enjoy life and I enjoy my fellow man. He is a fascinating and compelling creature. Even when he is at his worst he is an astonishing and challenging individual. I like the tumult of life. I like its problems, its ever changing stresses. I like the stimulation of it.

I have found it a healthful rule to close my business day with the setting of the sun. I have learned to put down and set away whatever the day has brought, and I have learned to find relaxation. To relax is to restore one's self.

It seems odd to be using the personal pronoun. I have no startling panacea for the spirit or blueprint for attainment. But being asked for personal philosophy I perforce have to make the reply intensely personal. It is an alien act for me. That being understood, and personal reference therefore condoned, I want to repeat all that I basically know, which turns out to be exactly what almost all of us know: love God, be loyal to country, be true to self.

Conrad N. Hilton

Beverly Hills, California
March, 1954

INTRODUCTION

Y̲OU may be one of approximately 25,000 persons resting tonight in one of more than 16,000 sleeping rooms controlled by Conrad Nicholson Hilton, a man who buys, sells and builds hotels from Cairo to Los Angeles. When it is impossible to buy—he builds. When it is impossible to build—he leases. When it seems propitious to sell, he does so immediately. He is a tall, slender, restless and indefatigable man who eats, sleeps and—most important—dreams hotels.

There are as many legends surrounding Hilton as there are facts. It is fair and reasonable to say that the facts often are more dazzling than the legends, and when the facts are brought out, he proves himself to be a fabulous human being. As you rest—and read this chronicle of a man who at 66 makes only the smallest concession to rest—you will learn for the first time the truth about an American with an insatiable hunger for trading, an incurable conviction that he would have been a great banker, an unswerving devoutness in his faith, an active firm belief that prayer is the wellspring of accomplishment.

And he is the owner of a small silver spade that has turned the first handful of earth from so many future hotel sites that it is wearing thin.

When Paul von Hindenburg was living out his last years in a twilight of reason, those who worked around the doddering old President of the German Republic had a fond but private little joke: "Don't leave any paper around on a desk, he'll sign it." This had some humor and not a little affection in it. The hotel trade the world over also has its humors, but they are colored by a little less affection. Among hotel management, the jest goes this way: "For Heaven's sake don't drive Connie Hilton past a vacant lot, he'll build a hotel on it." Hoteliers of the world have dozens of trade jokes about Hilton, but when you pin down a hotel man he'll own up to something far more respectful than the harmless jests with which the innkeepers amuse themselves: Hilton has brought more to the hotel business than any known practitioner of the hospice trade and his hotels are models of efficient, sensible and correct operation. He invented, for example, the unorthodox but healthy practice of making his managers almost autonomous business without exacting any investment except a manager's experience, honesty and zeal. It works out to a simple truth: a manager would be a fool to do anything but his utmost best in a participating formula of that kind.

It is commonly believed that Hilton buys and sells gigantic hotel properties the way most people deal in oranges. The uninformed visualize him as figuratively bouncing them in the palms of his hands a few times, pressing them between thumb and forefinger to get a notion of how much juice they have in them and then making a quick deal. Like most stories surrounding the lives of exceptionally successful men, it is mostly nonsense. Hilton, to be precise about it, gets a notion about a hotel before undertaking any action, devotes days and nights to thinking out all of the possibilities, good and bad, reduces all of his thinking to mathematical certainties on paper and then, and then only, begins what has become famous as the Hilton Stalk.

The executive manager of a large New York hotel not owned or controlled by Hilton has put it into words:

"Connie Hilton has got to the point where if he walks by a hotel at night and glances into the lobby through the front door he automatically elates half of the staff and depresses the other half. He is notorious for walking around and around a hotel he wants to acquire. He studies everything: how many men and women come in and out, how many are smiling, how many are frowning, how many have chauffeur-driven cars waiting for them, how many climb into taxis. If there are 64 light bulbs framing the marquee, how many are burnt out? What is the quality of the clothing worn by people coming in and out. How eager for their trade are the waiting cab drivers? What is the attitude of the doorman? Does he do his job straight out, or does he do it with one hand out? How crisp and fresh are the uniforms of the bellhops bringing luggage out to the cars at the sidewalk? He stalks a hotel in which he is interested, like a lion stalking a giraffe. And when, and not until, he knows everything there is to know does he begin the long, involved, elaborate and exhaustive trading sessions. He learned to haggle at the pine counter of his father's country store. And he still haggles. He learned to stalk fair game as a kid in New Mexico, and he still stalks. It is a fascinating process. I knew he wanted the Plaza months before Wall Street or the banks or his own intimates knew it. I used to watch him stalking it at all hours. I once saw him leave St. Patrick's Cathedral at 6:30 one morning and walk up toward the Plaza, keeping to the opposite side of Fifth Avenue. He never crossed over for a closer look, he never made a note in a little book, he never betrayed a thing on that astonishing, mobile face. But I knew the Plaza would be his—he had just prayed for it. And over the years I have watched it work out: what Connie prays for he always gets. Maybe because he invariably goes back and gives just as fervent thanks for what he got. He's even got me doing it."

Hilton does indeed stalk, he does indeed inform himself down to the last grain of ascertainable fact and he does indeed pray, with unquestioning faith that his prayers are heard and, if righteous, answered. He never enters a deal without prayer and he abandons any deal in which he feels his prayers have gone unanswered. He believes that lack of answer signals lack of rightness.

When he bought the Waldorf-Astoria, after months of delicate and detailed negotiation, his associates and advisors were gaunt for lack of sleep. They had their jobs to do and they did them until late at night, but no matter what time they went to sleep they were routed out daily at 6:15 in the morning by Hilton and led to St. Patrick's for an half hour of earnest, sincere prayer. The night that the Waldorf became Hilton's, his associates went to bed early in their suites in the rearing towers of that great hotel. They snuggled down for a long, hard-earned rest, content in their belief that they could sleep until noon. Instead, their telephones began tinkling again at 6:15 the next morning.

Twenty minutes later they gathered sleepily in the huge lobby. Hilton walked briskly toward them.

"All right, boys," he said, "let's go to church."

"But, Connie," one cried, "you've *got* the Waldorf!"

"You can't pray for something you want," said Hilton quietly, "and then not give thanks for it when you get it. Let's get started."

Later, in collaboration with the late Fulton Oursler, he wrote a prayer expressing his humble devotion to God and his intense love for America. When Oursler died, his widow, Grace, went to Hilton and told him that one of Oursler's last injunctions to her was to tell Hilton that the prayer belonged to him in its entirety.

"Connie thought of it, he felt it, he believed it, he practiced it," she quoted her husband as saying. "Tell him it is his. All I did was to put a stone into a beautiful cathedral. I want him to have what is really his."

Hilton first uttered the prayer in substantially its present form at the close of an address he made to a large group in Chicago. His peroration, followed by the prayer, was deeply moving to his listeners and it has since been reprinted thousands of times. The Hilton Hotels make it available to any one who writes in for it. It is printed suitable for framing and not less than 200,000 American homes have it framed on their walls.

". . . America on its knees . . . not beaten there by the hammer and sickle," he said that Chicago morning. "Freely, in-

telligently, responsibly, confidently, powerfully, America now
knows it can destroy Communism and win the battle for peace.
We need fear nothing or no one . . . except God." And then,
bowing his head, he said:

"Our Father in Heaven:

WE PRAY that YOU save us from *ourselves*.
The world that YOU have made for us, to live in peace,
    we have made into an armed camp.
    We live in fear of war to come.

We are afraid of "the terror that flies by
    night, and the arrow that flies by day,
    the pestilence that walks in darkness
    and the destruction that wastes at noon-day."

We have turned from YOU to go our selfish way.
    We have broken YOUR commandments
    and denied YOUR truth. We have left YOUR altars
    to serve the false gods of money and pleasure and
      power.

FORGIVE US AND HELP US.

Now, darkness gathers around us and we are confused
    in all our counsels. Losing faith in YOU,
    we lose faith in ourselves.

Inspire us with wisdom, all of us of every color, race
    and creed,
    to use our wealth, our strength, to help our brother,
    instead of destroying him.

Help us to do YOUR will as it is done in Heaven
    and to be worthy of YOUR promise of peace on earth.

Fill us with new faith, new strength and new courage,
    that we may win the Battle for Peace.

Be swift to save us, *dear God*,
    before the darkness falls."

One of Hilton's friends is President Eisenhower. When they have time, they joke together, argue together, play golf together and at odd moments have been photographed together. They differ widely on many points of view, as strong-minded men often do, but Hilton and the President agree completely on one thing: the forces of prayer are incalculable, mysterious and to be summoned only in the humblest spirit of devotion.

The President of the United States often reads the Hilton prayer and, in a mood of contemplation, adds his own supplication to it. Although they are of different faiths, they are mutually Christians bound in spirit by their joint devoutness and their personal credo that without God and His guidance the will to peace for all peoples is without real substance or probability of achievement. They recognize in each other a man of human needs and vast accomplishment but, withal, a humble man ever conscious that without the help of Divine Power no man is ever truly a man or arrives at anything that is truly good.

In his hours of most afflicting despair, and they have been many since he left the little adobe house in which he was born in San Antonio, New Mexico, Hilton has turned for help and direction to his faith. This simple acceptance of the presence of God has brought him through six disasters: three that befell his father and three that have punished and bruised him.

He wasn't born poor, he had a relatively unclouded boyhood, he was excellently educated, more often than not in private schools, he was a commissioned officer in World War I and he was for one term a legislator in New Mexico, a whirl with politics from which he emerged without any visible scars. If he learned anything at all as a young and somewhat bewildered politician it was that the easiest way out of a speech is to avoid it altogether and unless you have a burning addiction to politics the only course for a man of sense is to get out before the voters throw you out. The only possible plus he gained from his short romance with New Mexico politics was the secret of how best to deal with politicians.

This knowledge did not become valuable until later, when he began to acquire hotels as most men acquire neckties. The purchase of a hotel is much more than a real estate transaction. It has a curious personality not found in any other kind of transaction and, since it customarily involves real estate on important municipal sites, it often runs against the grain of entrenched politicos who either want it for themselves or their kin. What Hilton discovered has nothing to do with pay-offs, side deals or palm-greasing, which are blunt and common approaches to the political problem. He discovered a simpler, cleaner and much more orderly approach to what could often be a painful situation: he merely let it be understood, with enormous affability and his usual self-confidence, that he simply could not understand what politics had to do with his purchase of a hotel. Was it not clear that the best possible management for a city's major hotels was Hilton management? Of course it was. And did not Mr. Blank, the hovering politician, want the best for his city? Of course he did. All men of good will want the best possible for their cities. It was good to understand each other.

And thus shucked, Mr. Blank had no graces left save the grace to retire from the proceedings and stop making a nuisance of himself.

Affability and self-confidence are two sure arrows in the Hilton quiver. The others include a rugged honesty based on the early teachings of his mother, who did not flinch from a well-worn saying when instructing her children. If the old saw said that Honesty is the Best Policy, then at any cost Honesty *is* the Best Policy. Putting the maxim in less abstract terms, Hilton discovered early in life that a banker will listen to almost anything you suggest. He may not accept what you suggest, he may turn it down with cool hauteur, but he will listen. Hilton was barely out of his teens when he learned that bankers are remarkably patient and helpful people so long as they are not being asked to condone armed robbery. All they ask is honesty—and courage. Bankers have a lively dislike for people who set up a financial obligation and then, when times change and they cannot meet the obligation, run away instead of coming in and talking it over sensibly. No banker expects every loan to be liquidated with complete freedom from trouble. Our financial structure almost automatically makes room for trouble. But if a person who has an obligation at a bank will come in and be candid and try to work out a way of settlement beneficial to both sides he will find bankers the most co-operative persons imaginable. Some people never learn this and fear bankers. Others are belligerent and never avail themselves of banking benefits. Hilton learned it all early and it helped him to arrive at his present stature. He gave himself a motto in six plain words: Never try to outsmart a bank. The result is a career in which banks have been of inestimable help.

Indeed, he became so fascinated by banks as a youth that when he was old enough and had about $3,000 of his own to swing the deal he established a bank, only to have it yanked out from under him. This so irritated him that he set doggedly to work rounding up enough proxies to get it back—and did. Later, in Texas, he tried to acquire another bank and, when that didn't work out, he decided to buy a hotel.

The result of having a banker in Cisco, Texas, refuse to sell is an organization of hotels without parallel in the world. At this writing he owns or controls 18 hotels, with more than 16,000 sleeping rooms in them. He has hotels across the United States, Mexico, Puerto Rico, Spain and, any moment now, in Turkey. He is building or planning in Cuba, Egypt, Mexico and Italy. He has owned hotels in other places, including an unhappy period when he had hotels in Bermuda. The sun may shine and the sands glisten for tourists in Bermuda, but for Hilton neither of these pleasant things happened. He took a licking.

He has toted the silver spade to Istanbul, to Cairo, to Beverly Hills in California, to Mexico City and Rome. He dreams of sinking its bright blade into British soil in London. When it was revealed that we had a vast air base at Thule in Greenland, a rival hotel magnate smiled grimly and said: "I hope that Connie Hilton doesn't read this. He'll be flying that damned spade there to break ground for a hotel."

The truth is that his greatest excitement in life is opening new hotels. Once opened, he leaves them in skilled hands and goes on to open others.

"It is a thrill to dream of a hotel, set its construction in motion, watch it grow, attend its splendid opening and then start dreaming all over again," he said recently. "And when you can't build one, there is the thrill of another kind in starting negotiations for one already built. I've got hotelitis right down into the marrow of my bones."

He relaxes when he talks about hotels. He is like a practiced collector of old masters, no longer twitching with excitement but, rather, happy in what he has, appreciative of the value and ready to talk to any one who has another for sale. The relaxed attitude ends when a new hotel begins to take shape after having been only a dream. Then twenty hours a day are not enough. From dawn to past midnight he is planning, talking, sketching, totaling columns of figures, looking at blueprints, chalking off salable space in the lobby and public rooms, making decisions as to furnishings and decor, harrying the help over future menus and otherwise keeping a hundred men hopping.

Menus are a mania with him. He learned in his first hotel in Texas that it is suicidal to farm out the dining room on a catering contract. He insists that the cuisine in his hotels be managed and operated on the premises.

"No one profits contracting out the dining room," he explains. "The caterer wants to squeeze every nickel he can, naturally, and this leads to bad meals. Bad meals lead to unhappy guests. Unhappy guests are in no mood to figure out the culprit. All they know is that they had a bad meal for the money. They blame the hotel. The hotel can't go around wearing a placard reading: 'We are not responsible for the meals.' Of course the hotel is responsible. A manager would look like a fool telling a guest that he was sorry, but it wasn't the hotel's fault. No hotel has any business renting out the dining room. It's true that dining rooms don't make large profits—but they make great hotels. And it is nonsense for any hotel man to argue that he can't make his dining room pay. If a $2 meal costs the hotel $1.89, it still has profited by eleven cents. We often serve meals with a one-cent profit margin. But we have made X-number of guests happy, haven't lost anything and created the kind of advertising you can't buy—men and women traveling the world over saying to friends: 'You get wonderful meals at a Hilton Hotel.' "

It all goes directly back to Minimax, which is a personal invention of Hilton's.

But that comes later.

The life of Conrad Hilton has frequently been featured in slick magazines, sometimes with optimum accuracy and sometimes with minimum, but the major dates and accomplishments have always come out even. It is a life reasonably easy to describe. It had a formulated background, and the sources of information concerning the last ten years are manifold. Naturally, the story of a man who built a $5,000 nest-egg into a multi-million-dollar hotel corporation has defined episodes and milestones. The name of the first hotel, what happened to succeeding hotels, the hard times and the disasters, the present-day plans, the plans for the future. These are essentials, albeit repetitious.

The plans for the future are the most important thing in Hilton's life at this moment. He is expanding into a world-wide operation, with ideas ranging as far as Indonesia and India. There has been talk of a hotel in Pakistan, hotels are going up in Mexico and Cuba, he is negotiating for a hotel in Manila and three in Canada.

After sixty-six years, of which better than fifty-five years have been passed in work of one kind or another, Hilton has no intention of retiring, turning the corporation over to trained aids or of sitting in the sun and taking life with ease. One has only to consider an average ten days in his life to know that he is a man of incessant action.

Recently he moved busily and purposefully through a ten-day period not perceptibly different from any other ten days in his life. But these ten days will serve to illustrate the point that he cannot be still or long inactive.

On a Sunday night, in February of this year, he boarded an airplane in Los Angeles and flew to New York, where he landed in the morning. He conferred all day with executives of his hotels and, Monday night, had dinner with the President of Turkey. Hilton is opening a hotel in Istanbul this summer and the dinner was more than a courteous formality. He and the visiting President had much to discuss concerning that hotel and its affect on the economy of Turkey. Monday, at midnight, he boarded another plane and flew to Washington, D.C.

Tuesday morning he attended the opening of the Supreme Court, escorting Virginia Warren, daughter of the Chief Justice Earl Warren. Hilton is an old friend of Warren. Tuesday afternoon he conducted hotel business at his suite in the Mayflower Hotel and Tuesday night he attended a dinner with some friends.

Wednesday noon he had lunch at the Vandenberg Room in the Capitol with a group of senators and representatives, followed by another afternoon of work on hotel business. That night he dined with respesentatives of nations in which he hopes to build hotels and who, in turn, hope he will build with them.

Thursday he had lunch at the White House, following the second annual Prayer Breakfast that morning. This breakfast was attended by the President, Vice-President Nixon, members of the cabinet, supreme court justices, senators, representatives, and many others. After lunch, he went back to his desk and worked until 6 o'clock, the hour at which he likes to stop working.

Throughout Friday he met with officials of embassies of countries in which Hilton hotels either are under construction, are already open or will be open within the next eighteen months. Friday night he dined with top representatives of these embassies.

On Saturday he conducted hotel business all day until 6 P.M., when he had dinner with old friends in Washington.

Sunday morning, after Church, he boarded a plane and flew back to New York. He assembled notes that afternoon for his work the next day in meeting with guests from London who were to discuss in detail the final plans of a projected hotel there. These notes included working plans for the hotel, ways to change two London streets to give traffic freer flow and guests in the hotel a better view, and alterations in the original plans, particularly as they concerned what had been a proposed roof structure.

Monday morning he met with the men from London and passed the entire day, including lunch, going over these complex plans. The City of London does not allow new structures of vast size without a thorough study of not only the architecture but the decor, its relationship to existing design in the area and its probable impact on people, traffic and business in the area. The conference broke up at 6 P.M., and on Tuesday the long, strenuous discussions were renewed.

Wednesday, the tenth day of our arbitrary sampling, he allotted six hours to a rehearsal for a transcontinental television broadcast for the American Inventory of Faith, a program he shared with Peggy Wood, the actress, and a magazine editor.

It adds up to a crammed, active, demanding ten days, yet it

is an average. He is constantly in meetings, constantly traveling, constantly at work to improve his business, promulgate faith and arouse a sentiment for prayer.

What kind of background results in such a man? What was his heritage, his childhood, his young manhood? What kind of environment bred such an American? More important to a biography than the simple relating of facts and last-minute information on the most recently reported hotel purchase is the man himself and the factors that shaped him. They all come together in an astonishing story of an American life, and to fully understand it and follow the steps which made it what it is today, one must start at the beginning.

CHAPTER ONE

THERE was nothing on that Christmas morning of 1887 to indicate that the new baby screaming in the room back of the adobe store owned and operated by Augustus Holver Hilton would one day own a bank, and in turn a group of hotels. Nor that he would fight a war, grow tall and erect, marry twice, have sons, or ever earn his keep. He was averagely small, crimson and noisy. He had a heritage of generations of sturdy European stock to help him get started, culminating in his Norwegian father and his German mother. San Antonio, New Mexico, took no particular notice of Gus and Mary Hilton's first-born son. If he caused any ripple whatsoever in the raw, brawling frontier town it was because Gus Hilton was out front in the store giving his regular customers two fingers of "Nelly's Death"; one for Christmas and one for the newborn baby, and not counting the cost as the level in the keg fell lower and lower. Up and down the muddy street the word was passed from man to man: "Get to Hilton's store as fast as you can. He's putting up drinks on the house."

Among the ginghamed women, sitting behind the curtains in their rude huts and adobe cabins, the word was gentler and a bit dismayed: "I'd like to go see if I can do anything for Mary Hilton, but all of those men there swilling Gus's drink, I don't know but what I'd better wait."

"I don't know, I just don't know," another would say. "I think I could be a help to Mary, now that her little girl has a new brother, but Mr. Hilton is celebrating the event by giving the boys a drink around. I'm fearful of drinking men."

It was not as fearful as all that. Gus Hilton was a robust man and a loud one. He liked to laugh and clown with the men and tell jokes. But he was also a frugal man and smart with a dollar. He had literally fought his way up to what amounted to means on the frontier. Brought to the United States at seven, he had worked hard and long and westward, Fort Dodge had helped him for awhile, but he fled from its necklace of saloons and fancy women. Pushing west, he finally settled in San Antonio. It needed a store, it had some thin coal mines nearby where a man might hack out a living, it had frontiersmen and miners and they needed supplies. Gus started in business with a keg of whiskey, not because he yearned to be a saloon keeper but because in those days in the bare West it was a commodity with a fast turnover. If bolts of calico or bags of salt or leather hames had sold as briskly, he would have started in business with them. Whiskey neither attracted nor violently repelled him. It was simply merchandise.

In tapping a Christmas keg in celebration of his second child and first son, he was in a way symbolizing his life in the West. A keg for the boys was the proper means of celebrating important events. Also, it was good business. Gus was held in esteem as a merchant, a host and a citizen.

San Antonio was the fourth town in New Mexico which Gus had tried to crack open for himself. Santa Fe was forbidding, because the already settled merchants wouldn't let him get his foot in the door. He strode into Albuquerque and found it a muddy sprawl not near enough to anything to promise rewards. His third stab at earning a New Mexico living was at Socorro, a boom town of the moment. Gus was doing nobly there until the Indians drew a bead on him. The family chronicles do not detail that Gus Hilton left Socorro because an Apache took a shot at him one day and missed. But since four other men fell dead when the Indians attacked, it is scarcely to be wondered if Gus decided to go down river on the Rio Grande and find safer, if not richer, pickings.

He was in a hurry. He was bethrothed to Mary Laufersweiler of Fort Dodge and in Gus's heart Mary was a girl worth beating your brains out to win. He already had wasted precious time. How long could you expect a girl to wait, particularly a girl as attractive as Mary? He therefore shipped in his keg of whiskey and tin-cupped it into further merchandise. Inside of 60 days Gus had a horse and a stock of goods. He would load the animal and take off into the Mimbres and the Mogollon to bring food, tobacco, tinware and other commodities to the miners sweating in the mountains. He also served trappers on the route, bringing back minerals and furs. By this hard routine Gus kept alive, put a few dollars by and got his feet firmly on the San Antonio ground. At the end of two years he braced a friend for $700 and with it he built and stocked the adobe store with the two little rooms in the back. The store was across from the railway station, a clutch of unpainted boards into which passengers stepped when and if any detrained at such a forsaken hole in the plains as San Antonio. When the roof was snug over his mud store, Gus went back to Fort Dodge and was married to Mary on Lincoln's Birthday in 1885. While in Fort Dodge, Gus sold what little property he had there and put the money into a buckboard and a second horse. It was scarcely a honeymoon cottage of roses and vines and lacy curtains at the window, but Mary Laufersweiler was a frontier girl. She hadn't expected board floors and turkey carpets. She hadn't exactly expected long weeks of loneliness, either, but they became her lot. Gus took to the hills with the buckboard and some merchandise. He also drove into ranches, stopped people on the trails and conducted business however and wherever he could. By the time Conrad was born, Gus had property, money, standing in New Mexico and was, probably, one of the territory's most beloved men. He was to have eight children, all told, and for each as it arrived he would add one room to the wandering adobe structure that was his kingdom. From those eight primitive rooms young Conrad Hilton would, on a day when a dollar was sorely needed in the family, make his first hotel.

It is, therefore, safely within the bounds of fact to describe the world's foremost hotelier as having been born in one.

Conrad grew up with the native children of the area. From them he learned certain natural Latin graces and a fluent command of a beautiful language. Like everything else he stored away in his brain, he never forgot it. Rather, he improved it. Sixty years later he would charm Madrid on the opening day of his hotel there by responding to local speeches and toasts in flawless, elegant Castilian, correct in every detail including the sometimes perplexing grammar.

The children grew up under the influence of Mary Hilton. Gus was too busy creating security for his growing family. Mary gave them faith in God, devotion to honesty and a love of truth. In time, Gus subjected Conrad to store-keeping and was somewhat abashed to discover that his first son was plainly more attracted to religious concepts than to bargaining and selling. He need not have given himself any anguish: once Conrad got the hang of store-keeping he became the greatest haggler on the Rio Grande.

He never let the teachings of his mother fall away, but he embraced the calling of his father with eagerness after discovering the old-fashioned joy of taking part in a two-man tussle of wits over the buying and selling of a piece of merchandise. He learned to back and fill, to show indignation without ever actually losing the customer and to seemingly give ground without ever really doing so. Years later he would bring this training to bear on bankers, real estate brokers and recalcitrant hotel owners who had no intention of selling this sapling anything—but who always, somehow, ended up doing so.

The boy was almost nine before Mary gave him up to what formal schooling was available. It wasn't much and she knew it and it gave her anxiety. She didn't want an ignorant boy on her hands in an area growing so fast it would demand the utmost of training from each young citizen. She let him go

4

through what amounted to four grades of schooling in both Spanish and English. When he was nearing his thirteenth birthday she sent him off to a military school in Albuquerque. It wasn't much better than the education he had been receiving at San Antonio, but he probably would have completed high school in Albuquerque if the building hadn't burned down. She thought things out for two weeks and then sent him to St. Michael's in Sante Fe, a parochial institution which satisfied her on two counts: it was Catholic and it was strict.

Among the talents he took to St. Michael's was an indifferent mastery of the cornet, and even membership in the school band did not transform him into a convincing musician. But, a year later, in the New Mexico Military Institute, then and now at Roswell, he perked up when he discovered that a cornetist could become a bugler and a bugler rated an extra fancy uniform strewn with gold braid and glittering tassels.

"It made me a happy boy," he relates. "I loved that uniform with its gold dingles all over it. I loved it so much I wore it back to San Antonio where, if it dazzled anything, it dazzled the gophers and the rattlesnakes. No one else paid it much attention."

A buckboard driver at the station took a momentary glance at the resplendent adolescent, spat musingly over the offwheel of the buckboard and said his say.

"Guess it'll tone down some in the sand."

His father was even less impressed. He simply told Conrad to go put on a pair of plain pants and a shirt and come to the store. The boy's vacation was passed behind the counter: three months at $5 a month wages.

"Of course," his father reasoned, "you have a shot at advancing yourself. You can earn maybe up to $10 a month if you show the right git."

At fourteen, in those days and in that locale, five dollars was a lot of money. It still remains a respectable sum in Hilton's opinion. Although he has moved millions of dollars around in

5

crate-sized bales, he can sit in contemplation of a five dollar bill and rattle off the goods it will buy in relation to life. The handling of titanic sums has not eroded his respect for the basic value of a five dollar bill.

If Conrad had been casual in his attitude toward his father's business before going off to school, he shed his indifference at once and delighted his hard-working father's heart by showing signs of knowing what a store was for. He also invented ways of increasing his income, such as selling produce from his own garden to his father's store at prevailing market rates, and sprucing up the stock on overtime. He put away better than $50 clear that vacation.

When his second vacation came around, his father looked forward to having the boy with him in the store.

"Greatest head for business I ever saw," Gus told Mary with pride. "Think maybe he'll get somewhere some day."

Gus didn't live to see his prophecy begin to come true. But Mary did.

During the third vacation, his salary rose to $15 a month. After a family conference, Conrad decided not to go back to Roswell. On the strength of this display of lasting interest, Gus raised Conrad to $25 a month. It was 1904 and things were rolling for the Hiltons. The store was booming and Gus put away $135,000 after selling some coal mines he had acquired a few years before. He was a man of conspicuous wealth. Gus celebrated by giving his family a trip to Chicago. Conrad left several days later and rode alone in the then crude Pullman. He had his first taste of extra fare railroad travel. In Chicago he put up at his first hotel—and on the same day had his first ride in an automobile. He was thin as a rat's tail and lean, rather than tall, for his age. It made him look less robust but it was a deceiving appearance. He was as strong as a whip. He walked with a brisk, firm stride, his chin in the air. It is a walk he has never lost and the trip to Chicago gave him tastes he has never lost, either. He still loves luxury travel, good hotels and fast automobiles.

The happiness built up in the trip east soon died. His mother became ill and Gus decided to move her to California. He studied all of the coastal cities and decided, at last, that Long Beach would be good for her. It had sea air, a soft climate and no intolerable shifts in temperature. She took her children along and her first act, once she had settled in a house selected for her by Gus, was to install the children in school. Conrad completed his elementary education when he graduated from the high school at Long Beach. His mother's health was improving, he was developing a love for Southern California that he would never lose and he was casting about for a career when, in 1907, the financial panic which was to destroy so many men came along and took a hearty wallop at wealthy, secure and, for the first time, relaxing Gus Hilton. He waked up one morning without a dime.

He looked at a mountain of stock no one could buy. He had bought it at wholesale at higher prices than he could hope to get at retail. Every sale he made, and there weren't many, was a loss to him. He was saddled with a huge inventory and he was broke. He sent for the family and they came as quickly as the transportation of the period allowed. When they were all assembled, Gus made a short, terse and illuminating speech.

"We had it," he said. "We haven't it any more. I've been broke before this, and it doesn't scare me. Your mother is well again, and that's all the treasure I think is important. But we have to live. Up front there is a store loaded with goods. We won't go naked for a long time and we won't starve for awhile. We can live off the shelves. But we have to pull together and get our feet up out of the wreckage. Any ideas?"

At that moment Conrad Hilton went into the hotel business. He studied the floor for awhile, rubbed his thin chin a couple of times and looked at his father.

"I have an idea," he said. "Let's take five or six of our ten rooms and make a hotel. The place needs a hotel. There may not be many drummers in and out during the panic, but sooner or later someone will come along. The girls and mother can run the kitchen. I'll hustle the baggage. For ourselves, we can double up. I'd say about two dollars and a half a day for bed and found would make it fair all around."

There was no argument. It was the beginning of a way out and it was the beginning of the most relentless hard work Conrad ever did in his life. His mother and the girls ran the hotel. He and his father ran the store. Conrad slept in broken doses. He would close the store at 6 o'clock at night, get a light meal for himself and go to bed. He got up just after midnight, slicked himself up and was on the platform with a smile when the train came in at 1 A.M. He solicited guests, took their luggage in both hands, assigned them rooms, checked to see that they had clean bedding, soap and towels, asked them what they wanted for breakfast and what time they wanted to be called. He would make a careful record of the last two wants, then wash up again and meet the 3 A.M. train, repeating the services earlier guests had received. When the last possible guest was asleep and the house quiet, Conrad managed another three hours sleep until 7 A.M., when he got up, checked the guests for their needs and then opened the store at 8 o'clock.

Inside six weeks word spread throughout the Territory and all the way east to Chicago: "If you have to break up your sales trip, break it at San Antonio and try to get a room at Hilton's. They serve the best meals in the West and they have a boy there who is a crackerjack at making things comfortable for you."

There are no better advertisers for a hotel than the traveling salesmen who patronize it. Hilton to this day can't say for certain whether his early attentions to small details of guest comfort were born of instinct or the realization that if he captured the salesmen for his hotel success was assured. He only knows that they began going out of their way to register at Hilton's . . . and that the hotel picked the family up off the floor to which the panic had dashed it.

"Everyone got something out of our hotel," he says. "Travelers got cleanliness, comfort and a good table. We got profit out of their $2.50 a day, even though we served three bountiful meals. We all worked hard, and no one harder than my mother. I wouldn't take a million dollars for what those days taught me . . . and I'd give a million dollars for one of the suppers she served."

There had been plans for higher education for Conrad in the East. His own heart was set on Dartmouth. When the family fortune was erased, Conrad knew he would never get to Dartmouth. But by the fall of 1907, thanks to the little hotel, he found it possible to enter the New Mexico School of Mines, where he remained for two years during which he learned a little about mining and a great deal about social graces, such as dancing, tennis, picnics and moonlight walks. If he takes a moonlight walk today it is to case another hotel he has in mind for purchase. He isn't much of a hand at picnics any more, principally because of lack of time, and he will own to playing a less than able game of tennis. But the dancing he learned in 1908 and 1909 is still a talent with him today and he will dance long and joyfully although his mind is burdened with a thousand details of the hotel business.

"You can put it down in plain talk," he says. "Conrad Hilton likes to dance and most particularly he likes to dance with a pretty girl. There must be something wrong with people who don't like it."

Within two years Gus was clawing his way back to solid economics. He was dabbling in real estate in Hot Springs, New Mexico, thinking of organizing a bank there and he had a lot ready for the building of a new house. The lot was in the once hated Socorro, where the School of Mines was located, and Gus offered Conrad a swap: the family would move to Socorro

9

and Conrad could go back to San Antonio and run things there. He offered salary plus a share in profits, and the final inducement was Conrad's own idea: Socorro offered much better social opportunities for his sisters. He shook hands on the deal and went back to where it all started.

"What I have learned I learned there," he says. "I learned to trade straight, to take a long chance after weighing up all of the probabilities, to use a lot of sense and a little daring. And mostly, I think, I learned that you never get anywhere by sitting down. It's easier to be knocked down if you are standing up, but also you can walk to where you are going instead of vainly waiting for someone to carry you there."

He had to use all the sense he had on hand. The people who traded with him were used to bargaining. It was part of the joy of going to the store. He had to be able to hold his own in these bouts of trading and he owns up that he lost a little hide and some hair in the process of learning all there was to learn. He learned, for one thing, that man is mortal. He once backed an old prospector on what looked like a sure thing in mining, only to have the old man fall dead in his tracks without a trace of claim to anything. Conrad not only lost his considerable investment but had to dig the grave as well.

The experience cured him of exactly nothing. To this day he listens to hard luck stories and has a soft heart for less fortunate men, particularly within the ranks of his own hotel staffs. He is demanding in the management of his hotels and keeps his staffs on their toes at all times, but cannot harden himself to an incompetent. His executives plead with him to get rid of deadwood and he earnestly promises to do so, but he invariably winds up advancing the weakling some money and finding another job for him.

"Mr. Hilton has the best organizational and operational brains I ever encountered," one of his top executives says, "but he can't fire a man who deserves it. Often we have to do it for the good of the hotels, only to learn that he has found out about it and has secretly set the man up in another spot. We have to build a wall around him to protect him from moochers and deadbeats and bums in tailored suits. He isn't a sucker by any means, but he finds it apparently impossible to think of anyone as totally no good. He tells us there is good in any man and every man and we must find it."

Not long ago, a young man was sent to him by an acquaintance as a candidate for the hotel business. He placed the youth in a job in one of the New York hotels and almost immediately the yells started.

"We aren't against new blood and young blood," the same executive continued. "We are mostly fairly young ourselves. We know that the hotel or any other business must attract able young men if it is to survive. We welcome new talent because it means new strength. But this boy was bad from the start. He was lazy, he was indifferent and the evidence seems to be that he was dishonest. He also drank more than he could handle, which is a basic impossibility in a hotel man. You can't tolerate a house drunk. We told all this to Mr. Hilton and asked him to fire the boy the most decent way he could. Three months went by and nothing was done. We went, several of us, to see Mr. Hilton.

" 'He's just no good,' we said.

" 'I know, poor fellow,' said Mr. Hilton.

" 'He's a drunk,' we said.

" 'He may get over that,' said Hilton.

" 'He's also, probably, a thief,' we told him.

" 'There must be a reason for that, no man is a born thief,' said Mr. Hilton.

" 'What do you propose to do?' we asked.

" 'Send him out to me in California where I can keep an eye on him,' said Hilton. 'There's good in everybody. I'll put him in one of the California houses and kind of guide him along. It's not in me to destroy the boy.' "

There is a natural question to ask in such circumstances. What has happened to the boy since?

"Well," said the executive, "it seems all right. He straightened up. Doesn't drink, attends to business. If he is stealing, we can't find it. He knew we had the drop on him, which is too bad. Now we don't know if we scared him straight or Connie Hilton's faith in his fellow man cleaned him up or if the kid just pulled himself together on his own. Maybe Connie did it."

As 1912 approached, Conrad got the political fever. He talked it over with a cousin, Holm Bursum, destined to become a United States Senator. Bursum talked it over with the Republicans and Hilton found himself in the state legislature just when the Territory was to be accepted into statehood. It was a wild time and the young man from Socorro County found it, at 23 going on 24, an astonishing experience. He observed one or two political *coups,* notably the one in which Albert B. Fall clinched his hold on the senatorship, was fascinated by the political machinations attendant to that event, but soon became intolerably bored by the daily and molasses-like proceedings in the legislature. It is on record that he introduced nineteen bills and nine of them became New Mexico law. Looking back across forty-odd years he feels neither great triumph nor great defeat in any of them. He did try to push through several bills for the good of the people, notably the divorcement of state funds from political management, but lost to the chicanery of the politicians. He was a losing young David pitting himself against a crafty Goliath. This time David got the rock in the head. He also sponsored a prophetic bill which prescribed highway markings to guide and control the movement of motorcars. This time David was allowed to win and the specifications he laid down in that bill are, to this day, the customary highway markings used throughout the United States.

But after two years he had had enough of politics. He didn't like anything he saw or heard. Some of it disgusted him, most of it angered him. What was left filled him with lassitude. Put

12

together it was more than he could comfortably accept or condone.

He said goodbye without any tangible regret.

He returned to San Antonio and for the second time within mere months learned one of the less palatable facts of life: when eager youth tangles with wily old age there is inevitably only one result: youth gets a swift kick in the seat of the pants. Hilton went back home clutching a dream. He would start a bank. He didn't have much money, but he knew a lot of people who did have it and these people trusted him. He thought, with the impetuous zeal of youth, that he had but to open his mouth and a sleet of money would come his way. Nothing at all like that happened.

The first person to show him the cold side of a shoulder was his own father. Gus was well up off the floor again and putting away a handsome sum of money. He had no major family problems. Two daughters were married, another son was away at Annapolis. But he was frosty toward Conrad's hunger to start a bank.

"What I want," he said, "is for you to stay in San Antonio and attend to business. You've got work enough doing just that."

"But San Antonio hasn't any bank," Conrad protested. "It needs one."

"Seems to have got along all right so far."

"All right isn't enough," Conrad argued. "It's a one-horse town. It needs to grow. A bank will make it grow."

"If it hasn't grown up to now," the old man said, "it isn't likely ever to grow. Banks don't make towns. Towns make banks. If San Antonio was due for a bank it would've had one. No two ways about it."

"I'm bound to start a bank," Conrad said stoutly. "If I can't start it in San Antonio I'll start one somewhere else."

His father stared at him incredulously.

"And leave the property go hang?"

13

"And leave it go hang."

It was their first real impasse. This was the moment that comes to every son of spirit and restlessness. He must knuckle —or be knuckled. Father or son had to lose a decisive battle of wills. They looked each other straight in the eyes. It was Gus who shrugged at last, and made a gesture of defeat.

"All right. It's important to me for you to stay in San Antonio and heed the business," he said. "Put me down for twenty shares. You said $100 apiece?"

"One hundred a share. That's right."

"Here's my check. I won't add a penny to it, no matter what and don't use me as a stalking horse for others."

Conrad didn't. He added $2,900, every cent he had or hoped to have for some time to come, which gave him a full 29 shares. The Hilton family was in for almost one-sixth of the contemplated $30,000 capital. Old friends, ranchers of substance, trappers who had put together the foundations of an estate, anyone with any appreciable money at all, all were approached and all discouraged the voluble boy. They saw no need for and no place for a bank in San Antonio. They told him so—bluntly and sometimes profanely. But he kept doggedly at the work of selling shares until, at last, he had sold 300 shares.

There was no joy in his achievement. They cut the ground out from under him. The shareholders named as president an aged former banker from Illinois, rapidly filled the board of directors with graybeards from the county and when the New Mexico State Bank of San Antonio was opened in the late fall of 1913 Conrad Hilton, hustler and dreamer, found himself fobbed off with the job of cashier for which he received exactly no salary and little pressure to remain on. He knew a cross-ruff when he saw it and got out of there with honor intact and feelings lacerated.

Back in the store, with time to think things out, he had to admit that they were right about one thing: he had no banking experience and was young. But he did not accept either circumstance as justification for the rough treatment he had received.

If he got nothing else from the experience, he decided he would have a curative revenge. He wanted a revenge that would poultice his feelings and teach the oldsters a lesson. It took him a full night of thought to figure one out. It was a beauty. He would haunt the post office until he saw notices of the annual stockholders' meeting sift through the mails. Since the post office was in the Hilton store he didn't even have to leave the premises.

On a Saturday afternoon, late, they began to show up, setting the meeting for Monday afternoon. Hilton harnessed his horse and climbed aboard after sending word to his father, through a friend. He rode until Sunday night, talking himself hoarse getting proxies. When he got back to San Antonio at dawn on Monday he had cajoled and wheedled and blustered himself into enough of these proxies to give him control. He washed up, changed his clothing and waited for four o'clock in the afternoon. It was after the noon hour when Gus came riding in.

"Anything going on down there?" he demanded.

"Only a run on the bank is all," said Conrad.

"First time I ever knew a man to start a run on his own bank," Gus cried. "Stands to reason the old man did it himself."

"Looks that way," Conrad acknowledged gloomily.

Old Gus smiled. He didn't tip his hand, not even to Conrad. He just waited.

The directors and the Hiltons walked in at four o'clock and sat down. The president rose and made it clear to all of them. They had come there to take a bank away from him. Fine. The only thing was: there wasn't any more bank. It was broke, flat and tight.

"The cashier," said the foxy president, "will give you a close-of-business statement."

"Business isn't closed for the day yet," said Gus. "Let's look at a statement as of this minute including a couple of deposits I have here."

He tossed two wires on the table. One, from the National Bank of El Paso, promised a $3,000 deposit in cash as of opening time the next day. The friends in Albuquergue had responded, too. Its First National wired a pledge of another $3,000. The old president glared at the Hiltons, picked up his hat and walked stiffly from the room. The directors and stockholders forthwith elected a new president and made Conrad vice-president. At twenty-seven he was a banker.

It wasn't much of a bank. It had almost ceased to breathe. He didn't have much time to exult. He had to get out and start fighting to keep it alive. He had dreamed a bank, the bank had become a reality. But a hideous one, a hollow, empty, barely alive bank in a small, hot, indifferent town. He literally wore out the roads tracking down new depositors. He pleaded, he prayed, he fought, he begged. Money came in heartbreaking driblets. Sometimes as little as five dollars. Once in a while Fate decided to give him a breathing spell and provided him with a $50 depositor. Grain by grain, dollar by dollar it grew with painful slowness. The rejected old officer used political pressure to cause the county to withdraw its funds. Hilton never was to see his county as a depositor again. But in three years he was able to rest—a little. His bank had assets of almost $135,000, or $105,000 more than the sum with which it had opened its doors.

The memory of it still makes Hilton wince. Sitting in his office in the Waldorf-Astoria a few months ago he detailed the entire wrenching experience.

"There is no rancor, of course," he said. "That would be useless. But I still regret the effort I poured into it. Why, I put together a three-cornered hotel deal, complete with tax struc-

16

ture and operating plans, down to the last fork and spoon and towel, with not one-tenth the work and worry. Actually, there is nothing to regret. I learned a tremendous truth from it: if you work hard enough and long enough for what you believe in you make it happen. Now that's a tired old saying, no doubt of that. But it's eternally true. It taught me to work tirelessly for what I want, it taught me to deal with difficult, forbidding people and it gave me such a sense of victory that the taste of it is still with me. It was the first major battle of my life and the first real defeat of formidable enemies. Unfortunately, none of it lasted long."

What Hilton meant was that economic disaster once more was creeping up on his father. At about the time young Hilton had saved the bank the elder Hilton was going under again. And before it ended the father was to lose almost everything he had.

"I don't think I was properly frightened by what happened to my father," he says today. "I was too lost in my elation over the bank. While he was beset by troubles, I was dreaming of using my experience and credit rating to open a chain of banks across the state. Older and wiser heads brought me to an abrupt standstill. There was a world war on and it was creating new levels of commerce and economics. No one knew what would happen or when or where it might happen. I couldn't have raised a nickel with a six-gun. The folks with money were holding on to it until they could get a clearer picture of events to come. Sometimes I can choose rather odd times to have dreams."

His plans for a garland of New Mexico banks shattered by circumstances over which he could not conceivably have the slightest control, he decided to become part of the circumstances. He applied for and was accepted by Officer Training Command. It was a close race between bankruptcy and young Hilton off to the wars to see who would lock up the San Antonio store first. Hilton won by a whisker.

17

He was commissioned in San Francisco and underwent further training in Florida and was promptly, because of his mercantile experience assigned to the Quatermaster Corps. They gave him a job and a short leave the same day. He sped back to San Antonio and used up his leave finding a buyer for the bank. He managed, with three days to spare, to sell it to the Socorro State Bank. He emerged from the proceedings with a profit. It wasn't a fat profit, but it was enough. And he reported back to duty and overseas assignment content that he had proved an enormous thing to himself and all concerned. He could make the most unlikely dream come true by beating his brains out in the attainment of it. He had entered the complex field of banking green and ignorant and had emerged from the experience whole-skinned, trusted by all and with a profit. He wondered as he crossed to Europe on a transport if he could do it all over again when the war was ended. He decided, in mid-Atlantic, that he could and he decided that again it would be in banking.

He carefully weighed all that had happened to him. He had impulsively advised his father to go into the hotel business and it had been a success. Modest, but a success. He had kept his father's store going and had been a success at that until greater events engulfed his father. He had built a bank from nothing more tangible than the indestructible will to do so and he had been a success at that. He was young and an officer of his country's armed forces and he was off to fight a war of and for ideals. When his transport touched shore in France he knew one thing that had crystallized from all of his thinking.

He never again at any time would have to fear anything but God and it was right to fear Him.

It didn't quite work out that way. Young men's dreams seldom do.

CHAPTER TWO

Hilton passed through World War I without any notable peril. Once, up in a mountain pass, shepherding a supply column on the way to the front, some artillery shells boxed-in his unit. Scurrying from rock to rock, he saw to it that men and supplies, in that order, were stowed away beneath sheltering overhang of rocks, but when the enemy artillery became silent, he reorganized his unit and delivered his goods to the front. His only clear memory of the front is an occasional stutter by a desultory machine-gun off in the distance across No Man's Land; a chatter that seemed not to cause the slightest alarm in the trenches to which he was delivering food and warm clothing. Since no other man in sight displayed fear, Hilton decided that he wouldn't either, although reminiscing years later he recalled that for the first ten minutes he was experiencing a tension.

"It wasn't really fear," he said. "I think only men who have been at the front in any war can describe it. It's a feeling of 'Well, maybe, it will hit me but I don't think it will.' But I was a big, lank officer and I wasn't going to let the boys who had been there for weeks see me worried. My actual memory was that I took a surreptitious gulp of air and then, forcing myself to lounge against the side of the trench with studied negligence, said: 'Any place around here a man can play some poker after he gets his work done?' It worked fine. They accepted me as a battle-wise officer and I began to relax. I could feel it happening. Nothing a man does when bullets are flying ever makes much sense, anyhow."

Later, in Paris, he got a good look at things, including plush Parisian hotels, and became close friends with Major Jay C. Powers, a man who later was to join Hilton in Texas as a partner and, for his portion, was literally to get a hole in the head. He was assassinated by a Texan smoldering with the conviction that Powers had brought him tragedy.

The first New Year after the war ended found Hilton in Paris with the responsible job of heading up a service purchasing commission. He had passed New Year's Day paying the proper calls to ranking officers in his branch and had gone to bed early. The next morning, January 2, he strode into his office with a feeling that, somehow, 1919 would bring him luck. It began with heartbreak. As he reached his office door a soldier sprang to attention and saluted. Hilton returned the salute and reached for the door knob.

"Captain," said the soldier. "If you . . . if you . . . need me call on me. I'm Southwest myself and sometimes . . . well, sometimes, one man has to stand by another, no matter what the rank is between them. I'll be right here by the door."

Hilton looked at him, puzzled.

"Sure," he said. "Sure. Fine."

"There's a cabelgram on your desk," said the soldier. "Maybe you better read that first."

Hilton went in, hung up his coat and cap without haste, sat down at his desk and looked for the cablegram. It crossed his mind that the soldier had behaved oddly. And then he read the wire. It was from his mother and told him that his father had been killed in an automobile accident on New Year's Day. Hilton was stunned for several moments, then rose and went to the door, opening it. The soldier stood at rigid attention.

"Thank you," said Hilton. "Thank you for what you meant."

"It's all right, Captain. I have three lieutenants lined up to do your job if you want to—well—go to your quarters."

"I have a better notion," said Hilton. "Let's you and I pitch in and clean it up."

For nine hours he and the private poured work on themselves, and thus he managed to erase some of the grief. In the years to come, when he would be plagued by wracking, tormenting problems of finance, problems which seemed to have no solution except complete disaster, he would follow the same formula. He would lock himself up in a hotel room and exhaust himself in work.

Five weeks later, Hilton received his discharge from the Army and, mustering out in New Jersey, started for home and what he suspected would be a mountain of toil. His instinct was that his father's affairs were in a deplorably mixed-up condition, but learned that before his death his father had suffered severe financial losses, and left an estate with diminishing assets but no debts.

"The train seemed to move with maddening slowness," he recalls. "Finally, as we passed Raton and started down the slope to home I knew what I had to do. I had to leave San Antonio. Big cities had ruined me for its shabby streets and poor opportunities. I was burning to sweep the debris into a pile and get out of there. I was consoled by the conviction that my mother would understand my impatience and encourage me. She did."

When the debris was in a neat pile, ready for sorting, it consisted of about $40,000 in the clear, which had to be cut up among eight children and his mother. His share, plus what he had put away from the sale of the bank, was just $11 over a tidy $5,000. A puny weapon with which to conquer the world and, as a merchant, Hilton knew just how puny it was, how frail and slender it could be in a world already agonizing over falling values and post-war economic bewilderment. Also, although he had guessed correctly and received immediate encouragement from his mother, he knew that his duty was to remain home and lay the groundwork of security for her and the three Hilton children still in their teens and going to school. The situation in Socorro was no better than in San Antonio and in Albuquerque it was even more feeble and disconcerting. In desperation, he tried to put together another bank but in his heart he knew it was wasted time. He was right. He found warm friends, offers of jobs, hearty backslaps and invitations to dinner. But no money. The old crowd was having it too tough keeping things as they were and had no intention of helping him throw together another bank.

"Connie," said one, "I'd trust you with anything I've got but I won't give you a penny for banking. You want to open a chain of banks across New Mexico. You are, by my figuring, just about five years ahead of the times. By 1924 banks are going to do fine. Until then, they're going to open and close like a yawning mule. Why, boy, if you already had a chain of banks I'd advise you to sell 'em, lock 'em up or give 'em away until the storm blows over."

Several other equally blunt interviews resulted in a decision to look around for something else. One evening, at the home of a girl he took dancing on occasion, he sat down and had a long talk with the girl's father, a man dying but unquenchable in his enthusiasms. He described the state of Texas vividly and with passion. He begged Hilton to get to Texas as fast as he could get there.

"There's nothing in all New Mexico for you, Connie," he said. "Nothing. Texas is floating in oil. Go blotter up some of it for yourself. If oil isn't your brand of cayuse, get to something else, but always in the neighborhood of oil. Oil is like a trigger on a gun. You fool around the trigger and there's no telling what will come shooting out. Real estate, merchandising, insurance, hoteling. . . ."

"I've had that," Connie said. "I'll let someone else meet the midnight trains and check the linens and see that the kitchen opens up on time. I've got my eye on banking. Maybe I could buy one down there."

"I've got to pry," the old man said. "How much have you got put away handy?"

"Sunny side of five thousand," said Hilton. "Give or take a hundred dollars."

The old man looked at him in consternation.

22

"Boy, if you have a pencil put this down in real big writing: I can't make many more speeches. I'm winding up the score on my life. But I can tell you cold turkey that you will never buy a bank for $5,000. It's not in the cards."

Hilton went home dazed and unable to sleep. His advisor was a man of means. He was old and wise and honest. Maybe the old man was right. Maybe Texas was it. Maybe, somewhere in that great stretch of land, he would find what he wanted. He got up at dawn, breakfasted and went back to get some more advice.

"I thought about it all night," he said. "Maybe Texas is my hay field. I'll take a chance. But I have to know more. You talk if you're up to it and I'll listen."

The old man described the new Texas as he knew it. He gave Hilton the name of a friend. L. M. Drown. He said he would write Drown and get them together. Drown saved them the trouble. He came to Albuquerque and the three passed hours talking about the miracle called Texas. It ended with Drown and Hilton shaking hands in an informal, unimplemented partnership. Hilton went around to see a schooldays chum named William A. Keleher. Keleher had a brandnew law office and lively ideas. He decided to go with Hilton and at least look at Texas. Not one other friend offered anything but condolences. They figured that the best Hilton could hope for was a trimming and a quick one. One or two even offered to keep jobs open for him. On that less than inspiring note he kissed his mother goodbye and departed for Texas, his $5,000 in a wallet pinned inside his coat.

He and Keleher stepped off the train at Wichita Falls and found themsleves in a town crazed by oil. It was a typical bonanza town, a daffy, noisy, spinning collection of oil riggers, panting real estate salesmen, the kind of women who follow loose money in order to grab it in exchange for their matching morals and, here and there, a banker taking a dyspeptic view of the petrolated carnival. Hilton lost no time at all: he went to see a banker. He had his shoes polished, his suit was crisply pressed, his tie knotted to perfection. He swung his six feet two of length past a crowd of depositors and found the president. After a few moments of polite conversation, Hilton threw his lance.

"What's the price tag on all this?"

The banker looked as though he might have to summon a policeman.

"The bank?" he asked frostily.

"The bank," Hilton confirmed.

"The bank," the banker said, "is not for sale and good day to you whoever you may be."

"No harm in asking," said Hilton airily, and went back to his hotel. He found a discouraged Keleher.

"I'm saddling up, Connie," he said. "It's a little high on the hog for me here. Wish I could see it out with you, but I think my place is back home in my law office."

Hilton tried to pump new encouragement into his friend, but it didn't work. Keleher went back home and Connie, after circling Wichita Falls for a week or so longer and finding no promising crevice into which to thrust a foot, took the train out for Breckenridge. He arrived hungry and looked for the neatest and most popular restaurant in town. He had a meal of watery vegetables, meat that tasted like putty and a wedge of pie that looked and felt as though it had been cooked down from an old school tablet. He asked for a glass of water to wash down this unappetizing mess and almost exploded. The water tasted like oil. He called the waitress over.

"All the water taste like this?" he asked.

"You mean that sort of oil-like taste to it?" she laughed. "Sure. Even the wells have oil in Breckenridge."

"The railroad has just sold itself a ticket," said Connie. "I'm heading out of here. I like water that tastes like water."

"They've took two hundred million in oil out of the ground

here," she said. "Reckon with that kind of money the water ain't so important. But everybody to his taste."

"That's right," said Hilton. "My taste is for pure water. So long."

The next train put him down in Cisco. It is not on record that anyone ever referred to Conrad Hilton as the Cisco Kid. No one ever thought of it at the time, and it would be pointless now, but the present immense Hilton organization, operating luxury hotels the world over, had its birth in Cisco, Texas, a small town where Hilton put down his valise in search of a glass of clean water, and he did not leave the town until, once and forever, he was a committed, utter, complete and practicing hotel man. It looked like poor ground in which to plant a little seed and hope for a flourishing, green and opulent vine. But if there isn't a plaque somewhere in Cisco attesting that it was there that Hilton began the long career he has distinguished, there should be.

He found a palatable glass of water a block from the railroad station and decided that Cisco might be all right. It had some oil, but not enough to turn the town insane, it had a placid, well-swept look and it had a bank. Hilton spotted it two blocks up the main street. He went in and looked around. He asked for a statement and got it. He hunkered down on a long bench outside and studied the statement carefully. It looked healthy. He walked back in and found the president. This time he thought he'd edge up to things instead of shouldering his way. He used up what he remembers as eighteen minutes before he discovered that the bank was for sale, the books were in order and that $75,000 was the asking price.

"Where can I make the deal?" asked Hilton, wondering to himself where he could find another $70,000 if his offer was accepted.

"You can't," said the bank officer. "Not here, that is. Man who owns the bank is in Kansas City. You could write him."

Hilton got the owner's name and address and decided to

wire instead of writing. He had a momentary twinge about the $70,000 that stood between his own bankroll and the selling price, but after thinking it over on the way to the telegraph office he decided he didn't have too much to worry about. Keleher might go for $5,000. Drown might go for another $5,000. His mother might throw her lot in with him and put up still another $5,000. In his mind it looked easy; once you could plunk $20,000 in cash on the barrel-head, you could negotiate the rest. With this as a poultice for his last doubts, he wrote and filed his wire offering to buy the bank and went to sleep that night convinced that at last he had things running his way.

The bellboy knocked on the door at 8:45 the next morning.

"Telegram," he bawled.

Hilton went to the door, tipped the boy and ripped open the envelope.

"THE PRICE IS EIGHTY THOUSAND DOLLARS AND DON'T BOTHER TO HAGGLE."

Hilton glared at the offending telegram.

"He could have got his wire inside ten words if he hadn't put that 'the' at the beginning of it," he raged to himself. "Probably not a sound businessman. Guess I won't do business with him on any grounds. Better tell him so in his own kind of talk."

He went down to the lobby and, as he was walking out, the clerk called him.

"Your time's up," he said. "I'll have a boy set your valise in the lobby. Your room is already taken. That will be three dollars."

Hilton looked at him in astonishment.

"What about registering again?"

"Full up," snapped the clerk. "Lucky you didn't sleep on a pool table last night. Won't have a thing for days. Goodbye."

Thoroughly affronted, Hilton banged his heels against the

26

sidewalks as he strode to the telegraph office. Savagely, he dashed off an answer to Kansas City:

"AMAZED YOUR INDIFFERENCE TO ALL CASH DEAL NO REPLY WANTED."

"That jasper must think I'm a greenhorn," he said to himself as he walked back to the hotel to collect his valise. As he entered the lobby he encountered turmoil. Men were leaning red-faced over the front desk demanding accommodations and getting only curt answers from the clerk. Hilton, unable to find a chair, sat on his luggage and watched the scene. In a few minutes, a man came over and eyed Hilton. He seemed suspicious.

"Meeting anybody here?" he asked.

"No," said Hilton.

"You see what's happening," the man said. "You haven't a chance for a room. We turn them over three times a day. Sorry, but that's how it is."

"Who are you?" Hilton demanded.

"I own it," said the man. "And if I had the brains God give a gopher I'd find me a man with some money and sell it. I'm cryin' to get out into the field and get my hands on some oil land. This is peanuts here."

"You've found one," said Hilton.

"Don't make me laugh," said the owner of the Mobley Hotel. "It's a new dodge, but it won't get you a room. Now let's make some space in the lobby here, shall we?"

Hilton stood up, towering above the hotel man.

"I said you've found a man," he said evenly. "What is the price?"

"A man with fifty thousand cash could push me right out the front door," the proprietor said. "Too rich for your blood?"

"Scarcely," said Hilton idly. "But I don't buy without the books. Let's look at them."

He examined the books carefully and did not dare betray on his face what he found in the fat ledgers. The place was

27

making more money than was either reasonable or decent, yet the books looked square. He told Mobley he wanted to count noses for a while and passed the rest of the day studying the flow of traffic through the lobby. He was wary of planted customers. He had heard of mines being salted and he knew no reason why a hotel lobby couldn't be salted. He had passed three hours going over the books with detailed care. That would have given the proprietor time to call in his friends and stuff the lobby.

When sundown came, Mobley walked over. "Better find yourself another bed or give me a check for $50,000," he said. "That will give you my room for the night. I don't think there's another in town."

"Thanks, I've already made my arrangements," said Hilton. "I'll see you in the morning." He walked out, sent Drown a wire to come running, had a leisurely if undistinguished dinner and bedded himself down on a bench in the railroad station. Drown came in the next day and with Hilton, went over the books again.

"Either this man is a fool or a rascal," said Drown. "If these books are honest, he is giving it away at fifty thousand. Grab it, Connie. I wish I could be in it with you."

"You are," said Hilton.

"There's something I didn't tell you," said Drown. "I'm broke."

"I knew that back in Albuquerque," said Hilton, smiling. "You're a part of the deal anyhow."

"Why?" Drown asked.

"Because I feel that way about it," Hilton replied. "Now, let's go find some money."

"Better find out what we need first," Drown warned. "No use to pester ourselves digging for what we don't need."

There probably are old men alive in Cisco today who remember the bargaining between Mobley and Hilton. Both were trained, astute, rejoicing traders, getting as much fun

28

from the battle of wits as from the end product of acquisition. Each had been brought up to hash over every dollar and look in detail at both sides of every dollar. Days of this titanic haggling went on, to an accompaniment of growls, shrugs, expressions of lacerated feelings and similar dodges of trading. At last, Mobley, claiming himself to be the victim of a brigand, said he would take $40,000 cash. Hilton, stoutly maintaining that he was being robbed blind, said he would pay $40,000 cash. They shook hands with mock ruefulness on both sides and Mobley reached for a pen.

"You can make your check out right here," he said.

"If you think I tote $40,000 in cash around in a part of the country strange to me you are crazy," said Hilton. "If you think I have that much in deposit in Texas banks I don't know anything about you are even crazier. My holdings are in New Mexico, my native state. I'll need a few days to negotiate a transfer of funds."

"Can't say I'd move that kind of money around loose, either," Mobley conceded. "This is Tuesday. Next Tuesday noon all right with you?"

Hilton nodded gamely and he and Drown walked out to the sidewalk. There they faced each other with wry grins.

"There must be $35,000 I can lay my hands on real quick," said Hilton.

"I can move $5,000 out of the way for you," Drown said. "I've been working on it ever since you cut me in for free. Figured it was the least I could do."

A telegram to Hilton's mother brought her wired pledge of $5,000 to follow by mail. A New Mexico rancher, friend of both Hilton and his father before him, answered another telegram with another pledge of $5,000 to follow by mail. Drown's friend came through with a third $5,000. Two days later, Hilton received the two checks from New Mexico. The partners now had $20,000 put together. All they had to do was find another $20,000. As they walked, pondering this

29

problem, they passed the Cisco Banking Company. Hilton's shoulders squared and his face brightened.

"You wait out here or go get a cup of coffee," he told Drown. "I have a feeling we have just solved the other half of the problem."

Briskly, he walked right in and straight to the president's desk. He fanned out four checks and laid them on the desk.

The old banker glanced down at the oblongs of paper and looked up at Hilton.

"I want to discuss the purchase of a hotel, here in town," Hilton said.

"Fine. Always happy to have new blood in town," said the banker. "What are your needs?"

This direct question took Hilton off his guard. He had planned to play it out slowly and here the banker was rushing him right into things. He decided to spar a little.

"I have negotiated the purchase of the Mobley," he said. "The consideration is $40,000."

"You got that gold mine for as little as that?" the banker cried. "I wish the banking laws would let me get in on deals like that for my own account. What is your position in the matter?"

"I can put up half of the cash at this moment . . ." Connie began, rushed into basic facts before he felt it proper to disclose them.

"For us you don't need to put up half," said the banker. "It's a spanking place. Coins money. Nothing short of the end of the world could change that. Now, let's get right down to brass tacks. I take it you want to arrange paper for the other half?"

"Well, yes, I do," said Hilton. "You don't know a blessed thing about me, but . . ."

"I know that you will own half of the Mobley and be on paper to us for the other half," the old man said. "That's good enough for our purposes."

30

In twenty minutes, Hilton had $20,000 of the bank's money. He was astonished at how easy it had been but, later, he would discover that Texas bankers had a lovely point of view: the purpose of banks was to loan money. Why else did they exist? And three days later his dream burst at the edges.

The rancher's check for $5,000 bounced higher than a rubber ball dropped from the top of the Washington Monument.

The notice of insufficient funds came to Hilton in the mail. Having been a banker he knew that he had no choice but to walk in as swiftly as he could and make the situation known to the Cisco bank. Briefly, he told the president what had happened. Time was running short.

"Well, now, you know that's too bad," said the banker. "It's a shame to have a thing like that happen just when you're ready to close a deal. Disconcerting. But let's think a minute. There must be some way out of this fix."

Hilton sat back in silence and so did the banker. They studied the ceiling and cerebrated together. Finally, the banker spoke.

"How is your friend fixed for things in New Mexico?"

"He owns his property," said Connie. "It's probably worth $20,000 at a fair estimation."

"Um-mmm," said the banker. "How would this work out? Suppose we loan your friend $5,000 until he gets himself back in a liquid position? That way we'll have his account here in the bank, the check can be honored and you can make your deal. Sound all right?"

It sounded fine. It flabbergasted Hilton it was so fine. He arranged by wire with his friend to have Hilton act as power of attorney for him on the $5,000 loan and the hotel sale went through. Months later, dining with the president of the bank, he asked him why it had been made so easy for Hilton to get his money together.

"If a bank doesn't encourage young men in a town," the

old banker replied, "there soon won't be any town and, consequently, no bank. As for yourself, I found out two things first off: you put your own capital in before asking any one else to participate and you came running like a turpentined dog when your friend's check failed to clear. Showed me you were honest. Wouldn't jeopardize other people's money unless yours was in the pot first and wouldn't run around the corner when things went wrong. Men like to help other men who own up to things fast. You put yourself in our hands. We had to go along with you as an example of how we treat men with character."

Three stones that are deep in the foundations of Hilton's fortune were laid that day:

1. Put up your own money first.
2. Treat bankers as you would a friend.
3. Make your manager a participating member of your business.

To this day Hilton does for other men what he did for Drown: he gives men a share in the business without exacting any investment from them except willingness to work and good character. Drown, who had not put one cent into the Mobley, became its salaried manager with a share of the business. The first thing that became clear was that Mobley didn't know much about keeping books. The Mobley was making a monthly profit far in excess of what the books had shown. It had been in the hands of four owners and a share-holder, none of whom knew anything about operating a hotel. They were innocent babes almost unaccountably in possession of the Cisco version of the mint.

About the only thing that his $5,000 investment did not bring Hilton was a bed. The traffic in guests was pressing and for nights on end he stretched his long frame out in a leather chair in the tiny office of the hotel. But this was a small matter. He was living for the present, the exhilarating, stimulating, money-raining present, and what he did in those first days of hotel ownership stamped his code of management for the rest of his life.

Hilton would buy and lose and buy again many a time before he reached his present stature as the world's most successful hotelier, but he put into practice in the Mobley, his first real hotel, a way of management that exists to this day whether his purchase be the famed Waldorf-Astoria in New York or the creation of a completely new hotel in any one of six other countries. He learned within a week that anything, including a packing box, has waste space in it and that waste space converted to earning space often is the difference between plus or minus in the operation of a hotel.

The eating habits of Texans, he discovered, were almost unbelievably simple. They wanted what they ordered, to be served hot and without effete trimmings. That being so, and Cisco being amply furnished with side and main street cafés who found meat and potatoes an easy menu, Hilton ripped out the Mobley's dining room and spaced it off into bedrooms. He cut the front desk in half, and added a shop. He took three chairs and a sofa bed out of the lobby and put in a newsstand. Years later, he would order a popular and powerful brokerage house off the first floor level of the Plaza in New York and put back into being the Oak Room Bar, thus upping the Plaza's annual take on the space from $5,000 to $200,000. He would then, coursing the Waldorf-Astoria for waste space, discover that four of its celebrated lobby columns were phonies of no practical use in supporting the building. These he would encase in polished glass and gold-plate and rent them out as *vitrines* to such jewelers and perfumers as could recognize a chic display space when they saw it. Hilton has what every successful American businessman has and must have if he hopes to endure: an abhorrence of waste space, waste motion and waste dollars.

The carpenters moved into the Mobley and hammered merrily away, while Hilton and Drown set about making Cisco

33

mean the Mobley. To drummers he made it plain that he enjoyed not only their business, but their talk. He would move around the lobby from early morning until late at night, soaking up conversation, stamping his personality on visitors and constantly inquiring what he could do to add to their comfort. Drown was equally zealous in mingling with the guests. Only the partner, whom Drown had found, held himself aloof from these lobby sessions, claiming that he didn't want any part of listening to some lonesome salesman airing his views.

"I got other things to think about," he said. "You and Drown can handle that end of it."

This nettled Hilton, who could not understand such cool detachment toward a Golconda. Before the year was out, and after consultation with the other partners and the bank, Hilton handed Drown's man a check for $10,000 and got in return a signed withdrawal of partnership. The bank wasn't fully in accord with this quick 100 percent on the dollar profit, but Hilton made it easy to understand and mollified the bank.

"He's chilling the place," he said. "Drown and I warm these fellows up to where if they are within fifty miles of Cisco they go out of their ways to register at the Mobley and then he walks through the lobby like Jack Frost. It's worth the extra $5,000 to thaw the place out."

The other department in which Hilton excelled was in making the help not only happy but proud to be employees of the Mobley. He transferred to the hotel a trick he had learned in the Army: make your men proud of their unit and you'll have the best outfit in the service. This memory of Army training brought back to mind the name of his commander, Jay C. Powers. Hilton, who had never stopped corresponding with Powers, knew that his old major was in Chicago at loose ends. He put the Mobley in Drown's hands and took a train to Chicago where, over a dinner, he asked Powers to throw in with the Hilton operation.

"I don't think I would interest you," said Powers.

34

"What do you think I came to Chicago to nail down?" Hilton argued. "You. Why wouldn't you interest me?"

"I'm not fat enough in the money department," said Powers. "I've got some, but not enough."

"Enough for what?"

"Enough for what you haven't put into words yet, but is plain as bees: you want to sprinkle hotels all over Texas, Connie. Now isn't that a fact?"

Hilton stared at him in astonishment.

"That's exactly it, Jay," he said. "But I haven't told a soul. I once wanted to put banks all over the place. It didn't work out. Now it's hotels. I want a hotel around every corner in Texas. How did you know?"

"You didn't come to Chicago just to shake my hand," said Powers. "I could smell the yeast in you before your train got in. You're smoking with it. I wish I could go along, but I can't pull my oar strong enough."

"You do *wish* you could?"

"Of course."

"That's good enough. Let's go. I'm going to attend to some other business around here. You pack up and hit the road. Find us a hotel like the Mobley and you're in up to your shoulders. We can work out the participation later."

Powers threw his clothes into a suitcase and went hotel hunting. Hilton stalked prices on hotel linens and silver in Chicago. He was adding another stone to the foundation of his business: know your supply market inside out and no one, not even a venal purchasing agent, can fool you.

Ten days later, Hilton had a wire from Powers asking him to hasten to Fort Worth. He had found a hotel for sale.

The Melba wiped the anticipatory smile from Hilton's face. It was awful. It had around 68 rooms and that was about all. The furnishings in the rooms were a wreck. The kitchen was coated with grease. The carpets in the halls were down to the cordage. It had only one virtue: the lease could be bought for $28,000.

Hilton went to see the loan officers of the Texas State Bank of Fort Worth and they were even more discouraged than was Hilton.

"You have a stout operation down there in Cisco," they said. "Why do you want to fritter it away at the Melba? There are only two things a banker can give: loans and advice. We won't give you the loan but we will give you the advice. Let the place fall down of its weight."

Hilton went back and reinspected the Melba with Powers. Drown came in from Cisco and was as appalled as they were.

"It needs everything from top to bottom," said Drown. "I don't know but what the bank is right."

"It needs our kind of management," Hilton countered.

"Plus some soap and water and elbow grease," said Powers.

"Can we put together $25,000 real fast?" asked Hilton. Drown and Powers said they thought it could be raised.

"I think I want to prove something to some mossbacks I met in a bank," said Hilton. "We may have to milk the Mobley a little, but it can stand it. Let's get into action."

They had no trouble at all raising $25,000 in cash, in fact some guests who had made the Mobley their headquarters wanted to buy in. Hilton got the lease price down to that figure and moved in an army of laborers. He sat in the office eighteen hours a day dispatching his companies of cleaners. First the soap and water detachments, then the moppers, then the de-greasers, then the driers and, finally, the painters and the waxers. The furniture began to gleam, the halls lost their musty odors, the woodwork was spotless and shining, the kitchen gleaming. He gave a contractor eight days in which to transform the lobby, including the elimination of waste space and the construction of sales counters for vending newspapers, tobaccos, magazines and novelties. They kept their

36

money in an old house safe for a month and when it began to bulge the three men held a business meeting.

"We'd better move this stuff into a bank," said Hilton. "I have an idea but I want to hear yours."

Drown suggested the bank in Cisco, pointing out that they owed it allegiance. Powers suggested a bank in the up and coming city of Dallas, thirty-eight miles away.

"Show these local jokers where they stand," he said curtly.

"We will—by using their bank," said Hilton, grinning. "I want to stuff their bad advice down their throats by banking with them. Inside of sixty days I'll have them eating from my hand."

He was right. The hotel began making a fortune overnight. Every dollar was banked in Fort Worth and every dollar gave the bank some embarrassment. It had given bad advice and had almost turned money away from Fort Worth. Hilton knew that when he again might need bank accommodation he could get it swiftly and without argument—right in Fort Worth.

In a few months Hilton was ready for his third hotel—and, it so happens, his first Waldorf. It was in Dallas, it had about 150 rooms as it stood and the price tag was $100,000.

Hilton wanted it, but not at the price.

"I'll get to trading," he said. Ten days later the Waldorf was his for $71,000. He and his friends put $40,000 in cash together and went to the bank for the other $31,000. They got it without opposition and without wasting time, justifying Hilton's hunch that if you curdle a banker's bad advice with fast profits, he is your man from then on. Of course, it also pays to be sure of what you are doing. Hilton was sure and proved it in exactly twenty-one months, when he gave the bank a check for $31,000—all saved from profits made at the Waldorf. The bank's officers began automatically smiling any time Hilton was within three blocks of the place.

Hilton now had hotelitis the worst way. It wasn't enough

that his three hotels were turning in between $5,000 and $7,000 a month profit. Nor was it greatly important, except as proof to Hilton that he was a born hotel man. He packed a bag and crisscrossed Texas looking for good, sound, bargain buys. He was across the state at El Paso when he received a telegram from Powers asking him to hustle home. When he got back to Dallas, Powers introduced Hilton to a man who had once been a dish washer and short order cook and had through the years saved his money and used his brains. D. E. Soderman at that point owned a string of cafés throughout the Southwest and had cash in attractive mounds. He had told Powers that the 200-room Terminal Hotel in Fort Worth was for sale. Hilton examined the old pile and decided the salvage squad could resurrect it. The three men pooled about $60,000 and bought it. Powers now was managing it and the Melba, as well as acting as money scout for Hilton.

The hotel business changed Soderman from an astute businessman to a lobby loafer and an alcoholic. Both weaknesses distressed Hilton. He didn't like idlers and he hated drunks. After long hours of thought he decided to strain his resources and buy Soderman out. He made the proposition to the man and was stunned when Soderman countered with a deal to buy Hilton out. He and Powers talked it over and decided to let Soderman have it his way.

"But you want hotels," Powers had argued. "Why let him have it?"

"I have a funny feeling this is no good for any of us," said Hilton. "It's making money, all right, but it doesn't feel just right. It gives me the creeps at night. I can't lay my finger on the cause, Jay, but this is a wrong place."

Soderman took over and promptly made chaos of a sturdy operation. He lost his money, became moody and, finally, went to Hilton. He offered to sell it back to Hilton and Powers for less than his investment. Hilton still was doubtful. Even with Soderman out of the way he had an almost psychic feeling that there was something wrong with the operation. He stalled until at last Soderman insisted that Hilton buy it back at a fraction of its worth. Hilton remained reluctant, but the bargain was irresistible. He and Powers bought it back at Soderman's price, but Hilton saw to it that a few extras were tacked on so that Soderman would not feel himself the victim of a cheat. Soderman wanted $35,000 and got $38,500.

It was no good. Soderman was resentful. When the Terminal, under the Hilton-Powers management, began to make money again Soderman drunkenly convinced himself that he had been victimized by two sharpers. His friends argued vainly with him that he himself had run the Terminal down hill and that he was lucky to have had a fair man like Hilton with whom to deal. His rage increased daily and, finally, he put a gun in his pocket and went looking for Hilton and Powers. Going into the lobby of the Waldorf in Dallas, Soderman called Powers on the house phone, saying that he wanted to see him. Powers came down on the elevator, and as he stepped from the cab Soderman whipped out the gun and shot Powers dead where he stood, one bullet piercing Powers' brain. Soderman went to the penitentiary and Hilton was left with the problem of taking over Powers' interests. He got the necessary money together and bought out Powers' holdings.

In 1926, four years after he murdered Powers, Soderman was pardoned and began looking for Hilton. Hilton's friends told him to get out of Texas for awhile.

"That's the worst thing to do," he told them. "No matter where I'd go, he could follow. That kind of suspense can drive a man crazy. Get word to him that I'm right here and I'm staying here. If he wants to come gunning, that's how it has to be."

Soderman came straight to Dallas and found Hilton in his hotel office. The killer sat down, allowed that it was a nice day, talked about mutual friends, idly asked how Connie was and in five minutes left without uttering a threatening word or making a threatening gesture.

"Poor man," Hilton thought as the human wreck left his office. "Poor self-destroyed man."

They never saw each other again.

CHAPTER THREE

THERE had been a sharp recession in 1921, it had evaporated in 1922 and the two succeeding years had been about as normal in a business way as men could expect. Oil was pouring in spouts from the Texas soil, business was active and hotels were busy. Hilton had added a little hotel here and there, sold another here and there. He was becoming the foremost hotel man in Texas. Banks welcomed his accounts, drummers on trains gave him free advertising by advising their fellow salesmen to patronize Hilton hotels. He had bought a little hotel down in Corsicana and it was making money, the fifth house in his operation. He had built a wooden hotel in Wortham on the promise that oil would be coming up there in fountains. The wells and the new hotel were facts on about the same day. The wells spouted muddy, brackish water and the hotel spouted debts. Hilton rid himself of it for the cost of the lumber and decided to toe up. What his books showed salved his hurt over the disaster in Wortham. He controlled a hotel principality. Not yet an empire and a long, long way from a kingdom. He had his name impressed on 541 rooms which had cost just about $220,000. His personal investment was $100,000, and all of it safe, secure and afloat.

He made a humble, sincere prayer for the soul of the dying man who had, back in Albuquerque, commanded him to go to Texas. In four years his total fortune of $5,000 had grown by twenty times and none of it, not a dollar of it, but what was sanely invested. Not a wildcat dime lay restless in the bundle. His friends had become modestly well off, the citizens of Texas respected him. He was a happy man.

And then he decided to play with a million dollars.

41

Most men never get within looking distance of a million dollars. War, inflation and our growing national economy have changed the size of the dollar and have taught us to be casual about expenditures running into billions, but the phrase "a million dollars" still has an almost alchemic affect on mankind. Millions of people never see a fraction of a million dollars, and thousands see only that sum or its equivalent in other material forms: bonds, jewels, art treasures or goods. And of these thousands, a relative handful get to the core of things and not only touch but handle and eventually accumulate the magic sum. Hilton, apparently, was destined to move into the select group. His mind worked in terms of millions at this point. Part of his conviction that he would become a member in full standing of the exclusive Millionaires' Club arose out of keen business acumen. He had evidence to butress his thinking. His own efforts had increased his personal holdings from $5,000 to $100,000, which as any one can tell you is one-tenth of a million dollars. His efforts combined with others had pushed a $20,000 syndicate to a point where it was within shooting distance of a quarter of a million dollars.

Texas was fabulous even then. It was not as fabulous as it is today, but it was fabulous for the times. Texans had not yet become so accustomed to wealth that they could be contemptuous of any sum less than $10,000,000. That had to wait a few years and until its oil spouted in millions of barrels in order to meet the needs of the automobile. There would come a day when Albin Barkley, the affable Kentuckian, would lunch in Houston with Jesse Jones, the Lone Star financier, and idly say over a cigar and coffee: "I hear so-and-so is a substantial fellow, is that right?" And Jones would explode in mocking laughter and boom: "Substantial? Why, the man never had $10,000,000 in his pants pockets at one time in his life!"

Texas was at a golden threshold. It had not yet become the subject of kind-hearted, indulgent jests regarding unusual wealth, but it had its foot in the door and, among those right up front in the department of high, wide and handsome dreaming was Conrad Nicholson Hilton, young, energetic, and possessor of an extraordinary gift known today as psi.

Hilton is a mystic in the better sense of the word. He is a human being born with psi. Psi, as it has come to be defined, is possession of a paranormal talent for looking ahead, for seeing into other people's minds. The great prophets of old had it. In our time it has belonged—to name one—to the late Henry Ford. For all his mechanical ability, for all that he was an authentic genius within his complex field, Ford was a mystic. Those who knew him recognized his mysticism. A close friend, the late Arthur Hopkins, a sensitive and brilliant theatrical producer, was privileged to be with Ford on many occasions when designers and engineers would bring him an incomplete and seemingly unsolvable mechanical problem related to the automobile. They would confess their inability to master the problem and put a sketch on the desk before Ford. Ford would close his eyes, bury his face in his opened hands and for ten or fifteen minutes would remain in that position, silent, motionless and obviously lost to all around him. He seemed almost not of this world during such times until, eventually, he would lower his hands from his face, pick up a pencil and sketch in the idea that would solve the problem.

"It was much more than concentrated thought," Hopkins once said. "It was true mysticism. He would appear to have taken his soul and mind to other—and to us—unknown realms. He would return with the answer. If ever I met a true mystic, in the fullest sense of the word and its definition, it was Henry Ford." Since, in a sense, Hopkins was himself a mystic, his label for Ford may be taken as accurate.

No one possibly can argue against Hilton's mysticism. He, like Ford, has often gone into personal silences and emerged with the key to further personal growth. His convictions have a mystic nature. He was, for example, convinced that he would get $20,000 from the bank in Cisco. He was convinced that he would make his fortune in the hotel business, a business not notable for the creation of personal, enduring fortunes, and it seems accurate to say that the only times he has suffered sharp failures have been when niggling doubts in his mind have been brushed aside by a sudden surge of daring. The disaster at Wortham was one such example. He says today that he was not wholly convinced but did feel that at this moment in his life he was invincible. He had a surge of daring—and paid for it. If he had heeded the doubt put into his mind by his psi factor he never would have lost out at Wortham. He further implements the thought by saying: "I have had to learn to discipline myself. I have to quell the urge to dare and heed the warning which my mind supplies."

Psi gave him a picture of a Texas that would grow wealth the way most ground grows weeds. He had a foreknowledge that Texas would bloom and shine and shower down its wealth. His foreknowledge was absolutely accurate. Where trouble crept in was that foreknowledge is not a calendar. It has no dates of a specified nature.

He started to play with a million dollars—at the wrong time. There is to be said in consolation: he had a host of associates in one of his few wrong guesses. Many men guessed wrong at that time. And, in admiration, along with the consolation, let it be recorded that he deserves "A" for effort. Most men never have the imagination, courage or gumption to start a wrestling bout with a million dollars.

It is said that for most mothers little boys never grow up. Mother Hilton may or may not have held to this, but one day when she was in Dallas she observed Hilton doodling on paper and making crude drawings of a towering building.

"Are you taking up architecture?" she asked, seating herself in his office.

"I'm building a hotel," he said. "New one."

44

She was aghast. She had lived both hard and well on the New Mexico frontier of its day. She had been part of several boom towns: Fort Dodge, Socorro, Albuquerque. She had had a happy life with a man who would be rich one week and broke the next and who had had the misfortune to die during an almost broke period. She therefore had caution.

"Connie, you've already got hotels," she said. "Don't press your luck."

"This isn't a hotel, it's a HOTEL," said Connie, using a Texas form of speech. "This one will brush the sky and cost maybe a million dollars. It will be Dallas. When people the world over speak of Dallas the picture in their minds will be this hotel, the symbol of a rich and growing city."

"How do you plan to pay for it?"

"I'll get a notion on that," he said. "Main thing is to think it out. I know where I want to put it. That's a start."

Mother Hilton was gravely doubtful of the whole enterprise but since he had not yet even purchased the site, she decided not to worry too much. Also, her pride in him held back her warnings. As an original member of his syndicate, she had not lost anything in a money way.

Her belief in him was not shaken, but she went to her suite upstairs perturbed. Hilton had no such qualms. He folded up his papers and went down to the corner of Harwood Street, where it meets Main. A rickety old building stood on the plot. It was owned by George W. Loudermilk, a self-made man who had followed a course common to at least one person in every community: buy land where there is nothing and let the city come up around it. Loudermilk was talking in terms of $40,-000 for the land and the useless structure on it. That struck Hilton as a form of brigandage, but he decided to take an option nonetheless and haggle later.

The next step was to submit his rough drawings to professional architects. They listened to him for half an hour, looked at the drawings and computed for another half hour. Hilton waited while they figured.

"At today's market in labor and materials, this building ready for business will add up to a million dollars," they told him. "It might, due to unforeseen things such as weather, strikes, a dip in business or just plain cussedness, come to a million two hundred thousand. It's considerable of a building."

Any way you bale it, stack it or frame it, a million dollars can only be one of two things: a blessing or a porcupine. Hilton didn't know it, but he had a porcupine on his hands.

His first act was to pick up the option—with a string on it. He suggested to Loudermilk that he not buy but lease the land for ninety-nine years. Loudermilk wanted no part of it, but finally was induced to accept the deal; a monthly income for ninety-nine years with this protection, that if the installments weren't paid he got back the land and the hotel on it. But, in return for such a princely gesture by Hilton, he demanded that Loudermilk allow him to borrow on the land. Loudermilk's outraged yell could have been heard in Denver.

"You are the craziest man I ever heard of," he cried, "and I've heard of some prizes in my life!"

"Hold on, now," said Hilton. "Let's go at it A-B-C. First, for land for which you are asking $40,000, I'm offering rental fees of $31,000 a year for ninety-nine years. Comes to about three million dollars. Second, if I ever fall down in the payments you get your land back, plus a million dollar building, modern as this morning's sunrise. Third, if I borrow half a million toward the hotel—and the land—and default on that loan you have only to pay the default and own both the land and the hotel. The worst that could happen to you is that for half a million dollars of defaulted loan you would have a beautiful million dollar hotel and your own land. That's fifty cents on the dollar any way you figure."

"You're a smart scutter," Loudermilk grumped. "Too smart for me to follow your trail."

"I'm not smart," said Hilton. "I only know when I'm right. I'm right on this, legally, ethically and mathematically. You think up any objection you can and I'll answer it. Get help if you need it."

Loudermilk got help from wily real estate men and private financiers. They not only could not confound Hilton's ideas but had at last to advise Loudermilk to let "that fool boy hang himself."

Hilton found $500,000 in the National Bank of Commerce in St. Louis. He also found its president, W. L. Hemingway, to be a cold, hard-headed banker. He told Hilton that the loan would be paid piecemeal as the structure took form and that if he ran into trouble the bank would call his loan quicker than he could whistle "Dixie."

"You get yourself the whole sum before you stick a shovel in that ground," Hemingway warned. "I don't fool with money in any form, particularly my bank's money. Gird yourself, boy."

Hilton found $50,000 in a Dallas bank and from the contractor to whom he gave the work of erecting the hotel he got $150,000, a deal which left the contractor stunned but co-operative. He had never had to put up money to get a contract, but this time he did—or he wouldn't get the job. That was plain.

Of the remaining $300,000, Hilton went back to his basic philosophy: you can't expect others to put up money if you don't. He put up $100,000, which was his total fortune. He didn't have a personal nickel when he plumped that into the pot. His syndicate put up the final $200,000 and if they felt the chill of fear, he warmed them by pointing out that they still owned four hotels against which they could borrow.

Hilton picked up a spade on July 26, 1924, and rammed its edge into the Dallas earth, at a point where a small garden adjoined the old Loudermilk structure. He pressed down, picked up a gob of soil and flung it over his shoulder.

"Okay, boys, tear her down," he said. Hot or cold, rain or shine, win or lose, he had spaded into his first million dollar enterprise. He celebrated the event that afternoon by playing golf and turning in his first 92 for the round.

It was clear from the start that a million dollars wouldn't open the doors. This kind of news beats the wireless for swiftness of travel. The hotel was within four stories of completion when Hemingway came in from St. Louis and reiterated his warning: a finished, complete, open and operating hotel within the limits of money specified—or his bank would call the loan and take over.

Hilton's answer was to riffle through the bills to date and exhibit them—each one marked "Paid." Hemingway wasn't fooled.

"Just don't forget," he said. "I may cry sometimes in my life—but the tears are ice-water."

It was the plumbing contractor who brought things to a head. He and the Dallas bank moved together to destroy Hilton. The bank called its $50,000 loan, on the basis of distressing rumors, and the plumber walked in on a Saturday morning and demanded settlement of his account or his crew wouldn't show up Monday morning. Hilton, with a show of blithe self-confidence, had been able to hold the Dallas bank off a week, but the plumber didn't react to a firm, confident tone of voice. He only wanted money.

"I have money coming in Monday from St. Louis," said Hilton. "I don't write checks I can't honor. But I'll do this: I'll write your check this minute, seal it in an envelope in front of you and put it here on my desk. The St. Louis money will be deposited Monday here in Dallas. Then this check will become sound. Monday, at noon, I'll hand you this envelope with the check in it."

The plumber was not happy, but he accepted the alternative.

"I'll be here at noon," he said.

And Hilton knew that before noon he had to get $50,000 in cash into the Dallas bank or else it would move in and if it moved in Hemingway would move in and if Hemingway moved in, the entire beautiful dream would be blown apart. He left his office to get some fresh air and think. Somehow, he had to find $50,000 by Monday morning, less than forty-eight hours away. On an impulse, he walked into his office at the Dallas hotel. He looked on his desk—the envelope containing the plumber's check wasn't there. Alarmed he buzzed for his secretary.

"I left an envelope here on the desk," he said. "Did you—"

"Oh, yes, Mr. Hilton," the secretary said. "I saw it was addressed to the plumber so I mailed it. I figured you wanted him to have it for his payroll."

Hilton almost fainted. He had enough to pay the bank. Or he had enough to pay the plumber. But not both. He had pledged the bank he would meet his loan Monday morning. The plumber would have a signed check Monday morning. One way or the other, Hilton was ruined. If the bank honored the check to the plumber it would demand its loan money. If it took the loan money the plumber would hold a dishonored check, and nothing could be worse than that. It not only violated every principle dear to Hilton but was certain to cause disastrous talk in Dallas. He was, literally, almost crazed. He could not think any relief plan through to its end. Finally, in desperation, he went to see a friend.

Harry Sigel was a good friend who believed in Hilton and had never had to put up a penny to certify his admiration for the go-getter. To Sigel, Hilton abjectly confessed his dilemma.

"What do you want from me?" Sigel asked.

"I want an introduction to the postmaster," said Hilton. "I'll put the facts on the line to him as I have to you. I have to get that letter back or I am ruined, broke, and have ruined every one dear to me including my mother. Her money is in this up to the hilt."

"I won't do it," said Sigel. "It would be the most foolish act of your life. If you got the letter back, which I doubt because to give it to you would violate Federal postal laws, where would you be? An unpaid plumber? In ten minutes every craft on the job would walk out, knowing you were broke. That kind of news gets under way fast. If you break your word to Thornton at the bank, you are equally ruined. Banks move in on people like you even faster than carpenters and plumbers. You have no alternative, no choice of action. You pay *both* of them!"

"That's insane, Harry," Hilton cried. "I have just told you that I haven't got enough for both."

Sigel, smiling to himself, was making out a check. He signed it and handed it to Hilton.

"Now you have," he said.

There was a long silence, at the end of which Hilton, his eyes brimming, muttered "Thanks." Sigel waved his gratitude away.

"Finish your hotel, Connie," he said. "Any way you can."

Promptly on Monday morning, Hilton walked into the Dallas bank and up to the desk of Robert Thornton.

"Here's your money, Bob," he said briskly. "Let's get this settled and then have a bite of lunch later. You've been a mighty help to us. I think I owe you a lunch."

"Sit down a minute and tell me how things are going." said Thornton.

"Can't, Bob, I just can't," said Hilton. "I'm busier than a bird dog. Getting near completion, you know."

"Relax, relax," said Thornton. "You can take it easy for ten minutes. I've been thinking over the weekend; that's going to be a beautiful addition to Dallas. It excites me."

"Me, too," said Hilton. "Well, I'll be seeing . . ."

"Connie," said Thornton, "I think maybe we can wait a little bit. I think an extension can be fixed up. No need to hurry these things."

50

Hilton's face betrayed not one emotion.

"Good gracious alive, Bob," he said. "You're like a flea on a hot rock. First you want your money pronto and then you talk extension. Make up your mind! I'm busy, awfully busy. Do you want the money or not?"

"Well, we don't need it this minute," said Thornton. He didn't say that Hilton's prompt willingness to pay had given the bank new confidence in the hotel builder.

"If that's the way you feel about it," said Hilton, "let's put together a new note for $10,000 more. I could use it for a few days."

Hilton had the $10,000 additional accommodation plus his untouched $50,000 now. He felt like a giant.

And three days later believed himself to be a midget. A frightened midget, at that.

Final calculations had shown him with merciless exactness that he would need $100,000 to finish the hotel. He knew that Thornton would never advance another nickel. He knew that Hemingway would move in like a conquering army. He began telephoning and wiring friends all over the Southwest and not a thin, worn dime came back. Not only was his back to the wall, but his face was pressed against another wall. He was caught flat between two blank barriers. In ten days it would all be over. The plumber, held off only momentarily, would be around in ten days for another payment.

He went to the bitterest spring in Dallas to try for a gulp of water. He went to see Loudermilk.

"You'll have to meet the rest of the payrolls," he said bluntly. "Either you do or you have an unfinished hotel on your hands and you can argue with the banks and the con-tractors. I've been broke before and picked myself up off the floor. I can do it again—"

Loudermilk's anguished scream broke into this array of icy facts.

51

"Get out, get out!" he shrilled. "Get out of that door and never—"

"A pleasure," said Hilton. "I'm glad it's over."

He picked up his hat and started for the door.

"Wait a minute," said Loudermilk. "I won't buy a word of what you have to say, but I'm curious to hear it. Talk."

Hilton came back and sat down.

"Just don't interrupt me," he said. "Just listen."

"Maybe," said Loudermilk. "Start."

"Now," said Hilton, settling back in the chair. "It goes this way. If you meet $100,000 worth of payroll and material bills we finish the hotel. I'll give it to you. I will sign a lease at $100,000 a year to operate it for you. I also will furnish and stock it with linens, silver and all the rest. You get $100,000 a year, I get the rest. When you have received $1,000,000 in ten years you will be well in the clear, so will the house, so will I. We still will owe you $31,000 a year on ground lease for the ninety-nine years. What I can make for myself and my syndicate is ours above the $100,000 a year lease for ten years."

Loudermilk grimaced.

"It's the most horrible thing I ever heard of," he said. "Just plain horrible. I'm stuck all the way. What if the hotel fails? After all, Dallas has a lot of hotels and some of them are building additions."

"If the hotel fails you are in the soup," said Hilton. "If you don't finish it for me, you are in the soup even more. You'll have an unfinished building on your hands. The other way you will at least have a hotel to play with and I'll show you how to play with it."

"Give me ten days," said Loudermilk, inexplicably calm.

Hilton had exactly ten days in which to meet the next plumbing payment, but it didn't show where Loudermilk could read it on his face.

"Take your time," said Hilton. "Take all you want. You'll

think it over and see that I am right and my deal is square. I'd rather fail than offer any other kind of deal."

"That's the only reason I didn't throw you out of here half an hour ago," said the old man.

Hilton went out, hoping desperately that Loudermilk would arrive at a decision in under ten days. He did. He arrived at it in nine days. He accepted the deal. The plumber was paid and Hilton signed a ten-year operating lease at $100,000 a year. He also went to the Dallas bank and withdrew enough of his own funds to repay Sigel. He ordered furnishings for the hotel and laid plans for a gala opening.

He was personally stripped, he was burdened with obligations, he was tired and worried and relieved, all at once. But something, some indefinable something, kept nagging at the back of his mind. It wasn't money, because he believed that it would come to him and his backers in truckload lots. He had been scrupulous in his dealings. He had almost had the hide taken off him, he had lost sleep and frayed his nerves and jangled his soul, but he had fought a valiant fight for a million dollars and had won with clean hands. Not one man or woman in the world could claim that he or she had been burned for as much as a cent.

He would go to bed at night trying to grasp the illusive thing that was worrying him. At last, one morning at 3:40 a.m., he waked suddenly and knew what it was. He had wanted a slogan for his business and there, almost as though written in letters of fire on his bedroom wall, it was, all in one piece and complete: "Minimax." Half asleep he muttered it over and over and over. The word fascinated him. He was not yet ready to decode it. But the word was there for him.

At breakfast that morning it unfolded for him. Minimax meant "Minimum charge for Maximum service."

He still likes it, although he doesn't use it as the slogan of his business. He made it his own, he made it part of his operating philosophy, he drilled it into his staffs and for twenty years those five words meant Hilton Hotels. The philosophy still guides his managers and staffs, but he has dropped it from his organization's ads and stationery.

"You don't have to claim what the public already knows," he says.

The Hilton Hotel in Dallas was opened on August 4, 1925, a marvel of cleanliness, convenience, service and comfort. All of Texas pitched in to make the event memorable and for a minimum of a dollar and a half and a maximum of three dollars any guest could command elaborate, constant and sincere attention. From Hilton down to the bus boys, the staff extended itself in providing such hotel spirit as had never been seen in Texas before. The public responded. It became almost impossible to get a room except by reservation well in advance.

There was the inevitable banquet celebrating the opening. The happiest faces at the tables, next to Hilton's, were those of the general contractor and the plumber. Thornton didn't look grieved, either, and a St. Louis emmissary of Hemingway's may be said to have beamed. The usual speeches were made and the only odd note was struck by Hilton who, in the midst of a carefully prepared speech, departed from text and said to the contractor:

"If it's humanly possible I want one more thing from you. I've just thought of it. If you can find it, I'd like the spade with which I turned the first shovel of earth for this beautiful hotel."

Three days later, with a silver plaque attesting Conrad Hilton's million dollar dream screwed to the wooden handle, the spade was delivered to Hilton.

"Connie," said his mother, "what on earth do you want with that shovel?"

"I may build another hotel, mother," he said.

"Not just yet, son," she said quietly. "Pray heaven not just yet."

She knew the physical toll that building the first true Hilton

Hotel had taken and she didn't want to see it repeated for a long time to come, if ever.

Mother Hilton need not have worried. It would be two years before her son immersed himself again in the agonies and buffets of building a hotel. For that long he attended strictly to the care and nurturing of his new hotel. It was a compact, impressive and lasting course in major hotel operation. Every sheet and towel and pillow case and bar of soap, every fork and spoon and dinner plate, every rug and light globe and pound of coal was an item to be considered and thought about and carefully bought. The hotel, as well as Hilton himself, carried a burden that had to be lightened. The hotel was profitable, it promised to remain so, but it allowed for no careless nickels. It didn't even allow for a frittered penny.

Hilton and his staff learned a sparkling, new kind of hotel management which combined earnest, detailed management with the best possible return for the guest. He learned how to make a hotel desirable, how to run it so that persons having a choice of hotels to patronize would automatically think of a Hilton hotel. He learned how to run a dining room so that meals could be calculated to the fraction of a cent and yet be a rewarding adventure for the guest. Later, when his horizon widened, he would take all of these lessons with him to bigger hotels in larger cities. In short, he learned his business inside out and his present organization of distinguished hotels attests the soundness of his learning.

By 1927 enough of the load had been lifted from the Dallas Hilton to justify Hilton in again actively pursuing his daydreams. Chicago beguiled him. He thought that one day he'd like to own and operate a Chicago hotel, but he turned up next in Abilene, Texas, a long distance from Chicago. Abilene wanted a hotel and was willing to build it if Hilton would assume a leased operation of it in return for which they would call it a Hilton hotel. There were no financial fish-hooks this time. All that he had to do was warrant efficient operation on a sensible plane and that code of conduct was natural to him. He was never plagued or badgered or bored. When it neared completion he arranged the furnishing contracts and took Drown with him to open it. Drown remained on as manager after Hilton went back to Dallas. There now were six Texas hotels in his personal care and, later that year, at the behest of Waco, which put up $50,000 as an inducement, he built a hotel which ran twelve stories, cost about $823,000 and had the happy aid of Thornton and Hemingway in the money end of things. Neither banker pushed Hilton, since by now the Dallas Hilton was fulfilling their fondest dreams and solacing their bankers' hearts. Hilton surprised the citizens of Waco with a thing just coming along: he put air-conditioning machinery into the basement and conducted its benefits to the lobby and the dining room. But, as a gesture toward guests roasting upstairs in the bedrooms, a fate afflicting guests anywhere in any hotel in the country during the summer, he had iced water piped into every bathroom. Between the two innovations, Hilton became a local hero of Bunyanesque proportion.

One aged native seer, basking in the cool atmosphere of the lobby, uttered a prophecy which reached print:

"We'd better treat Connie Hilton right while we can. He's going to be too big for Texas and move on to greater glory."

In spite of Thornton and Hemingway, the Waco project cost Hilton more personal money than he had planned. He recalls now that at the moment the citizens of Waco were singing his praises the loudest, his bank balance was at its lowest.

"Scientists who talk in billions and the square root of billions have a phrase," he said recently. "They say that a certain figure 'is on the order of' such and such a total. My bank balance on the day Waco drank the iced water and relaxed in the air conditioning was on the order of $33.58, a sum not likely to give a man delusions of grandeur."

But he had clothes to wear, a bed to sleep in and a dining table at which he could sit in any one of now seven hotels and, inside of a week, it was obvious that the Waco hotel would coin money. Indeed, it was so profitable that fourteen months later, early in 1929, he was watching eighty new rooms being added to it.

Bleak and formidable days lay ahead of Hilton and millions of fellow-Americans that year. A pitiful few could see that far ahead but Hilton's psi factor was not accurately at work. He had the hotel virus raging in his veins. Money was coming from seven directions. If it also went out in seven others as payments on his bank obligations, he did not count that as a warning. No one did, including the best bankers in the United States. Few men in the higher brackets of finance foresaw the blizzard over the horizon. If Wall Street could not foretell the storm, how could a hotel operator in pulsing Texas do so?

He gave a thought one day to Wichita Falls and remembered that it had not been hospitable to him when he came to Texas from New Mexico. Maybe a Hilton hotel would make those who had spurned him think twice about discouraging able young men in the future. He traded back and forth in the old, joyous way of country store traders until he got a hotel there for $60,000, but this was only to keep his wits sharp. His real concern was the assembling of a deal which would cost $2,450,000 and bring him four hotels. He remembers now that he often sat in on business meetings having to do with this deal and blithely talked in millions while having less than $15 of his own money on deposit anywhere. He would negotiate in the hundreds of thousands while rattling as much as eighty cents in his pockets. People were eager to invest with him and banks were heartening in their cooperation. Nonetheless, he closed no portion of any deal until the first sum of cash on the line was his own money. He had stuck to that practice from his $5,000 start and he never intended to depart from it. He might go to sleep tonight with less than a dollar in his wallet, but the morrow always brought him his share from the working hotels and he would use that cash share to buy the first piece of anything new.

The spade now slashed four holes in the ground. In Lubbock, in Marlin, in San Angelo and in Plainview the contractors went to work on the four new Hilton hotels. When the last tile was set in the bathroom floors and the last towel folded away in the linen closets, it would be 1930 and despair would have settled over America. Hilton didn't know about that when he turned up a shovel of Texas earth four times in succession and waved his hand, signaling: "Go ahead."

He could have consulted the best financial brains in the country and they would have signaled the same "go ahead."

As the four structures rose floor by floor and local townspeople walked by in the cool of the evening to see how much progress had been made, Hilton was leap-frogging across Texas in search of more opportunities. He found a good one in El Paso, where the best site in town, right on the old plaza, was a mass of cinders and charred upholstery which were all that remained of a hotel. He decided what the site and El Paso needed was a Hilton hotel costing $1,800,000, more or less. He had incorporated now into Hilton Hotels, Inc., and lawyers were putting together some consolidation papers. It seemed silly to have twelve hotels under his care, with a thirteenth in project, and not have it all together in one neat corporate bundle. It was like having a herd of mixed cattle and not branding any of them.

Hilton expressed his earnest in the El Paso deal by signing a ninety-nine-year lease on the ground. He smiled wryly as he uncapped his pen. This was how all that shattering business in Dallas had begun. He prayed to himself that no such torments lay ahead of him in El Paso. He signed, he blotted, he handed over the papers.

And in just under three weeks some one twitched the rug out from under Wall Street. The twitch was felt from Maine to California, from the Canadian border to Mexico, and it did pass by Conrad Nicholson Hilton.

Almost a year after the November crash of 1929, the El Paso Hilton was opened. It was a spectacular opening at a spectacular if forbidding time. Hilton had managed by prudent care and cheese-paring to hold costs down below $1,700,000, a feat which delighted his investors. It was a lot of hotel, with nineteen floors and some rooftop suites. Later, much later, such dwellings in the sky would be called penthouses, an effete Eastern word, but in Texas in 1930 they were "exclusive suites on the roof."

But the depression moved in on Hilton as it did on every man of whatever economic station. He went over things with a collection of friends, examining his position with an unprejudiced mind. He wanted to know where he stood and he wanted sound advice. Bankers, too, sat in on these surgical meetings. Hilton did not invite them in to mollify them or calm their fears. He sincerely wanted the best financial advice he could get and his sincerity was mirrored in the considerate way in which all who took part in these meetings treated with him.

One thing was clear: a decision that had been an essential one when it took place was a saving one now. His leases on land were less involving than land purchase would have been. It became possible to reduce things down to where the payment of interest on obligations would keep him going.

He felt better. His bankers felt better. But, again, they were only men like any other men, and they could not foresee the grinding, twisting depression that had yet to reach its deplorable depths. Reservations were the first to decline. As they declined revenues withered. Hilton sped from hotel to hotel using every resource of his inventive mind to chink up leaks. Hotel holdings withered with revenues and, soon, any man who had any money, and there weren't many, could pick up hotel paper at fifteen cents on the dollar of investment. Here and there it became simply impossible for him even to meet interest charges. Here and there taxes became delinquent. In one swoop, a local telephone management removed the instruments from the rooms. It was a staggering blow to Hilton's pride. He shut off all the current he could short of making the hotels look like caves. He saved on heat, on light, on every extra in the book. On linens he refused to budge.

"A man has a right to a clean bed for his money," he said. "Try to get the laundries to cooperate."

J. B. Herndon Jr., a one-time banker and long a friend of Hilton's, was in the organization now and fighting tooth and nail to save his associate. Herndon placated creditors, begged for time, abased himself in as manly a way as he could, and staved off the wrecking crews.

Through it all Hilton doled out dimes and dollars where they would do the most good. He once had owed a hotel furnishing firm just over $100,000. By careful, painful payments he whittled until it was down to $178. The firm threatened suit. Hilton was indignant after his record of faithful if slow payment. No argument prevailed. They sued to collect.

"I think that was the most humiliating moment of my life," he recalls today. "It was total humiliation. It made me see the hopelessness of things. I had swung millions, created a hotel corporation, improved cities and towns, created employment, given civic pride to communities. But the serving of that suit for $178 crushed me. It was the first severe blow to my human dignity. I had never lied to or cheated a man in my life. It seemed a monstrous thing to do to me."

It was only the beginning, but nothing that followed was ever as lacerating to his pride. There came at heartbreaking last the day in which nothing availed. Hilton was swamped with debt and there was no way out. He had pledged his word, his dwindling assets and his insurance. If he could have pledged his clothing he would have done that. He was fighting for his good name. He had never done anything to injure that name. It was Thornton, in Dallas, who helped heal that sore.

"Your reputation as man of principle isn't at stake," he said. "Many a man has gone under because he couldn't help it. It's a bruising thing but not a killing thing. Your honor is not impugned, Connie. They just want their money."

"In my book, my honor is at stake," Hilton replied. "People invested money on my reputation. They will probably lose it. It shames me. This will all be different some day, Bob. I'll come back. I always have. But who would trust me with a dollar after this?"

"I would," said Thornton, rising. He put out his hand and took Hilton's firmly. "I would."

This simple, warm gesture made all that followed supportable. It was from Galveston that the final blow came. W. L. Moody and his son owned an insurance company to which Hilton owed a lot and could pay nothing. They foreclosed on the Hilton interests. They not only foreclosed but asked Hilton to come to Galveston and go over the debris with them. Hilton couldn't even raise the railroad fare.

A friend loaned Hilton the money and he went to Galveston to face the Moodys, father and son. It was a harrowing experience from which Hilton emerged with some triumph and a little money. The Moodys kept his hotels but gave him an operating contract over their National Hotels which were staggering along. He would be allowed to operate the Hilton hotels for the Moody account, too. Obviously, they believed Hilton was a great manager and a terrible owner.

"I was neither," he says. "I was a good manager and an honest owner. The depression gave me a licking. Without it, I could have saved probably ten years in my career. But it put iron in my soul and put me among the men instead of

61

among the boys. Those were whacking days in which you were a man of iron or you went all the way under and stayed there for keeps."

The Moodys put Hilton through the wringer. He couldn't buy a dozen sheets at a bankruptcy sale without justifying it to the Moodys in long, chilling arguments for which he had no heart at all. They sensed his discouragement over their way of business and sued to break the management contract they held over him. This was literally the last straw. Hilton flared up like an August haystack. He might be broke, which he was; he might be humiliated, which he was; he might be yelled at and browbeaten by the Moodys, but they would have a fight on their hands. He had kept to the letter of the contract. They had no right to humble him down to the ground. In plain, one-syllable talk he defied them to break the contract and filed a counter suit. The Moodys decided they did not want a protracted court fight. They gave way, and when the smoke cleared Hilton had all but two of his best hotels and $95,000 in cash with which to pull himself up financially.

He used the $95,000 to buy time. Time to breathe normally and not jump every time the phone rang or someone knocked at the door. He spread it around sagely and bought what he wanted. He got time to be his own man again. But not much. Not nearly enough.

It was 1933 and a barely discernible breath of promising wind was beginning to blow over the land. Smoke was coming faintly from chimneys which had long been cold. Machines began to hum. Some men went back to work. Men began slowly to edge out from New York and Chicago selling goods. The nation was showing some signs of life, but it was labored striving. Hilton felt the wind and took heart, only to receive another blow. The owner of the land on which the El Paso Hilton stood decided to seek legal recovery of what amounted to $30,000 in ground rental arrears. He took the hotel building and then dangled it over Hilton.

"You get me some money and I'll give the hotel back to you," he said.

"I'll get it," said Hilton. "You aren't going to keep my hotel or anything else I have built by sweat and work."

"Brave talk," said the man, glancing at the calendar. "Come back in exactly six weeks and we'll see how it stands up."

Hilton used up five weeks and three days looking for $30,000. He was fighting night and day to survive in business. Never again in life would he pass through such trials. He scarcely slept, he seldom ate except on the run. On the next day his searching was equally fruitless and he went to Dallas. There, with forty-eight hours to go, he found rescue. If their names are not up in gold on the lobby walls of the El Paso hotel it is because six people do not want them there, but Hilton will go to his grave eternally grateful to them. They put up the money. One was his mother. Whenever she had it, whenever she could, she put her faith in Connie Hilton.

This was the turn. It can truthfully be said that all that Hilton is today, all that he controls, was made possible by $30,000 put up by five men and a woman who never for a moment, in the blackest and most disheartening era our nation ever saw, lost their belief in him or for a single moment hesitated to make their confidence in his personal character tangible.

Slowly, almost invisibly, this $30,000 held back the flood. Little evidences of growing strength in the nation became an almost daily occurrence. But they were very little. In Hilton's case, it was a matter of fourteen guests one night instead of, say, twelve. A difference of six dollars in a hotel's revenues. Slowly he repaired his finances. He renegotiated in El Paso and with Loudermilk in Dallas. He paid his six saving graces back in six months, adding a 50 percent bonus as his evidence of real gratitude. They spread the word.

Bob Price of Dallas put it into words:

"I gave Connie $5,000 when it was his business life or

death. I got it back with a present of $2,500 extra in less than 180 days. No man can tell me that Hilton isn't all man and a credit risk sceond to none in Texas."

Hilton's troubles were not over, but they looked less harsh. Under the comforting embrace of 77(b), the Bankruptcy Act amendment which saved many a business man from fiscal drowning, he carefully and devotedly put some of the hotels back together. He lost some hotels and saved others. Some investors lost all they had put in, but many others got back everything, dollar for dollar, and would back him again today. They had trusted a man who wouldn't bankrupt, who wouldn't cheat and who wouldn't lie down and quit. No one will ever know what those years did to Hilton. You can't measure such things. Personal unhappiness was only part of the price. There are men in America today worth millions because they refused to quit when engulfed by the depression. Hilton is one of them. They refused to tarnish their honor or compromise their manhood.

Loan by loan, bank by bank, individual by individual, they all got paid. The investors who didn't are the ones who got out early in the battle for survival. Those who stuck by Hilton and saw him through reaped rewards for their patience and faith.

As despair turned to hope, Hilton did a little hotel trading just to justify his faith in himself. He was, actually, flexing his newly freed muscles for the move that would take him into international prominence as a hotel man. He bought the Paso del Norte at depression figures. It was in El Paso and a good hotel. He passed it on to W. L. Tooley, one of the six who had helped Hilton when things were most dire. He bought one or two others and traded back and forth. There was no longer any pressure on him. He had fun in these deals and they were more an exercise in free enterprise than an acquisition of means.

The deal in the Paso del Norte, which added nothing much

to his organization and involved only a small amount of cash, focused Hilton's mind on a residual factor of the depression: fine, well-built, established hotels could be bought for a fraction of their true value. Hotel stocks had not yet begun the climb back to normal position. Sometimes as little as ten cents on the dollar would bring hotel attorneys on the run, eager to complete a sale. And hotels throughout the country had built-in attorneys, the result of foreclosures and other financial blows.

Hilton took a long time to think it all out and arrived at the conclusion that if ever there was a chance for a man to become a hotelier on a national basis, this was it, an opportunity not likely to be repeated. Carefully, still nursing painful bruises, still wary of being suckered, he began looking around. However, it wasn't a search for a hotel that took him to one of the most delightful and beautiful cities in America. He needed to rest and heal his fiscal wounds. He decided that the salubrious climate of San Francisco offered the most of what he needed. Invigorating air, new surroundings and the hustle of city life, in the midst of which he could sit back undisturbed and plan the rest of his life, seemed a home-made prescription of the most sensible kind. He checked his hotels in Texas, found that the lobbies contained guests once more instead of process-serving sheriffs, put some money in his pocket and departed for San Francisco.

It was 1937 and for the first time in seven or eight years he wasn't on the run for something, toward something or away from something. That was a long time to be clubbed, and he couldn't remember a week in all that time in which Fate hadn't clubbed him. He settled down in the train and felt good. Really good. Already, before ten miles had been swept under the train's wheels, he felt better. He had never really run away from anything except, on cruel occasion, his own despair. But, he reflected, watching the Southwestern landscape rush by, no one could say he had ever run from obligation. That alone was enough to bolster his tired spirits. And as he crossed Texas to New Mexico and Arizona, on the way to his first rest in years, he remembered that felling moment when everything, including his own estimation of honor, had seemed gone and Bob Thornton said, shaking his hand, "I would trust you." He fell asleep to the rhythmic clatter of the train wheels and the clean feeling of a battered but uncompromised soul.

CHAPTER FOUR

HE arrived in San Francisco on one of those days which only the well-worn words describe. It was wine-like, crisp, the air was invigorating and the sun paved every surface with that especial gold which is the hallmark of Northern California. To the South the sun is hotter and more brassy in color. The sun of Southern California is essentially a desert sun, but from San Francisco northward it is a stimulating, inviting and medicinal sun, calming to nerves, clearing the vision and giving the skin a tone. He breathed deeply and determined to do nothing at all until all of the kinks were out of his system.

He took walks through San Francisco's inviting streets, paused to admire the flower sellers on the corners, noted that people went about purposefully and, for the most part, with smiles on their faces. He fell in love with San Francisco.

By force of habit, Hilton studied the hotels. He made mental notes of the human traffic in and out of their doors. He noted the kind of traffic. Which hotel drew the best-dressed trade, which attracted the most cabs, which had the most private cars driving up and away. The one that drew his greatest interest was the Sir Francis Drake. It was imposing. It reached up more than twenty stories, had a clean façade and looked like real money. He didn't have to come to San Francisco to know that it had housed great names and had famous public rooms. It went without saying that it had a distinguished cuisine. No hotel of any stature could exist in San Francisco without having a splendid kitchen turning out viands instead of meals. San Franciscans were picky about cooking. They had dozens of renowned restaurants to choose from and no hotel could offer less and hope to keep its dining room alive.

He stalked the Sir Francis Drake. He was like a man who owned a Chevrolet but longed for a Cadillac and had reasonable information that the Cadillac dealer would, because of slack business, listen to a sales suggestion.

He completed stalking the hotel after getting all of the information he could get short of walking in and asking for it. He felt that this would be a foolhardy operation, inviting upon himself a hornswoggling and a trimming. He took his time, he pieced together bits of gossip, he added up figures and when he was ready for direct action he had an almost complete picture of the situation. The most obvious fact was that the creditors were weary and impatient and the hotel was festooned with debts of all shapes and sizes and kinds. Debt hung on the hotel like Spanish moss.

Hilton waited and nothing happened. It was by now known that he was in town yet no one had approached him. This puzzled him. By all of the rules, the managing arm of the hotel should have come to him hat in hand. Finally, in the late fall, he grew as weary as the creditors. The way to buy something, he reasoned, was to buy it. Besides which, he had enough information now to protect him against a rooking. He made the first overture and was almost knocked over in the rush.

They almost gave it to him. They handed him, in fear lest they lose him, a hotel worth more than $4,000,000 for less than $300,000. Of course, it would have a mortgage of $1,500,000 on it, but for less than the worth of one of its entertainment rooms alone, he could have his first big city hotel. He kept the long distance and Western Union wires smoking with calls and wires back to Texas. It was no trick at all to put together a $300,000 syndicate into which, as always, his own personal cash went first. He decided on twenty-five percent as his piece and had $75,000 transferred

68

to his account in San Francisco. When it was all wrapped up early in 1938 he had $25,000 with which to turn around in at the Sir Francis Drake, a paid up leg of $275,000 on the hotel and an extremely painless mortgage of $1,500,000 asking less than four percent for sustenance. Some idea of how far $275,000 in cash went in those days may be drawn from this: he liquidated a $500,000 second mortgage for $75,000. For $50,000 he got better than $1,800,000 in common stock. The remainder paid for equally large obligations against the hotel.

It was a giddy ride at a giddy time in the nation's financial affairs. He took the remaining $25,000 and set about his habitual task of reducing waste space and converting it into income-producing space. Shops and sales counters and lobby shadow boxes. The bar was redecorated, the Persian Room made more inviting. Money began to come indoors and much of it found its way into the till.

Once the carpenters had departed and the paint was dry, Hilton sat back and matched receipts against obligations. It was all right. They matched up and left some over for the investors. That was all any one could ask of a hotel or even a fruit stand. That for every dollar it was in hock at least $1.10 be coming in. Preferably $1.25, but $1.10 was the difference between sagacious management and stupid operation.

And now Hilton turned his eyes to home country. It probably was Herndon who helped direct the Hilton gaze to Albuquerque. It was his home town and he wanted the Herndon impress back on it. Hilton wanted to put Hilton back into Albuquerque, too. Neither had to convince the other. They moved in and looked around. They found a site, had a year of haggling before ironing out some homemade difficulties, and ended with the Albuquerque Hilton, a brand new hotel on a site leased for forty years, a hotel designed indigenously and a credit to the city. Since nothing except fortune has ever happened to it, it has no dramatic interest. It was built with a minimum of struggle, has never had a day's financial strain and top executives of the Hilton operation call it "school." They started there as eager youngsters and were able to learn quickly and they moved up fast. Hilton has an abiding affection for it. He loves it as the hotel that has given him the least concern. After all he went through, a pain-free hotel was certain to be a beloved one.

It is. And it reflects his contentment with it in every facet. It is a gleaming house.

It has been mentioned that one of Hilton's ground rules in operating a hotel is to make the staff part of the team. He learned it early in small Texas hotels. He realized that none of his management ideas would work perfectly in terms of guest comfort and management profit unless the entire staff from top to bottom went along with the boss in everything he thought and wanted. It began when he purchased his first hotel, the Mobley. He called the staff in, introduced himself, described what he planned to do and how he planned to do it and made it plain that he welcomed suggestions and hoped for cooperation. He made every man and woman on the payroll feel a personal allegiance to the operation and it is factual to say that Hilton hotels have always operated with a minimum of labor trouble.

"You can't have five hundred or more employees circulating through a large hotel with personal grievances and real or fancied troubles," he says, "without communicating this unhappy spirit to the guests. There has been a lot of folk poetry and pep speeches written around The Man With A Smile, and some people hold that we in America overdo this facet in human relations, but the way I see it a willing, contented staff is probably the best advertisement a hotel has. A sullen bellboy or a grumbling linen maid, and most certainly a flippant clerk, can undo more in a few minutes than a year of careful management can accomplish."

When economic pressures mounted upon him until he was

bent almost double under their weight, he learned vividly the rewards of strongly established employee relations. Men and women in even the humblest jobs came to him and offered to work without pay until things were better for him. There were times when meeting the payrolls in full was almost an impossibility but in each of the depressed houses under his management he insisted on the blackest days that the staff salaries be paid to some extent and, in the lower salary brackets, he ordered managers to pay in full—even if the manager had to wait or do without.

"You fellows earning the top money will just have to stand still until the floor maids and bus boys are paid," he said. "You can sit it out a few weeks. They can't."

To this day his eyes moisten when he recalls one deed of generosity that took place in the bleakest, most hopeless days of his struggle to save something of what he had fought so hard to create. Only two men knew about it until Hilton told it to the Moodys in Galveston when they foreclosed on him but gave him hotels of their own to manage—with a $500 advance on his salary. They had no sooner pushed the money across the conference desk than Hilton sprang up and started to leave.

"Reckon we ought to talk things out," growled the younger Moody, a man of frosty attitudes and relentless business judgment.

"Plenty of time for that," Hilton replied. "We'll have a mort of talk before we're through with each other. But I'm going back to Dallas right now and level out with two people I am most beholden to."

"Creditors, I suppose," said young Moody mockingly.

"These people," said Connie, "have a lien—on my heart."

"That's one thing I never thought about much," Moody acknowledged.

"I have," said Hilton, firmly. "One of them is my mother, who stood behind me all the way with all she had in affection

71

and resources. The other one is a lad named Eddie Fowler. You wouldn't know him. He's a bellhop at the Dallas Hilton. On the day when things reached their bottom he walked alone into my office and put $300 into my hand. He didn't ask for paper or a signature or even a handshake. 'Just eating money, Mr. Hilton,' is all he said. I'll never forget Eddie Fowler as long as I live—and I'll never rest until I pay him. He gets the first $300 out of this $500."

Hilton walked out of the Moody office leaving a dead silence behind him.

On two other occasions Hilton had an opportunity to make evident and public his point of view toward those who worked for him. He had bought, renovated and put together a ram-shackle eyesore of a hotel in Long Beach, California, evicted squadrons of pigeons, shored up the building, painted it, and ripped out an old attic to make a top floor lounge with a view of the sea. Friends had pleaded with him to keep away from the derelict, but he was fascinated by the rehabilitation possi-bilities it offered. He got it for almost nothing and, in the end, the cocktail lounge alone was netting $200,000 a year. Or almost a dollar for every pigeon he rooted out of the tilted old barn. Just when it was all coming to a head and he had hopes of at least getting his plumbing and painting expenses back, the unions struck the place.

It was settled in exactly one hour. Hilton asked the union officers to meet with him and they agreed. When all had as-sembled he stood up before them and made a short speech.

"Gentlemen," he said, "I don't believe any man ever strikes unless he feels convinced he has been mistreated. It is a seri-ous thing to strike. It hurts both management and labor. Even with increased wages won by a strike it often takes months merely to regain wages lost during a strike period. My books and my problems are open to you. I want you to examine my position and acquaint yourselves with it. I want to examine your position and acquaint myself with it. It is entirely possible that we are both right. Let us get together like honest men and work this out based on the needs of both sides."

Both sides studied the conditions involved and the strike ended, with fairness to all, before it actually got underway.

Eventually, Hilton decided to sell the Sir Francis Drake as a result of a disagreement with the Hotel Employers Association, and sold it to a San Francisco syndicate at a profit of several hundred thousand dollars.

A dozen gaudy propositions were put before Hilton but he evaded a lancing and began, instead, to buy up hotel stocks at an average of a dime on the dollar. Finally, to escape panting opportunists, he fled to El Paso to visit old friends. He scarcely had unpacked his luggage when he received a telephone call from A. S. Kirkeby in Chicago.

"Connie," he said, "I have come upon a pretty little thing in New York, but I can't swing it alone. It might interest you. Grab a plane and look it over for the two of us."

He named a hotel in New York. It didn't interest Hilton to any extent, but anything that Kirkeby considered of value might conceivably be of value. Hilton flew to New York, studied the hotel inside and out during the latter part of December, 1941 (the Japanese had attacked Pearl Harbor on the 7th of that month), and arrived at the conclusion that this hotel was not for him. He took a train to Chicago, met Kirkeby, and launched into a detailed recital of why he, Hilton, wouldn't go along on this hotel.

When he had finished, Kirkeby looked out of the window and across the buildings of Chicago. Finally, he took a deep breath and turned back to Hilton.

"I'll sell you the Town House," he said bluntly.

Hilton can assume the blankest expression known to man when he wants to do so, and this time it was blanker than usual. He determined to show nothing to Kirkeby on his face, but inside his emotions were spinning.

"Well, what about it?" Kirkeby cried.

73

"What about it?" Hilton demanded.

"I'll sell it to you, is what."

"I heard you," said Hilton, and left Kirkeby with nothing to go on.

It was—and is—one of Los Angeles' most beautiful hotels. It cost a mint to build and had an exclusive reputation. If you were of California society the Town House was your Los Angeles residence. It took money to live there and sometimes just money wasn't enough. The management was choosy about its clientele. There are wealthy movie stars, for example, who can tell you that attempts to register there were politely but definitely discouraged.

It took Hilton exactly an hour after he arrived in Los Angeles to discover what was biting Kirkeby. The Town House, thanks to war panic on the West Coast, was virtually empty. He wandered through its lush gardens, its polished corridors and by its turquoise swimming pool without encountering anybody except a stray gardener (non-Japanese by that time) or a lonely looking bellboy.

Hilton drove to a home he had purchased in Bel Air, alongside Beverly Hills, and shut himself up in the library. He did for the next few hours what pitifully few Americans, and more especially Los Angeles Americans, had the wit to do: he thought out as best he could the war problem to the total of its probabilities. He arrived at a conviction that it just wasn't possible for the Japanese to land troops in mass on the West Coast. The enormous problems of distance and logistics just didn't put that possibility in the cards. He figured that the war would be long and heart-breaking but that not a belligerent shot would be fired on California soil. He was partly wrong. Two shots were fired from a submarine up the coast beyond Santa Barbara. For the rest of it, he was right. And then, ruefully, he implemented his thinking by the realization that if the Japanese did invade California, no one would have anything anyway. Conquerors are not moved or touched by the investment of hoteliers. Their usual course is merely to move in and the management can lump it.

He advised Kirkeby, who was in Chicago, that if the price was right Hilton might consider buying the Town House. He didn't care much either way. This was the old-fashioned country store trading technique at work again.

"You wouldn't want the deal I'd offer in today's uncertain conditions," he said quietly. "I'm just making my manners by calling you. It's touch and go out here and I'm not burning up to make a deal. Thanks, anyway."

"Hold on, hold on," Kirkeby cried into the telephone. "We might get together. Why don't you name a figure? Just something for me to chew on."

"I think not," said Hilton. "It's a big risk. My friends think I'm crazy even to talk to you."

"Just say a figure, Connie," Kirkeby persisted. "Just say some numbers."

"Seven and a half," said Hilton idly, and in his mind was a clear picture of that three million dollar jewel box, a true gem of hotel building and prestige.

There was a long silence on the Chicago end of the wire.

"Nine and a quarter," said Kirkeby. "I'm a mood to be robbed today."

"See what I mean," said Hilton. "We're miles apart. You're not being realistic. People are scared stiff out here. Leaving on every train in sight. I'd be insane to buy a mess of empty concrete."

"Nine," said Kirkeby.

"Eight," said Hilton.

"And a half," said Kirkeby, adding hastily, "But cash."

"Deal," said Hilton. "I'll mail you my binding check for one and a quarter."

Thus, although they didn't know it and would have foamed at the mouth if they had, San Franciscans helped enormously to finance Hilton's purchase of the Town House. He took

$125,000 from the half a million dollars they had paid him to give back the Sir Francis Drake. He began telephoning the boys and girls in Texas and they came through with sixty percent of the money in a syndicate arrangement. The remainder was Hilton's own money. The syndicate gave him $40,000 to go about his habitual job of changing things. This time it is acknowledged that his psi factor worked. He foretold the change that would come to Southern California. When the last dab of improvement had been completed we were gaining our first victories in the Pacific. The war receded from California to distant atolls and palmed islands. People began rushing back to the Golden Desert. Kirkeby's books show that the Town House had an operating profit in 1941. It was a wan $33,401. Hilton's books show $201,000 for 1942 and it has topped a quarter of a million dollars ever since. The jewel box on Wilshire Boulevard may have looked empty when he bought it, but it wasn't.

Deals like that become known in hotel circles the way a rumor of mumps becomes known in a kids' summer camp. The telephone began ringing with every Tom, Dick and Harry in Christendom trying to foist a house on Hilton. He was busier saying "No," than he was putting the Town House deal away for keeps. But, one noontime, two gentlemen from Mexico came to see him in person.

Luis and Julio Laguette came from sturdy and distinguished Mexican stock. They were true *caballeros*, proud of their heritage and their name. They wished to discuss "un punto with Senor Hilton": would he operate for the family a new hotel rising on ancestral ground in Chihuahua? He replied in Spanish that he might, which left the visitors so delighted that recess was called for a three-hour lunch. Before the lunch was ended, Hilton's Spanish had improved and the Laguette delight in the entire proceeding had risen to joyous heights. Hilton, they decided, was *muy simpatico*. He was, indeed, and he rejoiced in this chance to effect his first international deal.

76

It was a Laguette inspiration to call the hotel the Palacio Hilton. It was a Hilton inspiration to insure full occupancy and consequently profit by setting up bus tours to Chihuahua from El Paso on an all-expense basis, the cost of a ticket covering transportation, native food, a tinkling native orchestra and a guided walk through the colorful sections of Chihuahua.

Hilton organized a leasing arrangement at the Palacio Hilton, with land and building remaining in the Laguette family possession. By this time he knew leasing arrangements inside out and North to South. It provided for compensation on both sides.

"It was my first cross-the-border deal," he says. "It was the beginning of a dream to manage or build hotels in other countries. There is an old and impressively wise saying in geopolitics: if business does not cross frontiers, armies will. I hold with the most sincere conviction that hotels are the best insurance of good neighborliness and warm international relations. Currencies interchange, people interchange, points of view are swapped. It is a good thing. The Bible has it one way: Love thy neighbor. Modern life has it in different words but much the same meaning: Know thy neighbor. You can never hate a man you know. We have never been told to beat our swords into hotels, but it is a good idea."

By this time his old friend Drown had a bright, energetic son working in the combination. Joe Drown, a personable, intelligent man, was in California and scouting for Hilton. Meanwhile, Hilton, on his own, picked up a Los Angeles hotel worth about $3,000,000 for exactly $400,000 and just at the right time: the government tagged it as a fine place for troops to stay in while moving about from one war zone to another. Hilton estimates that during the war period it profited—because of one hundred percent occupancy, not because of excessive charges—by close to $1,000 a day, day in and day out. Joe Drown came in from a Nevada trip about that time and asked for $35,000 to buy a hotel in Las Vegas. Hilton

77

didn't quibble or question. He didn't go over the books or even look at the building. The El Rancho Vegas was a pig in the poke as far as Hilton was concerned and he never did like it. He gave Joe the money and the deal was made. The casino figures embarrassed him; he didn't cotton to legal gambling in the United States. At the end of fifteen months, they received an offer for the hotel, and he was neither elated or surprised when Joe came in with the closing papers and calmly announced they had racked up another million dollar profit.

Hilton still had personal ambitions to invade New York, but believed that the move should be made in two steps. California to Chicago and then Chicago to New York. Conditions created by the war upset his systematic approach to New York. The fact is that he bought two New York hotels before doubling back to Chicago. By this time his fame as a hotel trader had swept the country and it became difficult for him to make his business moves without detection. Nonetheless, following a careful plan of approach, he began buying hotel bonds for his own account. He found a block of Stevens Hotel bonds at 25 cents on the dollar and bought up almost half a million dollars worth of the securities. He looked at New York, found that the Waldorf-Astoria bonds were lying still at 4½. Thus, although this is the first time it has become known, he had two swings at the Waldorf. His first haymaker was the acquisition of $500,000 worth of its bonds at the low figure. Later, a long time later, he would buy the gigantic hotel itself, but not until he had sold the bonds he bought at 4½ for 85, thus quelling for all time a Wall Street opinion that he sometimes didn't think straight. Brokers hooted when it was rumored in the financial district that the "Western high-roller was bagging up those no good Waldorf bonds." It is not on record that Hilton hooted when he sold them at a profit of 80½ points on the dollar. He is not by nature a man who hoots or crows, but he owns to a human delight in prov-

78

ing himself sometimes smarter than the so-called smart money. While buying up Waldorf securities he also purchased the round side of $1,000,000 in Sherry-Netherlands bonds at 25 and, amazingly for a bargain hunter, put down enough cash to acquire Savoy-Plaza bonds at 60 to the tune of $160,000.

While brokers chuckled about "that jasper from Texas," Hilton harvested bonds. His zeal for buying hotel bonds was genuine, but it was also a cover for a little hotel-buying stunt he put together all by himself. He didn't fiddle while financiers giggled. Instead, late in the afternoon of March 31, 1943, he leased the Roosevelt Hotel in Manhattan's midtown and lacked only a few hours of being able to say to Wall Street: "April Fool!"

Six months later, he bought the lovely Plaza, itself a jewel box as authentic in its social claims and traditions as the Town House. Even more authentic because it represented generations of Eastern society and entrenched wealth. He bought it for $7,400,000 in October, 1943, and sold it for $15,000,000 in October, 1953, a profit of $750,000 a year for ten neat years.

These purchases stimulated the entire hotel securities market, and it may be said that he more than any one else provided the adrenalin which invigorated hotel finance.

"It is completely fair to credit Connie Hilton with teaching us all a thing or two," a famed broker said recently. "His faith in hotel securities and hotels themselves, his wise, tasteful operation of them, his devotion to them, all combined to give the financial world a new and respectful point of view toward hotel business. We all smiled broadly when he came East and he took the smiles right off our faces in less than a year. People sometimes are inclined to call Hilton a lucky man, and that's ridiculous. He learned his business the hard way, he slaved for it, built it painstakingly and honestly. You can't made deals like the Plaza deal or the Waldorf deal by sitting in the sun and waiting for luck to tap you. You get in there and hustle and plan and beat your brains out. Some of us thought he was a knucklehead. I know one of the real knuckleheads now—every time I look in the mirror. We're worse than a small town here in New York, more provincial. We get delusions of superiority just because we are the financial center of creation. It's healthy for a stranger to come along every now and then and cut us down to size."

Hilton was in no mood to hew anything down to size when he bought the Plaza. He only felt humbled and hoped desperately that he could dovetail his personal plans for it and the militant attitude of a lot of solid, important New Yorkers who were determined that he would not alter a venerated inch of it.

Mainly, he cleaned it. Beautiful old wood was covered by years of New York grime. Exquisite bronze fixtures worthy of a museum were dingy. Storage space in the cellar was collecting only cobwebs. A broker paying $100 a week on the lobby floor was put on the second floor and his vacated office turned back to that most mellow and inviting of New York bars, the Oak Room. He spent no less than $600,000 cleaning and refurbishing the Plaza. The basement space became the Rendezvous Room, earning $200,000 a year. The Oak Room grosses about $200,000 a year. He kept the early decor of the lobby floor, brought a gleam to the beautiful bronze lamps. The floors began to shine. Worried lest these improvements harrow the old residents, he kept within eyeshot of the elevators and watched their faces carefully as they emerged and saw what was happening. No one complained and, when it was all done, they came to him and told him they were proud of what he had done for the Plaza. He would rather have heard that than make a million dollars.

As he bought larger and more important hotels he became, willy-nilly, something he never had thought about to any extent. He became the biggest employer of dance bands and floor show artists in the world. The Plaza had a supper room, the Roosevelt had had Guy Lombardo since, as one Manhattan wag put it, "they trucked up the first load of steel." He met with his managers and decided on a course of action: he would continue these entertainments in the quality already established and, if that quality wasn't enough, he would improve it. When he bought the Waldorf, the Wedgwood Room and the Starlight Room were part of the house. So was a luncheon and dinner room in which a Hungarian band leader had held sway since the beginning. He disturbed nothing except the lobby, which had begun to attract a large group which treated it as a private club, spent nothing and passed entire days wearing out the upholstery and reading newspapers. This gave him some annoyance. He believed that any hotel has to extend a certain amount of fee-less hospitality. It keeps the lobby alive and is good advertising as well as good will.

But the same profitless faces used the Waldorf lobby daily, drifting in around nine in the morning and sitting there until after six o'clock at night. They brought their own newspapers and magazines and when lunchtime came they scuttled out for a quick, cheap meal somewhere on Lexington Avenue and then rushed back to claim a chair or couch.

It took Hilton some time to arrive at a way to dislodge the Haunt Club. When the idea finally presented itself, it was perfect. He didn't want to create a situation or embarrass the most persistent free loader. He felt it a violation of the tone of the house for an assistant manager to question the squatters. Dining alone one night he suddenly remembered the phrase: Peacock Alley.

Peacock Alley was and is a New York institution. It had been one of the virtues of the old Waldorf at Fifth Avenue and 34th Street. It was where ladies and gentlemen met in the late afternoon or early evening. If you did not meet your lady in Peacock Alley you were not of the purple. When the new Waldorf was built on Park Avenue, making it possible to tear down the old house to provide ground for the Empire State Building, Peacock Alley was recreated at the new stand. Hilton loved all that Peacock Alley stood for.

As the words entered his mind, he went down to the lobby and walked through Peacock Alley. No doubt about it, it needed refurbishing. Ladies and gentlemen sat at its tables and on its couches. They were happy people. Hilton said to himself that they deserved a redecorating job. Yes, sir, that would do it.

He called in the house carpenter and painter and outlined his plan.

"Put up a partition at the entrance to Peacock Alley," he said. "Install a service bar across it, make the back bar attractive and in the decor of the Alley. Give it a permanent look. I don't want any jerry look. Then we'll move all of the chairs and sofas out of the lobby and put luncheon tables there. Luncheon and dinner. When the bar niche is ready and service is available for the tables, we'll tear out Peacock Alley from stem to stern and redo it."

That did it. The Haunt Club had no choice but to take its loafing to the streets or to another hotel. The old expanse of comfortable divans and embracing, deep chairs vanished. Spotless linen on cozy little tables took its place. Peacock Alley got a face-lift, its bar service was never interrupted and habitues of the Alley, ladies and gentlemen who paid their tabs, were charmed with the lunching and dining out in the lobby. When the redecoration of Peacock Alley was finished, the paying guests moved back to it without disturbance and the lobby staff had a fresh start. It is easier to prevent the formation of a squatter colony than it is to expel an organized colony, in situ.

Another revered fixture of the Waldorf which Hilton did not touch in any way was the Men's bar, one of the preciously few public places left in New York where men can congregate without women. The Men's Bar had always had a clientele of substantial men. Substantial in income, substantial socially, substantial in appetite. The bar has always served cocktails in oversize glasses, glasses fit for a man's hand to clasp, and offers generous meals served at sturdy wooden tables with leather upholstered chairs. The famed sculptures of the Bull and the Bear, symbols of Wall Street, stand on the plain, masculine, austere back bar.

"I didn't come to New York to blow it up," Hilton says. "I believe in tradition. I believe in preserving it. I once built a hotel in Albuquerque and the first thing I said to the architect was that I wanted it to stand for the Southwest: in line, color and material. I visioned mellow sand-colored walls, red tile floors, polished smooth, native woods and tile roofs. That is the tradition of the area. The traditions in great New York hotels are something to be guarded and nurtured. It is a difficult thing to give a large hotel personality. If it has it when you buy it it would be foolish to disturb it."

The only major disturbance he created was in his trading. He bought the Plaza, as said, for $7,400,000. The cash consideration was $600,000 which was used to buy up both the common and preferred stocks as well as accomplish the retirement of $3,992,500 in notes. The remaining sum, roughly $7,000,000, was in a first mortgage. Hilton not only arranged a lower rate of interest but was granted a comfortable extension. It was no generous whim or scapegrace attitude toward money which brought him these benefits. It was simply that the mortgage holder had infinite faith and trust in him as the result of his credit record and his management of hotels. He had never, for example, taken a hotel over that it didn't show an immediate upswing in revenues.

"I was right, back there in the early, pressuring Texas days," he said, "when I was concerned for my honor and my credit. I was right to refuse to go into bankruptcy. Those things follow a man through life. The fight that any man puts up to preserve his credit is reflected later in trust of him. It doesn't matter if he was beaten to the floor, so long as he got up off it, paid what he owed and started again. It is the basis of credit. It would have been easy in Texas to go into bankruptcy—and hard ever again to get the credit I needed."

But he got the credit in enormous quantities and he preserved traditions. He also proved once again that his methods of operating hotels must have a common sense foundation. The Plaza, which had been occupied at about 60 percent of capacity, almost immediately became a house filled nightly, a house with only rarely a vacant room. This was done without flashy advertising or reductions in rates. Indeed, some suite rates went up. Whatever it is that Hilton brings to operation of a hotel, however it may be defined, it is now axiomatic that that house will begin earning as it never earned before.

Hilton was now putting into operation another of his inventions calculated to make acquisition and management of new hotels about as foolproof as human ingenuity can arrange. He would take the improved securities of the established hotels in his organization and apply them in the financing of a new hotel. This was like giving blood transfusion from strong sources. The Rosslyn and the Town House, for example, found their strengthened values acting together. They were purchased by the Plaza. The purpose of having the Plaza Operating Company purchase the Town House and the Rosslyn was to utilize the advantage of the Plaza's tax base. It had a very substantial invested capital and, therefore, had to earn a great deal of money before it was subject to excess profits tax. This, it was not doing. On the other hand, the Rosslyn and the Town House were earning a great deal of money and did not have the tax base and were subject to excess profits tax. By having the Plaza acquire these two properties, they could be paid for virtually out of the tax saving.

Later, when he would acquire the Palmer House in Chicago, another socially acceptable hotel, the methods he used at the Plaza would obtain. Act in good taste, move slowly, do nothing that isn't for the better—and observe tradition.

While all this New York activity was in fullest swing, Hilton clung to the hope of a Chicago hotel, preferably the Stevens because he had $500,000 of its bonds in his vault. The year before, in 1942, the Army had put a full stop to any dreaming about the Stevens. Under war-time rights it took the vast hotel, the largest inn structure in the world, and used it to house recruits destined for the Air Force. First mortgage bonds were retired at par, thanks to government money, and Hilton had profits on his purchases rather than an objective dream. He received word that the trustees of the Stevens wanted to sell the controlling corporation of the hotel with the multiple obligations against it. This interested Hilton for only one reason: if the armed services ever moved out and restored the hotel to civilian life, ownership of its corporate structure would allow him to be the first to get his foot in the door when full purchase time came. It was a complex maneuver, filled with corporate ifs, ands and buts and it was no happy day for Hilton when the trustees elected to ask for sealed bids. He didn't like sealed bids. Few men do. It is blind bidding instead of open trading and the best man often is euchered out of the picture by a man with a sharper pencil.

He pocketed his resentment and put in a bid for $180,000. The next closest to him was $179,800. By the sliver-thin margin of $200 he became owner of the corporation. It didn't mean a great deal and guaranteed him nothing as to eventual ownership of the hotel. It only gave him corporate ownership. But inside a year by collecting this and that delinquency and patching this and that tax and by eventually selling out the corporate ownership, he emerged with $2,000,000 profit from a less than $200,000 investment.

The corporation had a remarkable tax base with a very substantial loss carry-over. Recoveries on this proved to be advantageous to Hilton and his associates when the tax case was finally disposed of. Recoveries on refunds of real estate taxes and other contingent assets more than paid for the purchase price of the stock of Stevens Hotel Corporation.

Late in 1943, some three or four months after Hilton's profits on the Stevens became a reality, the government decided to move out, pay up and let the best man in sight get the Stevens for private operation. Hilton looked the physical plant over and decided not even to make a stab at purchase.

"Let's bide our time," he told associates. "It will come."

Today he believes that in the main he was right.

"I can't tell you how much it would have cost to rehabilitate. Manpower was at the bottom of the barrel. Labor was high, materials were high and in short supply. It would have been back-breaking to polish the old girl up again."

Stephen A. Healy, a wealthy contractor, came out of nowhere and bought the Stevens. He was indubitably the right man. He had a unique call on construction labor. He knew the materials market. He paid the whopping sum of $5,531,000 in cash for the titan.

It was a fantastic moment. Gravel diggers and steamshovel operators, sand trenchers and concrete mixers all pitched in for Our Boy. They not only patched plaster and dried up leaking pipes, but they waxed floors, washed windows and hung curtains. They made beds and swept halls.

"No one but Healy could have done it," Hilton says. "He had Chicago heavy labor in the palm of his hand. They loved him. They would do anything for him. Literally, not another man in Chicago could have rounded up such a force, or got so much done for so little. I know I am accurate when I say that a two million dollar job—at the least—was done for under one million."

When the job was done and the abused Stevens was once more a shining example of a modern hotel, Hilton guessed wrong for one of the few times in his life.

"It was my guess that Healy would get bored when it became a simple hotel operation," Hilton says. "It was an utterly alien job for him. He had shown Chicago, he had had his laugh at the crepe-hangers. I figured him ready to talk turkey. He wouldn't talk anything. He had learned to love running a hotel. I was the last man in the world who could fight him for that. I loved it myself. But I kept going back to him and I kept getting the brush-off. I let him know candidly that I wanted it. Mistake or not, I was frank about the whole deal. Maybe this stiffened him up, but I don't know. All I know is that he was stubborn."

At long, wearing last Healy gave in one day—he asked for a $500,000 profit. Connie jumped at it. They arranged to close the deal the next day and the next day Healy vanished. When he bobbed up again the price rose to $650,000 above purchase. Hilton kept accepting and Healy kept upping the figure. It drove Hilton nigh mad. Meanwhile, he was quartering at the Palmer House and studying every nail and wash-cloth in it. He decided to let Healy cool for awhile and see what indifference would do to the contractor.

He used the waiting time to arrive at a figure on the Palmer House—if it was for sale. Meanwhile, he let it be known in circles close to Healy that he, Hilton, no longer wanted the Stevens. He wanted the more distinguished hotel. It must have taken all of three minutes for this information to reach Healy and startle him. In four minutes it undoubtedly reached Henry L. Hollis, a gentleman eighty years old, a man of severest rectitude and a man who would not, if he could avoid it, waste five words on any other man whose rectitude was in even the slightest shadow. Hollis was the trustee of the Palmer estate.

Hilton went to call on Hollis and asked forthrightly if the Palmer House was for sale. Hollis replied that it neither was nor wasn't. Hilton interpreted this to mean that they would not throw him into Lake Michigan if he mentioned a figure, but neither would they spend a five-cent phone call to solicit his bid. He knew when he had met solid rock. He decided to be a supplicant. A well-heeled supplicant, to be sure, but nonetheless a man coming to them. He went down and said: "I offer $18,500,000, subject to examination of the books and obligations."

Hollis looked at him as though he were a strange sort of bug.

"Mr. Hilton," he said, "we are not without information on our own account. You are in a deal for the Stevens. The Stevens is opposition. You are in gravest error if you think we will submit our books to a competitive examination. Good day to you, sir."

When a man like Hollis says good day to you, sir, you have had it. That is it. You go. Hilton went. But before he went he said as simply as possible that the way things looked he never would get the Stevens. Hollis bowed silently and politely and waited for Hilton to take himself away.

Two days later Healy sent a friend to see Hilton and offered to sell the Stevens once and for all at $1,500,000 above what he had in it. Hilton scoffed. He had dealt with Healy before and said that he had as soon deal with a Mexican jumping bean.

The friend argued. He said that he didn't blame Hilton, that Healy had been less than steady in his dealings with Hilton.

"But he means it this time," the friend said. "He won't add another penny."

"Bring it to me in writing," said Hilton. A day later, it was all in writing. Hilton bought the Stevens at the price set by Healy.

It took several days, during which Hilton was up to his neck in arrangements, before the Stevens deal was all squared away. Hilton took a room in the vast hotel and lay down to relax. Suddenly he jumped up. He had told Hollis that the way things looked he never would get the Stevens. Now only a few days later he had it. He had no stomach for the impression this must have made on a man of Hollis' character. As a jealous guardian of his own character, Hilton felt compelled to move fast. He might never get the Palmer House but he could not rest until he had explained things to Hollis.

He dressed and hurried to Hollis' office. He counted it some sort of gain that he was received. It wasn't a cordial reception. A sensitive man would have felt a distinct frost. Hilton is sensitive. He plunged at his unhappy duty.

"Sir," he said, "I came to make an explanation and—"

"It is unnecessary," said Hollis. It was the iciest kind of dismissal. It stung Hilton.

"Nonetheless, I will make it," he cried with passion. "I had opened a negotiation with Healy. I had an ethical commitment to see it through. He behaved in an unorthodox manner. He made the delay, not I. When I told you it looked as though I would never get the Stevens, that is exactly how it looked. I did not color one syllable of that. I did not reopen negotiations with Healy. He sent for me. I felt a duty to complete or reject a transaction I had myself initiated. That is it. In full."

"That's plain enough," said Hollis. "Thank you for making me understand it."

It was evident in his tone that he had never expected to understand it at all. Nor particularly wished to.

"Is the Palmer House still open for an offer?" Hilton asked.

"I think so," said Hollis. "But the figure would have to be changed. I remind you that by your own explanation the situation has changed. Are you ready to make a new offer?"

Hilton looked across the polished desk at an aged man of firm mind, impeccable manners and utterly devoid of nonsense.

"I offer $19,385,000," he said simply.

"That testifies that you grasp the situation," said Hollis, "and have worked it out carefully." He studied the desk top for a few seconds and looked back up at Hilton.

"It's a just figure," he said quietly, "I accept," and put out his hand.

Within the compass of a few days Hilton had acquired the world's largest hotel structure and also had acquired one of the most distinguished. For the first time in seventy-five years the Palmer House had moved out of control of the Palmer family. It was an event and, for Hilton, it was also a bargain. Any finance house in the Middle West would have put at least $35,000,000 and perhaps as much as $42,000,000 of valuation on the property. The land value by itself was in the neighborhood of $20,000,000.

These figures are fancy and formidable, but they are not what Conrad Hilton particularly remembers about the entire transaction. What he recalls fondly and with emotion is the character of Hollis.

"He put his hand across the desk and shook mine," says Hilton. "He never picked up a pen or reached for a piece of paper. In less than a week he had other offers for the Palmer House, at least one of which topped me by a million dollars. He declined them calmly and without discussion. He had shaken my hand, his word was pledged. That was it. He was a great gentleman."

Hilton turned out to be a man of character, too, in this transaction. He gave his word that no press photographs would be taken of the closing session. None were. But there is a picture, locked away in Hilton's vault. It shows Hilton, pen in hand, signing his personal check for $7,500,000.

"I won't bore you with the story," he told Hollis, "but I'd like that picture for my own keeping. You see, I once almost lost my mind trying to find $30,000 in forty-eight hours."

"Of course, Mr. Hilton," said Hollis. He didn't even exact a handshake.

The tremors which had run through the old clientele of the Plaza in New York were repeated among the gentry of Chicago, patrons through the years of one after another of three successive Palmer Houses. What would this tall, restless, loose-jointed man from Texas do to them? The best families of Chicago looked at each other in alarm and although they never said so in so many words you may be sure that they would not have been at all astonished if Hilton had started branding yearlings in the lobby or drilling for oil in the pantry. He had no intention of doing anything but giving them better even than they had had. They didn't know it at the time, but the man from Texas was a great respecter of tradition. He knew that anybody with enough money could buy a hotel. He also knew that not anybody could move in on a tradition and not flurry a feather or ruffle a temper.

"We walked on eggs," he says. "But at the same time we made changes. The trick was to make them unobtrusively. I knew we had succeeded when one of the most critical ladies in Chicago emerged from the dining room one night and said: 'Good evening, Mr. Hilton.' That was the coronation of our efforts."

Hilton, however, was not completely satisfied. He was irked by a management problem. He had never wholly approved of two hotels under one management in one city. It seemed to him that they nibbled at each other with unhappy results for both. He determined that this would not happen in Chicago. He owned two hotels of totally different spirit and value to the community. He sat down on a weekend and thought his problem out. The Stevens was huge and efficient and brisk, whereas the Palmer House was settled and traditional and elegant. They did not in any way impinge on each other except that each was a hotel. They were two different houses and Hilton decided they must stay that way. He called in the executives and their staffs and mapped out an operating policy for them.

It has worked well. The hotels use a common laundry, but otherwise they are separate entities. There is no cozying up.

Both houses operate at capacity and there is an intense friendly rivalry between them. Hilton's plan of having his managers operate on an almost autonomous basis has spurred them to greater efforts to top each other. Off duty, the two managers are life-long friends. On duty, they are like opposing knights on the field of tourney. They do not confide in each other, swap experiences, or telephone in emergencies.

The success of the rivalry has given Hilton courage to set up two hotels in Los Angeles. One, the Town House, he has had for years. In early 1955 he will have the Beverly Hilton, farther out Wilshire Boulevard in Beverly Hills. He won't have to make the Chicago speech all over again. The men will know that he expects individual operation. Actually, the Los Angeles situation may be more acute than that in Chicago. The type of clientele attracted to the Town House will be much like the clientele reasonably to be expected at Beverly Hilton, whereas the clientele of the Conrad Hilton is somewhat more transient and commercial than that drawn to the Palmer House.

Associates of Hilton believe that Hilton's demand that he be heard was a major factor in mollifying Hollis and bringing the Palmer House deal to conclusion, but at least two of them, who decline to be quoted by name, think that Hilton capped it with an answer he gave to a shrewd suggestion thrown at him suddenly by Hollis.

"What do you believe the annual gross of the Palmer House to be?" Hollis asked.

Hilton screwed up his face, took an envelope out of his pocket, put down some figures on the back of it, crossed part of them out, added the total of what remained and passed the envelope over to Hollis. The old man studied it with growing stupefaction, and then looked at Hilton with amazement in his eyes.

"There are books and there are figures," he said. "The inside figures of any operation are never available until the new owner moves in. But you have come within $1,890 of the inside figure."

Neither 1947 or 1948 was notable as an Acquisition Year. Hilton became interested in the Ambassador in Los Angeles, but found out it was almost hopelessly involved in litigation. He nibbled at the St. Francis in San Francisco, but decided not to get involved in another round of protracted negotiation. In December, 1946, he had painlessly acquired the Mayflower, the social, political and diplomatic hub of Washington, D. C.

It was time, indeed, not to acquire but to take a reckoning, and to this purpose he turned to the completion of the structure of Hilton Hotels Corporation, an organization which would consolidate his holdings, make legal stock offers through existing exchanges possible and create an integrated form of financial management. It was a titanic job. The work of divesting each house of its independent status with justice to all investors concerned was one nut that had to be cracked. Preparation of a detailed, scrupulously accurate statement for the Securities and Exchange Commission was another. In the midst of his involved duties he fell and broke his knee. He hobbled from meeting to meeting for weeks, eschewing golf or dancing perforce, and often was in acute pain as a result of standing too long. His amazing grasp of every facet of his multitudinous affairs was demonstrated time after time as accountants, lawyers and executives burrowed through the mountain of information and, unable to find what they wanted, came to him.

"Oh, that's in the Plaza records," he would say. "Let's see. about page 116 of a book marked '1941 Inventory.' Just about there."

Often enough, "about" turned out to be "exactly."

In time, and after months of arduous compilation of records, the information report went to the SEC and was approved. Late in June, 1947, securities of the new corporation were offered on the New York Stock Exchange and, some weeks later, the Los Angeles Exchange admitted them for trading. When every paper had been signed and notarized and every bank statement scrutinized and every tax receipt recorded, all of the hotels except three were part of the corporation. The hotel in Longview no longer was his to include. He had sold it at a modest price to a combination of all his hotel managers who had been in the armed services during World War II, a sale that was in all respects a gift. To have given it to them outright would have involved them in tax obligations beyond their immediate freedom to pay. But he "sold" it to them at a low price and took notes from each for his share, these notes to be retired out of profits from the hotel and profits only. Thus not one man had to put up a dollar of his personal funds. It was the conclusion of Hilton and his advisers that the Palacio and the Roosevelt should not be included in the merger for many reasons. Management contracts were entered into between these hotels and Hilton Hotels Corporation.

Formal estimating services hired for the occasion placed the total value of the corporations holdings at $41,183,327, with Hilton the largest stockholder of securities valued at $9,193,-096. From a start with $5,000 this may be looked upon as a great American story of enterprise, ingenuity, steadfastness and the grit to rise above and beyond black circumstance. In the beginning of this book about Conrad Hilton, it was said that his story was not really a Horatio Alger story, since it transcended those modest fables in many ways. Any man who can build better than $9,000,000 on top of a $5,000 foundation has left Horatio and all his dewy-eyed boys far behind.

CHAPTER FIVE

WHEN Hilton got around, at last, to buying the most famous hotel in the world the transaction required, with all its complexities and ramifications, exactly one week to complete. It was his third pass at a hotel with the word "Waldorf" in its name. There had been the little Waldorf in Texas. There had been his purchase of Waldorf-Astoria bonds at 4½, which he later sold at 85, and now he was ready to look at the old girl herself, rearing up more than 600 feet above New York's Park Avenue, an empress of a hotel.

He had stalked it for weeks, after returning from Europe with the considered decision that he was not yet ready for Europe and Europe certainly was not ready for him. He soaked up everything he could learn about the Waldorf. Its physical plant, its economics, its complicated ownership, its traditions, its management. For several years a picture of the Waldorf had lain under the glass top of Hilton's desk at the Town House in Los Angeles. He had scrawled across it, with a pen: "This is the greatest of them all."

When, at last, he made the opening move it was not in effect the first move. He had several times before tried to open the door a crack and nothing much had happened. Not enough to give him the feeling that this time it was it. He settled himself in the Plaza and started holding conferences with Colonel Joseph P. Binns, a former manager of the Stevens. Binns and Hilton matched like a pair of good gloves. They understood each other. Binns had enormous respect for the thinking of Hilton. Hilton had confidence in the managerial and negotiating talents of Binns. For some time Binns had been managing the Plaza, with a side assignment of keeping eyes and ears on the Waldorf.

This was not a simple matter of approaching an individual and getting a defined "yes" or "no." The Waldorf was an intricate corporation child. The Hotel Waldorf-Astoria Corporation was organized to build the Hotel Waldorf-Astoria. It floated an issue of $11,000,000 of debentures and sold the debentures and stock to the public. The proceeds of these securities were used to pay its share of the cost of the construction of the hotel, which was built on leased property. The land was leased from the New York State Realty and Terminal Company, which is an instrumentality organized by two railroads to operate real estate. The New York Central has always taken issue with the statement that the New Haven has any interest in the fee ownership of the land, contending that under the many agreements between the railroads its interest is only a specified amount in the revenues received from the property. This matter is now under judicial determination with respect to two parcels of Grand Central property. Hotel Waldorf-Astoria Corporation was unable to pay its ground rent and interest on its debentures. It was reorganized under chapter 77(b) and then there had to be a further readjustment of the ground lease. When the corporation was in existence, it did not own the furniture nor any interest in the building except a right to operate the property. Hilton and his associates bought control of the stock of Hotel Waldorf-Astoria Corporation.

The two roads had the building and the land, therefore, and they also could toss a prospective purchaser right out on his ear if they didn't like the cut of his clothes or the polish on his shoes. Their authority to refuse any kind of approach or negotiation was vast. In four years Hilton had twice almost directly, and once subtly, made it known that he wouldn't run away if the railroads nodded at him. But they didn't nod at him. For one thing, they didn't like the idea of operation by a man with several other hotels on his mind. They preferred a man with nothing on his mind but the Waldorf. They thought that

96

was burden enough and obligation enough to occupy any fellow. They reckoned without Hilton, who has a tenacity all of his own.

Finally, a door was opened. Hilton went to see one man. He felt relieved. This was better than having to confront a corporation, which has a certain indistinctness about it. You can talk to one man and arrive at something, if only defeat. To argue with a corporation is like debating with a wall. R. E. Dougherty, vice-president in charge of real estate for the New York Central, allowed it to be known that he would at least listen. He didn't actually invite Hilton in, he merely implied that his ears were unplugged if Hilton wanted to talk. Hilton wanted to talk.

He took Binns with him and they entered upon a long, wearing and detailed campaign designed to convince at least Dougherty that they did not plan to convert the lovely Waldorf into an upholstered warehouse. The major problem was to make Dougherty recognize what they already had done in the way of managing hotels of tradition without disturbing any facet of the tradition. Hilton was lucky: he had the living, vivid proof of his deeds at the Palmer House and the Plaza to strengthen his hand. They were smaller editions of the Waldorf problem: how to keep the traditions of a historic house while aggrandizing its economics. Dougherty conceded that Hilton had done a beautiful job in both instances.

As the hours grew into days, Hilton directors began converging on New York. Hilton warned them, echoing what his lawyers had warned him: "Keep away from that place. Don't go anywhere near it. If you have to pass it, do so on the other side of Park Avenue and don't even look at it."

They followed orders better than Hilton did. Almost any dawn of that week would find him walking on Park Avenue, on the side opposite the Waldorf, shooting covert glances at it without turning his head.

Hilton and his corporation, together with syndicate participants, bought about 69 percent of the common stock of the Waldorf-Astoria Corporation for roughly $3,000,000. He made certain promises as to the nature of the operation and agreed to preserve certain traditions.

On the day the transaction was closed, Hilton did a typical thing. He called General Eisenhower, at that time president of Columbia University. He suggested a golf game for the afternoon.

"My boys are busy on a little matter," said Hilton, "and I want to get out of their hair for awhile."

Binns, Eisenhower and Hilton played golf on a Long Island course that afternoon with Jack Henessey, another hotel man not associated with Hilton. It was October 13, 1949, Eisenhower's birthday. When the game was over Eisenhower invited the other three to his home at the University for a birthday cocktail. They walked into the house at exactly 5:20 and were met by the housekeeper who said, "Oh, General, the most beautiful birthday cake I ever saw was delivered from the Waldorf-Astoria at 4 o'clock. It is their birthday greeting to you."

"Well, it looks as though some people know how to run a hotel, Hilton," said Eisenhower with a wry smile. "Those folks at the Waldorf have memories. I don't see any cake from the Plaza."

"What time did you say that cake was delivered?" Hilton asked the housekeeper.

"Four o'clock, sir," she said.

"May I use your phone, General?" Hilton asked.

"Sure, go ahead," said Eisenhower.

Hilton dialed a number, got it and whispered a question. His face lighted up and he said "Thank you," and put up the telephone. He came back into the living room.

"I wasn't going to say anything about it," he told Eisenhower, "but the fact is that I sent you that birthday cake. I took title to the Waldorf at three o'clock this afternoon and

your cake was delivered at four o'clock. I agree with you—
some folks have memories and also know how to run a hotel!"

When the smoke of the Waldorf deal cleared away, things
long obscure became apparent. The railroads had had the
difficulty of finding a man with two definite sides to his nature: enough money and enough taste. When they found
Hilton, they had their answer. The Waldorf, built in the depression, had never been a satisfactory revenue yielding hotel.
Its bonds withered and its stocks were profitless. The owning
railroads took no pleasure in bolstering the giant white ele-
phant with cash. But they deserve credit for their reluctance
to sell: many a time they could have sold for more money and
refused to do so until money was accompanied by a demonstrated talent for keeping the tone of the house.

Hilton at no time concealed his opinion that the Waldorf
could be made to yield much more money. When he assumed
the control of the Waldorf he had a world-wide assortment of
guests with fixed opinions. He had heads of great nations,
famed men and women of the arts, one-time monarchs and
men and women of a social stratum where impeccable service
is like air. It's simply there.

He accomplished economic miracles at the Waldorf. The
installation of vitrines in the lobby for a gain of $18,000
a year was only the beginning. There had been a legend among
hotel culinary workers the nation over that the theft of meat
and potables at the Waldorf amounted to about a million
dollars a year, give or take $100,000 either way. Hilton and
his staff went relentlessly into this rumor at once. They moved
fast and expertly. They found some leaks and, inevitably, a
few dishonest employees. They were not unduly shocked. You
can't employ over 1,000 men and women in jobs involving
the handling of millions of dollars in foods, liquors, linens,
tobaccos and other commodities and not have one or two easy-
money characters in the lot. It would be against human nature
for things to be otherwise.

Room waiters often find a fifth of Scotch left behind with perhaps an inch or more of good whiskey still in the bottom of the bottle. Multiplication of such findings by annual measurement could amount to an enormous amount of bulk whiskey and, presumably, such bulk whiskey could be resold to unscrupulous little side-street bars for a personal profit to the waiters. The investigators found almost no evidence of such practice.

When it was all boiled down and sorted over, the legend turned out to be just one of those things with which hotel workers in distant towns and cities bemuse themselves. They had the human frailty of getting some sort of odd enjoyment from talking about a large hotel in which theft ran to a million dollars a year. It was like saying "I'm only a little fellow in the game, but I work in a business which has possibilities so large that one house alone accounts for a million dollar heist each year." The purveyors of the legend got a mild lift out of passing the story along.

The other immediate task was to set the operating side of the Waldorf up on a basis where partial occupancy still would be profitable. Almost any hotel man will tell you that if his house is properly managed and cost-planned it can make money on a 75 percent occupancy. Strict controls are essential and in some Hilton hotels these controls are so carefully balanced that the houses could make profit on a 50 percent occupancy. He put $3,000,000 into the Waldorf and assumed a debt of $4,400,000. Since then, thanks to the excellence of the operation, the Hilton Hotels Corporation has increased its Waldorf holdings from 68 percent of the stock to 100 percent and has lease renewal options to 1977. For less than $8,000,000 and burdens to which he long ago became inured he has a property of incalculable value.

In the dining rooms the cost sentinels are doubly watchful. Some restaurant managers or owners will say out loud that no food establishment can run on food alone. It must sell liquors to turn a profit. Hilton describes that as nonsense. His menus in most cases, and up to and including the Conrad Hilton in Chicago, are designed on the cost basis of 31½ cents to the menu dollar. At such specialized houses as the Waldorf, the Plaza and the Palmer House the food cost basis per menu dollar is a little higher because in those houses the clientele is of a more international color and has sometimes bizarre food notions which 31½ cents to the dollar will not cover.

In the case of the Caribe Hilton, the Puerto Rican government built the hotel with Hilton providing operating capital and advice and benefits on architecture, building and furnishing. The government receives two-thirds of the profits and Hilton gets the rest. They are, as said before, tax-free and from his profits on the Caribe Hilton he is building his international hotel structure. In each case it is planned to have the government in situ, or well established local financiers, build the hotel with Hilton advice dredged from experience, plus an "expenses" investment of between $200,000 and $300,000, depending on locality conditions. This kind of arrangement keeps local capital intact, provides work for native artists and labor, gives the country an opportunity for national pride and allows for the trained services of Hilton and his international outfit. The hotel in Istanbul, ready for occupancy in July, 1954, will be the first to benefit from an idea that came to Hilton while flying between New York and Los Angeles. He set up a plan whereby young Turkish nationals, who also are college graduates and who wish to learn the hotel business, could come to the United States and work for a year in a succession of Hilton hotels at a succession of jobs. The first group has been graduated and has returned to Istanbul. They will go to work in the Istanbul hotel when it opens.

He would do the same for a projected hotel in Rome or London or anywhere else on the face of the earth. But Rome has been a problem. It wants a Hilton hotel, and would go out of its way to create one, but negotiations are so complicated that various barriers must be reduced one by one. The deal for Rome was signed in 1951 and the projected hotel even got a name . . . The Albergo Dei Cavalieri Hilton. Eventually, the Albergo will get underway. But not until Conrad Hilton goes over and turns up the first spade of Roman earth with that silver shovel he keeps.

Great foreign hotels have existed for years. Indeed, the American hotel business has learned valuable and lasting lessons from them. But Hilton has gone beyond them in his operating rules. The banquet business is one of the major facets of profitable hotel operation. It is one thing to attract banquet bookings, provide the room, chairs and tables, serve the food and retire from the scene. It is another to prepare the waiters for the event. At Hilton hotels the waiters are briefed before each banquet. Most hotels don't go that far. But at the Hilton houses the waiters learn all there is to know before a banquet is scheduled to begin. They are assembled in a large room and seated. The management gives them pertinent information: the nature of the organization that is banqueting, the reason for the banquet, the names of officers of the organization plus the names of distinguished guests. Brief histories of the careers of some of the officers and guests are supplied. If any officer or guest has food whims, these are described. Thus, if chocolate ice cream is going to be the dessert and the Hilton management knows that a guest has an allergy to it, the waiter assigned to the table at which this guest will be seated is told about it.

"When dessert time comes," he is told, "tell the gentleman that although chocolate ice cream is the regular dessert you will be happy to provide him with anything else he desires. Be sure to do that before you serve any dessert to any one else at your table. Don't put one order of it down before consulting him."

This attention to detail has resulted in a tremendous upsurge of banquet business in all Hilton hotels. Waiters bring both personal knowledge and personal interest to every seated guest. It goes to the extent of reading newspapers at the last moment. If a distinguished guest has become a father, say, in the last twenty-four hours, his waiter will find an opportunity to say quietly: "Permit me to congratulate you on your new son, sir." These personal touches, not too difficult to arrive at, make business men and community leaders warm toward Hilton hotels.

It is the result of behind-the-scenes planning rather than lobby smiles. Any manager can stand in a lobby and greet guests with a smile and a handshake, but if he does he is likely to have to neglect other things. Hilton managers work in their offices and keep things smooth for guests while assistant managers do the lobby greeting.

The briefing sessions with waiters always end with inspection of each waiter. His clothes are inspected for cleanliness and must be immaculate. His hair must be neat and well-cut, his hands clean, his nails freshly filed and clean. He must have shaved within four hours of banquet time. If he is ill with a headche or has a personal problem damaging to his mood, he is asked to say so and will be excused. The management does not want any brooding, unhappy or distraught waiters serving in Hilton dining rooms.

While these details receive attention in this country, Hilton lets his imagination range far afield. These thinking sessions have already resulted in hotels abroad, as already told here, and will result in many more. At this writing he has a total of fifteen foreign hotels in mind, about six of which are actualities or underway. At the end of the list as of now, is a hotel for Jakarta in Indonesia. The name fascinates him. He realizes that it will be a hammered-out job, with two points of view having to find a common meeting ground, but he believes in his destiny and he believes in Asia and emphatically he believes in prayer and the efficacy of prayer in arriving at world peace.

Besides which, there is a lot of prestige in being the first American hotelier to operate an Asiatic house. The British ran hotels in odd corners of the world for a long time. Hilton sees no reason why the job shouldn't fall to him.

It undoubtedly will and some of it already has.

When he contemplates a new hotel built from the literal scratch in the earth which his shovel makes he studies everything concerning the site: how many persons pass hour by hour on a twenty-four-hour basis, how many automobiles pass in all directions, what the prevailing wind is over the course of a year, whether the site is protected from weather or open to it, how accessible it is, how close it is to already established and popular hotels and similar intimate facts.

"If it were important to know how much cotton it would yield to the acre," an associate said recently, "I think he'd study that, too."

He broke ground on August 28, 1953, for the Beverly Hilton Hotel. This time the old reliable silver spade had a pair of glittering cousins. Miss Terry Moore, notable for the firm way in which she fills a bathing suit, wielded a gold-plated shovel and Lt. Gov. Goodwin J. Knight of California wielded another gold-plated job, suitably inscribed. Miss Moore was there because over the years it has been found essential in Los Angeles to have a film actress present for top occasions. They are not only decorative but they seem to add a touch of luck to the enterprise. Mr. Knight was there as the second executive of the state. The golden shovels acted as out-riders for the venerable old silver spade, wielded by Hilton in a gesture to tradition. The silver shovel bit in first and the two golden shovels took the second and third bites into the location at the triangular intersection of Wilshire and Santa Monica Boulevards. A few blocks down Wilshire Boulevard stands the Beverly-Wilshire Hotel and up the rise toward the hills nestles the Beverly Hills Hotel, both equipped with swimming pools, cabanas, class and a fancy clientele. The Beverly Hilton will make the third good hotel in Beverly Hills and by actual geometric location completes a triangle as defined as the corner on which it will stand.

Hilton came to the ceremony armed with his usual encyclopedia of facts, plus an extra piece of information supplied at the last moment by that tireless California historian, actor Leo Carillo, descendant of authentic California dons. The eight acres on which the $14,000,000 hotel will stand, hopefully open to the happy customers in the Spring of 1955, are part of an original Spanish land grant of 4,500 acres called El Rancho Rodeo de Las Aguas—the Ranch of The Roundup of The Waters. At one time its hard-pressed owner sold all 4,500 acres for $800—but not, alas, to Conrad Hilton. The price was considerably higher by the time he got around to acquiring his eight acre section.

The Beverly Hilton will be an eight story hotel with three wings, earthquake protected, and will have 450 rooms and suites, each with private balcony, a design he found practical and attractive at the Caribe Hilton. Specialty shops will occupy the ground floor on two sides of the structure and there will be an underground garage for 600 cars, plus landscaped outdoor parking space for 400 more.

There hasn't been much Hilton could do about parking and garage space in the established American hotels he has acquired. They don't meet his point of view about providing parking space for guests with cars, but except for the Waldorf there was no ground to be had for parking. The Waldorf has basement automobile parking to a degree. For that matter, it also has basement railroad tracks in the event a guest should want to run his private railway car under shelter and out of the way of the trains moving into and out of Grand Central Terminal. Hotels now being built by Hilton have ample parking space, since he himself is a dedicated motorist. Also, he has too often heard fellow travelers in trains or planes tell him why they have stopped going to hotels and now patronize first class motels on the rim of each major city and town across the continent.

"It's mainly," they say, "that I not only can run right in off the road and park alongside my own unit for the night, but I avoid a lot of extra fees and tips. Now look, Mr. Hilton: I pull up in front of a city hotel. No parking room. I pay a doorman to help me unload. I tip another man to take my car to a nearby garage. I tip again when a bellboy takes my luggage from the sidewalk to the desk and then to my room. In the morning the process is reversed: tip to bellboy, tip to doorman for helping me load up, tip to garage boy for bringing my car to me—and a garage fee on top of all that."

Hilton concedes that there is a point involved. He recognizes that magnificent motels, some with swimming pools, are a threat of a kind to the hotel business. He foresees a battle on the subject, with hotels having to provide many small, alluring extras such as free books, magazines and newspapers, TV in every room, sunlamps, ultra-violet lamps and many other doodads. He is too good a business man to shrug away the motel competition. Instead, he intends to meet it and top it. Ample parking space is only one facet of his determination.

He went over all this in detail when he assigned the Beverly Hilton design job to architect Welton Becket and he went all over it in renewed detail in his exploratory talks with Del E. Webb, head of the construction company which got the job of building the new hotel. Between them they estimated that for a 450 room hotel space for 1,000 cars was ample and would care for all possible contingencies including two banquets on the same night.

When the Beverly Hilton is opened it undoubtedly will be an event dwarfing all other events in fabled Los Angeles for the last twenty years. Also, attesting the personal popularity of Hilton, the social and motion picture groups will make it their new headquarters. And, as in the case of the Town House operation, many of them will be amazed but pleased

106

when they walk into their rooms for the first time and see evidence that Hilton was aware of their preferences in food, drink and flowers. He is a ready and enthusiastic dispenser of gifts. He was introduced once to a pretty girl at an afternoon party in New York and, as he walked her home in the dusk, they passed a pet shop. There was a gray toy poodle puppy in the window and she exclaimed over its cuteness. When he told her good night at her apartment door, he asked if she would dine with him the next night because it was a rather unusual day in his life.

"Birthday?" she asked.

"Oh, no," he said. "At my age there is nothing unusual in birthdays. But please dine with me."

She told him she would be delighted.

He called for her the next evening after a full day of business and golf, and put the puppy in her arms.

"Please call him Waldorf," he said. "You see I . . . well, I bought the Waldorf this afternoon. He might be a luck charm."

The afternoon had cost Hilton $3,000,400, with all but $400 being the price of the hotel. The puppy represented the rest. He is still called Waldorf and whether he brought luck is impossible to prove, but he didn't hurt the hotel at all. It has been a mint ever since.

He never impresses himself on the help at one of his hotels. The days when he had to assemble every employee in the place and give a talk on manners, cooperation and all pulling together so that they could eat at the end of the week, Hilton included, are long gone and far away. It is reasonable to think that perhaps as many as half of the employees in one of the giant hotels not only do not know him but would not recognize him as he walked down a corridor or through a lobby. Once, at the Plaza, an elevator door was closing just as he approached it. It nettled him for a moment that the operator did not reopen it for him. He jabbed at the bell . . . and then jabbed again.

He heard the elevator man say, "All right, all right," in an impatient tone. Hilton matched it with patience. He waited until the car came back down for its trip and had emptied. Then he beckoned the operator.

"My name's Hilton," he said quietly. "I think one 'all right' is permissible, but two kind of crowds things."

Many a tycoon would have stormed the place down until the man was driven from the premises. Hilton let it go at that and, probably, never thought of it again. He has an air of quietness and naïveté which fools many people into thinking it is easy to take advantage of him. It isn't. He has a Western courtliness and a total lack of ego because of his success. He still looks up to big men and not down on any one. He is to this day surprised that things have worked out for him as well as they have and when he asks a man of national stature a question it is with deference.

He once asked Herbert Hoover, long a tenant at the Waldorf, if the former President of the United States would honor him by becoming a member of the board of directors of the hotel. Mr. Hoover accepted with gracious gravity. Hilton went into the offices of his managers at the Waldorf.

"That was *very* nice of Mr. Hoover, *very* nice," he told them and added: "I am terribly *pleased* that he consented to do it for me."

It is easy to please him and difficult to thoroughly anger him. He has the relaxed manner that goes with most men of unusually tall stature.

There is one name for which Hilton has especial regard. It belonged to the late king of French hotel keepers, César Ritz. Ritz not only gave his name to the most plush hotels but his name became a synonym for rich elegance. Hilton isn't impressed by the word ritzy as such, but he knows what a truly great hotel man Ritz was and how his name came automatically to mean fine hotels, perfect service, flawless cuisine and total well-being. The preoccupation that Ritz put into hotel operation is not entirely Hilton's way. He has been too busy acquiring hotels and building others. But he constantly advises his managers to remember what a contribution to perfect hotel operation Ritz made and leaves unsaid what apparently is a private wish: he would like the great Hilton houses to come to have the same connotations.

His shopping for hotels is on an international basis now and this alone probably will hasten the day when the name of Hilton becomes synonymous with hotel operation on terms of the *grande cuisine* coupled with service that attracts men and women of international repute. He has it already in such hotels as the Plaza, the Waldorf-Astoria, the Mayflower, the Castellana Hilton, the Palmer House. Although the Plaza no longer is his, there is no guarantee that he will not acquire it again. When he sold it and bought the New Yorker, he traded away only a small portion of the enormous prestige that has come to surround his name in hotel management.

Those who hold that his entire energies and planning must have entered into his invasion of New York are in error. His thinking was much more flexible than that. He had had his eye on the Dayton Biltmore in Dayton, Ohio, and its acquisition on November 1, 1944 just happened to coincide with his activity in New York. He bought a fine house that had lost money in the depression. He bought it, as he bought so many others, just as the tide was turning. He had foreseen the turn, others did not. Almost from the day that he got the Dayton Biltmore it began to make money and has been doing well ever since. While settling back to watch this fine house begin to skyrocket its profitable returns he was looking at the Mayflower in Washington, a hotel which had housed and entertained fashionable and political Washingtonians since the day it opened its doors in 1925. He got the Mayflower at the end of 1946.

The Mayflower, with its traditions, legends, color and verve intact, came to him for about one-sixth of what it cost. It had cost approximately $12,900,000 to build. He acquired control for $2,600,000.

While dabbling in these purchases, which included taking over the Arrowhead Springs at the mountain and water resort of that name near San Bernardino, California, he sold the old Long Beach pigeon loft which he had turned into a scrubbed hotel with an all-glass top floor. His net profit on the Long Beach Hilton was $743,558, which all by itself proves for all time that it is often the part of common sense to shoo pigeons.

These adventures, together with other operations, have made him the subject of an unique experience in the hotel field. It is accurate to report that scarcely a week goes by that he is not approached or importuned to lend his name, money or management to a hotel somewhere in the United States and, increasingly, somewhere in the world. His name has aroused the forlorn, the involved and the battered to turn to him in the hope that he will consent to work a Hilton miracle. Obviously, he cannot give ear to a tenth of these suggestions and has steeled himself to avoid any deals which his own intuition has not created. There is very little that any hotel owner, banker or real estate salesman can tell him about any hotel in the country since hotels are his business and he makes it his business to be informed. He knows how other operators of system hotels conduct their business, he knows within a few dollars what each rival hotel is doing in revenues. As Mr. Hotel, he is in full possession of careful run-downs of all hotels except the hapless dogs to which no one in his right mind pays the slightest attention. He undoubtedly could walk into any self-respecting hotel in America, scribble a few figures on a memo pad and hand over to its management a close estimate of its total business broken down into room rentals, dining room revenues and liquor sales, balanced against its payroll, fixed financing charges and operating costs.

This kind of detailed knowledge has given him tremendous confidence in his own thinking both as to operation in this country and international expansion.

"I can honestly say," he told friends recently, "that international operation would be less of a mystery to me today than was the situation in Chicago when I dreamed of getting my foot in the door there."

Nor does he think of world expansion in personal terms such as overtook him in California. His entry there resulted in buying a house for himself for $55,000, selling it later to buy the beautiful Casa Encantada. When he bought the Arrowhead Springs, he also bought what he calls his camp, hard by the lovely lake cupped in the mountains. It is some hint as to the nature of this rural retreat to say that among other civilized things it has four master bedrooms and no one sleeps under canvas or does without running water. The camp is not far from the hotel. Nor does he count Arrowhead Springs as a resort. His suspicion of resorts is still live and powerful. He looks on Arrowhead Springs as a retreat. Its famed baths and golf course and lake may look like a resort to the public, they may be dubbed a resort operation by the opposition, but Hilton does not consider it a resort. It is a first-class hotel which happens to have mineral baths and a fine lake. His adventure in Puerto Rico led him to no private house purchases there, nor is he thinking of buying a house in Madrid, Mexico City, Acapulco, Rome, London, Cairo, Istanbul or Jakarta.

"I don't need any house except the one I have," he says. "Come to think about it I don't really need that. I could find a different bed to sleep in every night of every year for the next fifty years."

Well, to be exact it could be for the next fifty years and some odd months. After all, he controls about 18,000 sleeping rooms, all of which he is convinced are just about the finest sleeping rooms a man can find.

The chances that he will buy a quaint abode with wrought iron fence in Madrid are about as remote as his buying an estate on the banks of the Nile or on the shores of the Bosporus.

"I love the country I was born in," he says.

Besides which, look at the fun he has at a hotel like, say, the Waldorf in which 20,000 men and women move about in any one day. His fun is in providing the machinery and planning which will make every one of those 20,000 persons eager to come back again.

"You cannot please everybody always in every way," he says. "It is neither in human nature nor the cards. But you can work hard making a try at it and you'd be amazed how many people give you 'A' for just trying. You can tell by the wording of what few complaints you do get. Instead of rushing in all red in the face and shouting 'I want to tell you . . .' most people with a grievance, real or fancied, come in quietly and begin: 'I'm sure you don't know this, so I thought I'd tell you.' There's a whale of a difference. A process server once got upstairs in the Waldorf Towers and nailed a big film executive with a summons in a corporation suit. We thought the roof would come down. It didn't turn out that way at all. He merely said: 'I'd give a dollar to know how that joker got by those wonderful fellows on the elevators.' He puzzled over it for days. Naturally, we set up new barriers against such annoyances for guests. But all it did was puzzle him. And I take that as a real compliment to the house."

Occasionally residents of the Waldorf or any other great hotel become the subjects of Page One headlines, not always of a savory character. Then the management has a thin line to walk between customary protection of the guests and recognition that, in America, there is a free press and it is a precious freedom. Up to now the tender decisions must have

112

been arrived at with uncommon sagacity, because no head-lined guest has screamed and no reporter has gone away angry.

Andre Vishinsky has had occasion to register at the Waldorf and also to confer there on delicate international matters. As touchy as the Russian official is, he has never complained that the press was loosed upon him. When General Douglas MacArthur came back from Korea and took residence at the Waldorf reporters in squads followed every move he made. The hotel had to divide its sense of recognition between General MacArthur's privacy and the rights of the press to pursue the top story in America. The Duke of Windsor and his American Duchess almost invariably reside at the Waldorf when in New York. They come and go in freedom now, but it was not always so. There was a time when reporters stood five deep in the halls and waited for every fragment of information. The hotel was in an extremely delicate position. The Duke had, after all, been king of the largest empire on earth. The press had an authentic story to cover. It was the kind of situation of which every hotel manager in New York must have said to himself: "I'd like to have them as guests and I thank God they are not."

The Waldorf is annual headquarters for, among other things, a baking contest staged by a milling company to dis-cover and reward new uses for its products. The first prize is a comfortable $25,000. Ladies, and a few gentlemen, descend on the hotel from dozens of home kitchens and for several days bake their hearts out at lines of identical electric ranges and before the eyes of critical judges. This event, which could become a touchy thing with jealous ladies watching every cup of flour and wisp of butter used by their rivals for the grand prize, goes off not only serenely but with enormous good will. The hotel goes out of its way to make each contestant person-ally aware that the hotel has her or his best interests at heart.

The private files of the hotel are filled with items describing

113

the odd, the bizarre, the unexpected, but so trained and expert is the staff that nothing untoward ever is allowed to occur.

During the fall of 1953, as noted, Hilton sold the Plaza for $15,000,000 for a profit of $7,500,000. Not only did this sale net him a 100 percent profit, but it allowed him a continuing connection with the mellow, beloved old house. He emerged from this astonishing transaction with a lease to continue operating the Plaza for at least two and half more years. There is much to be said, far transcending the happy uses of mere publicity, for any hotel operator who converts a touchy, delicate operation into a property worth double what he paid for it and which he managed so skillfully that the new owners retain his skills for continuation of the operation.

Shortly after the sale of the Plaza he bought the New Yorker, a more than 2,000 room hotel a block from New York's sprawling, busy Penn Station. The skyscraper hotel had long interested him, and when the proper arrangements presented themselves, he wasted no time.

When Hilton bought the New Yorker he gave definitive evidence of his concern with the tranquility of man's soul. He ordered the installation of a meditation chapel in the hotel, adding that its decor be such that it could serve as an interfaith refuge for men disturbed by cares and problems. On May 9 of this year it was dedicated, with services conducted by Dr. Norman Vincent Peale, New York clergyman and author of inspirational books. The room, on the fourth floor of the hotel, is paneled in wood and has a small, raised platform at the end on which stands a simple table with a vase of cut flowers, changed daily. Behind that is a paneled wall with three leaded glass windows. An anteroom contains bibles of the various faiths, plus religious literature concerning them. Simple, comfortable chairs in the chapel, and facing the platform, make it possible for those seeking religious consolation to sit and lose themselves in prayer and thought.

It has been said that rival hotel men were stunned that

114

anyone would consider selling such a traditional house as the Plaza and acquiring such a commercial house as the New Yorker. In the first place, Hilton is a businessman and not a real estate dilettante. Any businessman with pencil and paper can determine in less than five minutes why Hilton made the deal. He made a 100 percent profit on the Plaza, he divested himself of a 1,060 room hotel and acquired a 2,000 room hotel, and he retained managerial powers over the Plaza. Also, in the sale of the Plaza was a clause permitting him to buy one-half of its real estate in twelve years for $400,000—if he chooses to do so.

The purchase of the New Yorker is another vivid example of his prowess for negotiation. He used stock of the Hilton Hotel Corporation instead of cash. In fact, the sellers, the Manufacturers Trust Company, handed him $500,000 cash with the deal!

The best proof that Hilton is an astute businessman is in the dividend statements of the Hilton Hotels Corporation. For a business which was notorious, until he came along, for being unstable and seemingly unpredictable he has set up a sound corporation with a healthy stock position. When he moves swiftly, as in the cases of the Plaza and the New Yorker, his first concern and sense of obligation is to the corporation and the stock it represents. It is not on record that the stockholders became restless or dubious about any Hilton deals when for 1952 the earnings per share were $2.74 and for 1953 they rose to $3.92. The New Yorker, which is worth much more as building and real estate, was acquired for $12,500,000 subject to a first mortgage of $5,303,905 and not a nickel in Hilton cash was involved in the transaction. It is fair to suggest that any rivals harboring or pretending to harbor reservations concerning the Hilton operations have an equal opportunity to go out and make the same kind of deal. It is significant that they don't. Either fear, lack of imagination or inability to come up with the proper economics, and possibly a combination of all three, would seem to be the inhibiting cause.

This definitive study of Conrad Hilton and his hotels is being written in the late winter of 1953-54. At its writing, Hilton controls the destinies of sixteen hotels in the United States, including the four largest hotels in the world, and has projected or under construction or open and operating, all abroad, eleven more.

The details of acquisition of all sixteen domestic hotels have not been told here because, in all truth, these details probably are not fascinating to the thousands who will read these words either by purchase of this book or by reading it in a Hilton hotel room. Some, as has been recorded, were difficult, complex and painfully detailed from start to finish. Others seemed to manage themselves with a minimum of discussion, haggling and bartering. One group wanted to sell a hotel, another group wanted to buy it. All that was at issue was a figure and the acceptable financing of that figure.

The sixteen Hilton hotels in the United States, together with the number of rooms and number of employees, follow:

Hotel	Locale	Rooms	Employees
The Plaza	New York	1,017	1,200
The Roosevelt	New York	1,100	1,000
The Waldorf-Astoria	New York	2,000	2,500
The New Yorker	New York	2,200	1,800
The Conrad Hilton	Chicago	3,000	2,300
The Palmer House	Chicago	2,268	2,200
The Town House	Los Angeles	300	205
The Beverly Hilton (April, 1955)	Beverly Hills	450	550 (est.)
The Mayflower	Washington, D. C.	1,000	900
The Dayton Biltmore	Dayton, O.	500	320
The Deshler-Hilton	Columbus, O.	875	615
The Hilton Hotel	El Paso, Tex.	293	205
The Hilton Hotel	Fort Worth, Tex.	300	200

Hotel	Locale	Rooms	Employees
The Hilton Hotel	Albuquerque, N. M.	167	200
The Hotel Jefferson	St. Louis, Mo.	800	600
The Arrowhead Springs	San Bernardino, Cal.	175	125
		16,445	14,920

Foreign hotels now operating or under construction:

Hotel	Locale	Rooms	Employees
The Palacio Hilton	Chihuahua, Mex.	124	100
The Caribe Hilton	San Juan, P. R.	355	494
The Castellana Hilton	Madrid, Spain	338	450

In construction abroad are:

Hotel	Locale	Rooms	Employees
The Istanbul Hilton (Nov. '54)	Istanbul, Turkey	300	360 (est.)
The Continental Hilton	Mexico City, Mex.	360	400
The Acapulco Hilton	Acapulco, Mex.	250	300 (est.)
The Havana Hilton	Havana, Cuba	650	800 (est.)
The Nile Hilton	Cairo, Egypt	400	500 (est.)
		2,777	3,404

In addition, there is negotiation underway for the building of the Athens Hilton in Greece, a hotel projected for 250 rooms.

The formula used at San Juan, Puerto Rico, has been, with little or no deviation, the formula used in all foreign agreements. In its essentials, this means that either the government or capital belonging to nationals of each country builds the hotel. Title to the building and land remains in custody of the government or participating nationals. Hilton furnishes and manages the hotel and the profits are divided two-thirds and one-third, Hilton getting the latter, with the larger portion turned back to either the government or participating nationals as the case may be.

The hotel in Madrid was two-thirds completed before Hilton was invited to come to Spain and examine the property with a view toward management. He liked what he saw and the terms offered and effected a long term lease plus the right to direct important changes in layout and room arrangements. These changes were made while the hotel was being completed.

In Istanbul he was able to obtain a twenty-year lease which was signed with the Ministry of Foreign Affairs of the Republic of Turkey. The government in this case is the owner.

When Hilton signed the complicated and still inactive deal in Rome, he did so in the Vatican itself, not because the Vatican owns the real estate or will finance the hotel but because the chairman of the Societe Generale Immobiliare, the largest real estate and contracting firm in Italy, is also the Treasurer of the Vatican and has offices there. Plans for the hotel have been completed and the putting of Hilton's silver spade into the soil of Italy awaits only final approval of the government and completion of local financial arrangements. Hilton's participation begins with the breaking of ground.

Planning, construction, furnishing and operation of all these establishments will be under Hilton direction with the exception of the Castellana Hilton, which was well on its way to completion when his participation was invited.

"Unusual problems present themselves in foreign countries," he said in New York in the fall of 1953. "Language barriers and many restrictions must be overcome. In most of the countries where we will operate, the level of hotel employment must be raised. Our hotels must measure up to Hilton standards and methods, but these results must be accomplished without shock to age-old custom, much of which is found to be contrary to sound business practice.

"In the months to come many Hilton Hotels executives will

be consulted for advice and counsel in the organization and development of these hotels. If we are to be successful, our American guests in Europe must recognize immediately that they are in a Hilton hotel. At the same time, our European and Asiatic guests, who will be in the majority, must be made to feel equally at home. This will insure the success of our hotels abroad and will contribute to the increasing success of our hotels at home."

Study of the plans for all of these hotels (with once again the exception of the Castellana Hilton) shows that he has found the architecture used at the Caribe Hilton best suited for management and guest. This means that every room or suite will have a private balcony closed off by a masonry wall from every other balcony. This amounts to getting two rooms for one since each balcony has three walls, two on the sides and one between the interior room and the balcony. The only open space is the one facing outward.

While these projects were either under construction or in final stages of negotiation, Hilton turned to his American hotels and continuation of his constant work of improving either the financial or physical structure of several. In the case of the Waldorf-Astoria he used profits to acquire sufficient control to enable him to dissolve the Waldorf-Astoria Corporation and place the queen of Park Avenue squarely in the Hilton Hotels Corporation. Furthermore, he delighted a great many early debenture holders, men and women who years ago abandoned all hope of ever realizing a penny on their securities, by redeeming $1,830,500 worth of income debentures at full value, plus accrued interest.

"I have looked upon my holdings as worthless paper for years," one investor says. "Now look. I get a check in full."

The controlling factor is Hilton. He is proud to have made such a showing in so short a time, particularly with a gigantic house about which every hotel man in the country used to say: "She's awfully pretty, but she's broke."

He is also proud of having set aside $2,400,000 for redecoration and refurbishing of the Jefferson in St. Louis and a like sum for the Deshler Hilton in Columbus. The governments of both cities acknowledge freely that this kind of lump sum, large-scale spending is of enormous benefit in terms of labor, income and civic improvement. The Jefferson got a new marquee, extensive interior alteration, reshaping of public rooms and a coat of paint in addition to furniture, fixtures and rugs. Much the same kind of renovation is being done at the Deshler. In effect he put almost $5,000,000 in cash into two American cities, with obvious benefits to the communities. Labor and artisans received wages, the wages were spent in the two cities for all kinds of goods and services needed by families.

CHAPTER SIX

BUT nothing that Hilton did in all of 1953 gave him as much joy or created as much amazement as the address he delivered in Madrid on July 14 when the Castellana Hilton was formally opened. The citizens and officials of Madrid expected the usual token speech, in English, later to be translated for anyone who might care to read it. No one, not even Hilton's own staff, knew what would happen when, at the inaugural dinner of the hotel, he would be called on to speak. When it did happen, his associates, even his many guests flown to Madrid from the United States, were stunned. He rose, put some notes down beside him, covered them with a napkin and began to speak in flawless Spanish with a Castillian accent. The translation was made . . . from Spanish to English for the benefit of his American guests.

"Spain to me, a boy who was born and reared in New Mexico," he said, "has always been a land of enchantment, a mother country of wonder and warmth. As I grew older and read and studied I came to know the tremendous contributions made by Spain to the great currents of world progress. Even in its beginnings your country gave to the Roman Empire some of its most illustrious poets and philosophers, Marcial, Lucan, Seneca, and under the Califate, Maimonides. From that day to this, the Spanish heritage has brightened the world. Murillo, Velasquez, Goya, Cervantes, Ignatius Loyola, Therese, Suarez, Ferdinand and Isabella; Madrid, Toledo, Granada and Sevilla . . . in human history these have been names to conjure with.

"And you did not hold to yourself your glory and culture. Your Spanish colonial empire transplanted your heritage over almost the whole of America from Florida and California down to Cape Horn. The warmth of Spanish culture spread over a large part of Europe and extended as far as East India, Australia and the Philippine Islands.

"As you may know, my homeland is in the southwestern part of the United States of America. On this occasion I am deeply conscious of the many sentimental ties that have bound your country and mine for hundreds of years. It so happens that my birthplace is in New Mexico, which was an outpost of the Spanish Empire for centuries. My native village is San Antonio, and county of my nativity is named Socorro, so named in honor of Our Lady of Help. The Spanish language is still spoken in my native village, as it was in my boyhood, and in many other areas in the Southwest. Since my earliest years I have known and understood the beautiful language of Castile, and have known of the many splendid things attributable to early day Spanish culture in my native state of New Mexico. My boyhood years were spent within a stone's throw of a river which bears a historical Spanish name . . . Rio Grande. Along this river centuries ago Spanish armies marched on their way to fight for possession of a new country for the Kingdom of Spain. Since my earliest days I have been aware of the intrepidity of the Spanish soldier, of the heroic self sacrifice of the Spanish missionary.

"In my native New Mexico there is a natural landmark honoring forever the memories of the Spaniards who came there centuries ago. In Valencia, New Mexico, a county named after Valencia in Spain, in a remote and sparsely settled area, there stands even to this day a great bluff or mountain of red and white sandstone, two hundred and fifty feet above the floor of the valley, known for hundreds of years by the name of El Morro. On the north face of El Morro, protected from wind and weather by recesses in the bluff, there is registered the passing by that place of many early day Spanish explorers, some of whom, using the point of a sword or dagger for a pen, carved out brief messages so that those who followed might

122

have a record of their expeditions. The words, 'Pasó por aquí' have become immortal in my country, because they were carved so many times at El Morro to announce epoch-making journeys. Bertolomeo Marsso, Governor and Captain General of the province of New Mexico, carved out a message for posterity on July 29, 1620, in which he said that, in serving his Lord and his King, he had passed that way to subdue hostile Indians at Zuñi. Juan Garcia de Rovas, chief Alcalde of Santa Fe, then as now the capital of New Mexico, passed by El Morro, and left a message on August 26, 1716, a half century before the American Revolutionary War.

"Despite the fact that many events have come to pass over the years, bringing in their wake the difficulties inevitable in the history of nations, Spain and the United States of America stand today firm in their mutual respect, trust and friendship.

"The Western World owes a debt of gratitude to Spain and her people for many things over the centuries. But in my mind, in this lovely summer of 1953, she stands on a glorious pedestal of the twentieth century for being the only nation in the world which has defeated Communism. Russia was swallowed up by this monstrous thing, so was Czechoslovakia, Hungary and Poland. Bulgaria, Romania and Yugoslavia fell with ease. Half of Germany, all of China, all of Tibet, half of Korea. But none of Spain. The Communist strategy called for the taking of Russia in the North and Spain in the South. Then the pincers were to close over all of Europe. The world should be tremendously grateful to Spain for the great sacrifice she made in hitting back so hard that the Communist time-table has been upset ever since.

"But this is a day of festival. I should be telling you of our home in far off California and thanking you for the charm and beauty of the Spanish architecture, Spanish furnishings and costumes which surround us in our homes in the New Spain of California. Our cities are a Litany of the Saints, you know: San Diego, San Francisco, Los Angeles, San Carlos,

123

San Mateo, San Jose, Santa Monica, San Fernando, San Bernardino, San Luis Obispo. Hundreds and hundreds of cities and towns which still breathe the perfume of Old Spain over our homes and our families and our children.

"Let us all unite today in expressing the hope that Castellana Hilton will be for many years to come a place of peace and comfort for all travelers of good will. Let us hope that Castellana Hilton will be so managed and conducted that it will reflect honor and credit on Spain as well as ourselves. Let us all hope that for many years in the future Castellana Hilton's guests will find here warm-hearted friendship and the true hospitality of the Spanish people. Let us hope that years hence it may be said that those who 'passed by here' as guests of this hotel will have been treated with courtesy and respect, and with the dignity that is due to people of good will in all parts of the world."

Spaniards jumped to their feet as he finished and in an ovation that lasted for minutes they expressed their admiration for a man who had come to them and addressed them in their own language.

Although he has not had the access to Turkish which he from childhood had to Spanish, it is certain that when the Istanbul Hilton is inaugurated this year he will rise, when called on, and utter at least part of his formal address in the language of the country.

"He is a dedicated believer in international amenities," an associate said recently. "He believes that any language can be learned sufficiently to master a few words of courtesy and that the least any American can do is try to bring those words into his command of language. In Havana and Mexico he will speak Spanish with the fluency that years of use has brought him. And I'll guarantee you he will spend weeks learning Greek when the time comes for the operation in Athens. He was a young man in Europe, in service, when he noticed that courteous Frenchmen always at least tried to speak English

124

when dealing with American or British officers and he never has forgotten the lesson. He has passed along this belief and most of us in the operation have some knowledge of other languages. At houses like the Waldorf, the Plaza, the Palmer House or the Town House it is imperative. These houses have a wide international clientele. I've found, as I expect he did, that even a faulty attempt to speak another man's language is respected and creates an immediate rapport."

Hilton is excited about the Instanbul hotel. He is excited about operating a hotel in Turkey. He considers Turkey the only truly successful revolutionary effort in our time and one of the few in all time. He vastly admires the strides that Turkey has made in the thirty years that it has been a free republic. He believes that much of the success of the young republic arises from the nature of its broad and democratic constitution which in a multiplicity of ways duplicates the Constitution of the United States. It guarantees every citizen freedom from molestation on religious, ritualistic or philosophic grounds, guards the sanctity of the individual and the home, provides freedom of conscience, thought, speech, press, assembly, association, travel, labor, private property, contract and incorporation. Special privilege is denied and primary education is mandatory for all citizens and is gratuitous in government schools. The wide freedoms constructed and given to the Turkish people by Mustafa Kemal Ataturk, first President of the Turkish republic, have been cherished since his death in 1938 and are receiving devoted guardianship by Mahmut Celal Bayar, the current President, who rose to power with his opposition Democratic Party in 1945. He was elected President in 1950, after thirty years of work as one of the leading architects of the new republic's political and democratic structure. Turkey is an outstanding member of the North Atlantic Treaty Organizations and from the beginning has fulfilled its obligations in this role. It is also a member of the Council of Europe as a strategic outpost of

Western civilization and culture. It provided brave and distinguished troops for the tragic struggle in Korea and has in every other way distinguished itself as a modern, free nation.

Of its 21,000,000 people, 80 percent are agricultural, 8 percent are miners and industrial workers, 7 percent are in public service and the professions, and the remaining 5 percent àre engaged in commerce and transportation. The revolution which created the armies of liberation whose successes led to abolition of the Sultanate has been a penetrating effort, reaching down into the lives of the most humble citizens. One of its major deeds was the emancipation of women, giving them equal rights and duties with men. The result is a legislature with a high percentage of women members and the professions of law, medicine, social service and air transport abound in women.

Under the old Ottoman Empire there was a high percentage of abject illiteracy. The republic's first task, directed by Kemal Ataturk, was to abolish this condition and set in motion a carefully planned, long-term public education program. It discarded the ancient Arabic script and substituted the Latin phonetic alphabet and modern characters. It created a plan by which gifted students are sent abroad at government expense to complete their studies and acquaint themselves with conditions and ethics and political concepts in the modern world. The majority of these exceptional scholars choose the United States as the country in which they wish to complete their educations.

In thirty years, the republic has transformed the land as well as the people. It has achieved astonishing results in every phase of cultural, political and technological progress. Without bloodshed, a revolution has taken place which has changed every aspect of life. Political Turkey is a country respected by every free nation. It is capable, as freedom from aggression has proved, of dealing with any eventuality in the firm conviction that Turkey is part and spearhead of the West, the bastion

126

of democracy in the East. In social fields, Turkey has advanced her standard of life considerably. At a time when unrest and uncertainty paralyze the world, Turkey is on her way to achieving a balanced economy.

Turkey has shown that her road has been the right one, that she can help herself if she can obtain the right tools at the right time, and that her concentrated efforts to achieve her healthy, free goal have been fruitful. Much has been accomplished in three decades. Much remains to be done, as any thinking Turk will concede. But already she has proved that she can be trusted to fulfill her pledge to work and fight for freedom, peace and democracy.

This kind of situation appeals to Hilton. He has a profound respect for free nations which intend to remain free. His abounding love for the United States encompasses smaller, newer nations striving for the same great results and he believes it his duty to contribute his share toward these achievements in whatever amount possible.

The Istanbul Hilton, overlooking the Sea of Marmara, is a dazzling white, ten-story oblong which seems to float on its supporting columns. When the negotiations for his management were completed, Hilton cabled his enthusiasm to Governor-Mayor Fahrettin Gokay:

"It is my hope that the Istanbul Hilton," he wrote, "will be an edifice of peace serving free men from all our nations which are joining together to create a world of hope and security for the future. It is with the greatest respect and belief in the future of Turkey that we will join with you in helping create an outstanding center of hospitality which will not only bring economic benefits but understanding between peoples."

Hilton's brother, Captain Carl H. Hilton, of Hilton Hotels International, while in Istanbul, discovered the first employee on the payroll of the new hotel. He was served luncheon at Istanbul's Park Hotel by a gray-haired, attentive man who, it turned out, had been a waiter at the Jefferson Hotel in St. Louis back in 1911.

Captain Hilton talked at length with the waiter, and as a result that he was hired to begin work the day that the Istanbul Hilton opens. He was the first Turkish national put on the future payroll.

Hilton's brother brought back not only a deep impression of Turkey but an appreciation of the nation's vast sense of humor. He told his brother about this, as displayed in cartoons, printed jokes and other ways, and Hilton recalled something once said by Theodore Roosevelt:

"In any kind of a battle, I like a man who laughs as he fights."

It was also discovered by American troops in Korea, who not only grabbed every Turkish comic book and cartoon in sight but noted with some amazement that Turkish troops waded into the toughest kind of fight wearing wide, amused grins which showed their teeth. They were tough, and seemed to take a hearty, boisterous and laughing relish in hand-to-hand combat.

Several chartered planes will fly American guests to the opening of the Istanbul Hilton as they did, a year ago, to the opening of the Castellana Hilton. The hotel king loves a party. He loves to be a host. He takes enormous pride in being a good host. When they arrived at the Castellana, Spanish workmen still were taking down some scaffolds, applying the last dabs of paint to murals, sewing together the seams of rugs in the corridors. But the rooms were ready and immaculate. He and his guests and Spanish friends were not abashed when Gary Cooper received so many telephone calls that the hotel's switchboard became jammed and for several hours could not handle any other communications traffic. These and other minor conditions, caused by bringing construction of a huge hotel to conclusion right on the dot, failed to dampen the spirit of the opening day and, indeed, guests found fun in watching artists work on murals and sculpture while seated at ease in the large triangular courtyard of the hotel.

The Castellana Hilton is on a prominent corner of the stately Paseo de la Castellana in Madrid. It is in the center of the embassy district, three blocks from the embassy of the United States. Not far away on La Gran Via, formally called La Avenida José Antonio, are the elegant ateliers of such world-famed fashion designers as Balenciaga and Pedro Rodriguez.

"Madrid has an altitude of 2,000 feet," Hilton says, "and has a short winter followed by a wonderful spring. The temperature never gets much higher in summer than the upper 80's and it is a dry heat, pleasant and most bearable. Spain is being rediscovered as one of the great potential tourist countries. The flow of visitors is increasing annually. They had an unofficial count of 100,000 foreigners visiting Spain in 1952. That was just about doubled in 1953. There is no sign of a saturation point. It can, and almost certainly will, go right on increasing."

The luxury hotel which will rise in Cairo is planned as a structure that will cost $6,000,000 and is frankly expected to take the place of the long revered Shepheard's in the affection of world travelers of all nations. The plans call for 400 rooms, with opening set for 1955. It will be air-conditioned and occupy a six acre site on the bank of the Nile on land at one time occupied by the Kesi el Nil barracks of the British Army.

Shepheard's was destroyed by fire in 1952 when anti-British mobs rioted through Cairo. It was in the center of the populous city. A landmark of Oriental splendor, the old Shepheard's was a haven. The Nile Hilton should, as the only luxury hotel in Cairo, become one also. The building, as are all of the Hilton hotels abroad, will be of reinforced concrete and steel and will use native architectural design while having American equipment. Hilton's agreement is for twenty years on a leasing arrangement with the Egyptian government. Egyptian funds will pay for the construction of the hotel and Hilton will, under the usual formula, provide furnishings, staff and management. According to present blueprints the hotel will be T-shaped and have ten stories. Native marble, rare woods and sandstone will be decorative features in the interior of the building. A large restaurant overlooking the Nile will be installed on the roof, with a view toward the pyramids. The lobby and main public rooms will be just above the ground floor and the acreage outside will contain a swimming pool, parking areas and tennis courts as well as those American foundation stones of modern hotel operation: a coffee shop and snack bar.

Although Cairo's climate has impressed itself on most people as being at its best in winter, the swimming pool outside and full air-conditioning inside will make the Nile Hilton a year-round operation.

Hilton, basing his thinking on his settled and lasting aversion to "resort" hotel management, will not consider any foreign hotel undertaking that has a seasonal flavor. He looks upon it as a bad and costly business, with such hotels jammed and jumping four months a year and yawning empty the other eight. It involves stresses on staff, seasonal layoffs which impress him as the worst possible kind of operation and dips and rises in economic graphs which fill him with distaste.

"It is a patently silly thing to assemble a fine staff, train it in the ways of a hotel and its spirit, inculcate loyalty and enthusiasm," he says, "and then have to turn it out for two-thirds of a year. You never get the trained men and women back, you are constantly having to hire and train new help and you are, therefore, constantly vexing the guests who have to endure insufficiently trained help. I like to put a staff together, assign a fine manager as its leader and hope to find the whole lot together five or more years later. That way you get a staff that has pride in its hotel and in its guest relations. Look out for those seasonal places with quaint names like 'Home In The Pines.' They have green help and generally terrible management."

Istanbul, for centuries a major city on the East-West trade routes, is not seasonal and neither is Cairo, the capital of Egypt. Mexico City is a full twelve months city and so is Havana. Madrid is a busy, bustling place around the calendar. Athens, London, Rome and all the other cities in which he hopes to erect and manage large, modern hotels are not seasonal.

It simply doesn't pay and hotel operation that doesn't pay is no good for Hilton or anyone else.

"The guest does indeed come first," he says. "That is axiomatic. It is the duty of a hotel to please its guests or it will not long have guests. But good management and pleasant guest relations do not mean you have to give the place away. I also have a duty to my stockholders and, up to now, they have received careful, business-like operation and consideration. Our dividends are mounting. I could not last in my business if I were not as firm on the business side as I am adamant on the guest relation side. I want happy hotels, desired hotels and popular hotels, of course, but not at the cost of my business. I would not command respect and stature in the business community with any other point of view."

Meanwhile, the silver spade has dug into the soil on the banks of the Nile.

The acreage he demands for new hotels will be generous not only in Cairo but in the other cities. The Istanbul Hilton will rest on fifteen acres of ground. The age of the automobile and tourists on wheels have brought about his concept that modern hotels must provide shelter and space for cars.

"It's not only a matter of car space," he says. "It is also a conviction that hotels must have landscaped grounds, give the feeling of space and park, with native trees and flowering shrubs to appeal to the eye. Give a man a choice between a

131

hotel huddled down in town or out a little ways in a gardened space and he'll take the hotel with gardens and paths every time. People like to feel free to roam about the grounds, to rest on a bench under a shade tree, to have something green and colorful to look at through a window. The cost of city ground prevents any such generosity of space downtown in most communities of any size. But you can always arrange to find economically feasible space if you go out a mile or so. Not even enough to make transportation into the heart of a city a problem. I think hotel men must consider this in planning future hotels. Part of the competition coming from motels is that, generally speaking, they are on the rims of communities where trees and formal planting and a feeling of unconfined space are available."

When he bought the Town House he acquired a hotel, well within a city, but beautifully landscaped. It is in the nature of several hotels in Los Angeles and Beverly Hills that their planners insisted upon ample grounds and garden space. Joe Drown now operates the Bel-Air Hotel in the mainly residential community in which Hilton has his Casa Encantada. It has magnificent planting, including a glassed-in tree and shrubs in one end of the main dining room. The planning of the Beverly Hilton was around space and landscaping. The Beverly Hills Hotel has winding paths and formal planting. Only the Beverly Wilshire is somewhat lacking in garden area and this has been overcome by a luncheon terrace in the open, overlooking a large swimming pool and decorative cabanas, giving the feel of space and open air.

Naturally, city hotels built earlier and acquired by him after their construction have little or no garden area. They are in the thick of business districts. But he has insisted on interior planting to provide greenery and a sense of openness. The days when a hotel lobby was considered finished with one or two peeling tubs of drooping rubber trees has long since vanished. Now whole sections of lobbies, long corridors

132

leading to public rooms and even the space under the marquees has opulent planting. The wide corridor leading to the Park Row dining room in the Conrad Hilton in Chicago has the effect of a greenhouse, with lush plants spreading wide their thick, green leaves. Hilton began tapping at the ornate beams and pilasters in the old room one day and discovered that as decoration they were old-fashioned and that structurally they were useless.

"Tear all these out and let's take a second look at things," Hilton directed.

When the dismantling was completed, the room was 15 percent larger. Hollow columns were gone, fat pilasters had disappeared and meaningless overhead beams had been torn away. He directed that five percent of the increased area be maintained and that the other ten percent be given over to plants and shrubs.

These swift decisions arise out of conditions created in the original architecture of hotels he did not build. They do not always have to do with increased space desires or with decorative plans. For months he gave thought to the laundry operation at the Plaza, the Waldorf-Astoria and the Roosevelt. It seemed incomprehensible to him that each house needed its own laundry. It didn't make sense. He set up a survey which brought him the answer he wanted: there was no reason at all why a central laundry could not handle the problem for all three hotels, thus providing valuable space at the Plaza and the Waldorf. The change has worked out efficiently and with profit. Anna Tynan, who for forty years has been first an employee and later in charge of the Plaza laundry, was appointed head of the consolidated operation. But that wasn't all. Hilton sent for Dean Carpenter, general manager of the Plaza.

"Dean," he said, "I think we have a party due. Any employee who remains on a job for forty years and grows in it and gives the kind of satisfaction Anna has given deserves a

133

little celebration. I'm going to promote Anna to full charge of the three combined laundries, but before she walks out of the Plaza to start work at the Roosevelt I want you to give her the best party we've had around here in years." She had an orchid corsage, received gifts from the management, an embossed scroll and a buss on the cheek from every member of the staff.

And a square of the original marble of the Plaza.

That final gift came about at the end of the party when Anna stood up to tell the rest of the group her appreciation. "There's something in this fine old house I have always felt belonged to me," she said. "My late father was the marble contractor when the hotel was built. It's been my feeling that at least one of the stones is mine."

Carpenter whispered to an assistant, who left the room. In ten minutes he was back. Yes, there was some marble down in the sub-basement, left over from a reconstruction job. Carpenter ordered a square of it washed, dried and delivered to Anna with the compliments of the house. It is now the top of a coffee table.

The Hilton hotels are filled with staff personality stories. An example is the story of Jack Lacy, Baltimore-born barman at the Mayflower in Washington. Lacy in his youth was an animal trainer, traveling with a leopard act in Keith vaudeville. When vaudeville became extinct, he learned the art of bartending and, after working several of the top clubs around Washington and in Palm Beach, went to work at the Mayflower.

One night, just at closing time, a motion picture director, in Washington to film local sequences for the picture, "My Son, John," starring Helen Hayes, came in and asked for a stimulant. Lacy was unable to serve him because by law it was time to close the bar. But he explained it so tactfully that the director remained merely to talk and, in conversation, discovered that Lacy had been in show business.

134

"That's great," said the director. "Solves a problem for me. I've been looking for someone who can play a senator with a keen, direct, piercing gaze. You've got it. Probably what quelled the leopards. You go to work in my movie tomorrow."

Lacy played the senator with the long, level look in his eyes and when his acting job was ended returned to the Mayflower as barman. Some months later, another unit was sent to Washington to film part of another picture. Lacy's work record on the Hayes picture was in the files and he was promptly hired again as an actor.

"But it was a demotion, in a way," says Lacy. "The second time they made me a representative."

There is also the story of the actual senator who, at the last minute before having to walk into a dining room as guest of honor and main speaker, discovered to his horror that his wife had failed to pack his cufflinks for his evening shirt. There was no time, literally no time, to borrow or buy any. An assistant manager provided the solution with a quickly arrived at idea.

"I hope you'll accept an idea, Senator," he said. "It will work."

"Of course I'll accept it!" the senator boomed. "I must be in that room in exactly fifty seconds or be rude to the President of the United States! What is the idea?"

"I'll staple your cuffs together," said the junior executive.

That night a famed senator made a historic speech—with stapled shirt cuffs.

The stately Palmer House also has its tender stories. Some twenty-five years ago, in Chicago, a man without a job was married to a woman who believed in him. Between them, they had 50 cents with which to buy a little celebration breakfast. It left nothing for bridal flowers or even the most modest gift for the bride. He lifted his cup of coffee in a toast and said: "On our twenty-fifth anniversary I'll take you to the Palmer House for dinner, the finest to be had."

They moved on to Minnesota and, in time, started a small restaurant in the town of Eveleth.

She became the mother of three daughters and struggled to bring them up and educate them. In 1942, Fred Klepitch died and the struggle for Ilma Klepitch became redoubled. She often told her children of the promise their father had made on his wedding day and, as what would have been her twenty-fifth anniversary neared, her daughter, Katherine, wrote a letter to Vernon Herndon, general manager of the Palmer House, telling him the story and asking for a Palmer House menu to put on her mother's anniversary table. Herndon wrote back by return mail, offering the hospitality of the Palmer House, including an anniversary dinner in the hotel and a room for as long as they cared to remain.

Mrs. Klepitch and her daughter went to Chicago, and walked into the Palmer House on a length of red carpet. They saw shows, were on "Welcome Travelers," where Mrs. Klepitch received many gifts, and at the anniversary dinner in the hotel was served a huge cake in the shape of a heart, for her anniversary was St. Valentine's Day.

"It's the way Fred would have done it," she told Herndon when she went to his office to say goodbye and extend her thanks.

Hilton can point to many honors extended to him. He takes reasonable pride in the fact that an organization of gourmets, Les Amis d'Escoffier, choose the Plaza for one of their annual and exacting dinners. Preparation and planning of this dinner exacts the utmost from every one in the hotel and most particularly from the chef. At the 1952 dinner, three chefs participated in a dinner the members of the group still talk about. Humbert Gatti, executive chef, worked with Raymond Bosquer, banquet chef, and Albino Bonardi, sous chef, on putting together a dinner which caused Robert W. Dana, an editor of the New York *World Telegram and Sun* to write:

"In the ten years I've been attending Escoffier dinners, I

136

can't remember such a conscious effort on the part of the host hotel going so all out to make this culinary event one to challenge the artisans of future spreads. To begin with there was a meal before you entered the dining room, at the magnificent buffet created by Chef Valdo Fattori.

"The first course . . . consomme double boreal . . . with les convives told to look for the constellations in the rich essence of chicken and beef, through the diced fresh vegetables and the star-shaped cooked egg whites.

"Came the trout of the next course, fresh flown from Pennsylvania, boned and filled with a mousse of turbot and lobster, poached in dry champagne and served with tarragon hollandaise sauce. The delicate dish had the extreme good fortune to have as its liquid running mate Pouilly Fume 1949, otherwise known as Chateau du Nozet.

"Next a classic, named after Talleyrand, one of the great French gourmets of the nineteenth century . . . the heart of sweetbreads, larded and braised in Madeira, garnished with tiny mushroom caps, truffles, ripe olives and a crescent-shaped crouton and served with new peas in sweet butter.

"With the sweetbreads was served a light and delightful Bordeaux wine, Chateau d'Estournel—St. Estephe 1947. This was a prelude to the roast baby lamb of the main course which had as its running mate Volnay-Clos des Chenes—Domaine Ropiteau 1937.

"The dessert served on illuminated blocks of ice consisted of scooped small pineapples filled with pineapple sherbert in Kirsch. The final touch was lent by colored spun sugar that gave the impression of Christmas wrapping and petits fours served from a sugar basket."

It is not reported that any participant raided his refrigerator for a bedtime snack when he arrived at his home that night.

The menus for the hotels abroad are a constant source of discussion within Hilton Hotels International. It is conceded that national dishes be available and constantly present on these menus but that, also, European generic cooking be a part of them together with certain dishes appealing mainly to Americans.

Decor of the public rooms receives Hilton's personal attention constantly. He long ago realized that you cannot design a room, build and paint it and leave it that way for years. The public tires of the same decor no matter how affectionately it may feel toward a popular room. One of the few exceptions is the men's bar at the Waldorf. To change that would be, in the fixed minds of thousands of men the world over, like scrawling on the walls of Mount Vernon or setting fire to the Lincoln Memorial. They don't want it changed and probably would stage a riot if it were changed.

Flying between coasts in an airplane, Hilton was reading a newspaper. He came across one of those little two-line fillers all papers use. It read: "The first official postoffice in the United States was in a Boston tavern owned by Richard Fairbanks."

Those seventeen words stuck in his mind and began to burgeon into an idea. He decided to create an Oak Room, a bar primarily for men, at the Palmer House. The Oak Room at the Plaza was an institution. The Palmer House should have one. The Oak Room in Chicago would be tasteful and decorative if it carried a postage stamp motif. There was nothing feminine in such a decorative idea and, also, most men are fascinated by historic stamps. Edgar Miller, a Chicago artist, was commissioned to design the walls of the room, with emphasis on a mural over the bar. He depicted American stamps and cancellations in colorful array, using the first five- and ten-cent stamps of 1847, the famous bank note issues of 1870 and 1871, the series of 1861, picturing Lincoln, Franklin, Jackson and others. As end pieces on the back bar, the hotel staff discovered two old whiskey barrels dating from 1805 and one of which was authenticated as having come from the counter in the Ship's Tavern in Brighton, England. The other was authenticated as 1806, when it was bought to form the pair now in the Oak Room at the Palmer House. The other three walls of the room are in massive oak panels.

Occasionally, an incident crops up which allows Hilton a burst of humor. It happened at the Town House at least once. A motion picture company was filming in its lobby some scenes for a picture called "Donovan's Brain." In the midst of things, two guests from the Middle West walked in after a shopping tour and were astonished to see cameras grinding, recognized stars acting and a famous director shepherding the entire proceeding. Hilton, standing to one side, was watching.

"Good Lord," one of the women exclaimed, "I've tried for two weeks to get my nose inside a studio door and here I've got the whole works going for me right in the lobby of my own hotel!"

"Hilton service, madam," said Hilton gravely, bowing slightly and disappearing into the manager's office to hide his wide grin.

Hilton is immensely proud of the individuals in his employ. A great chef, a self-reliant manager rising to an occasion, a woman with a record of forty years in one hotel, deeds of good heart, examples of skilled operation, all these give him pride. He is also proud when his payroll shows the name of a man who has contributed to hotel benefits. One such is George Dennis, veteran head of room service at the Mayflower in Washington. Dennis is the inventor of two devices which have done more to make room service a true service than anything else imaginable. Back in 1932 Dennis perfected and received a patent for the folding, rolling, ball-bearing table which makes it possible for room waiters to whisk meals in and out of rooms with ease and with a minimum of struggle for all concerned. The second design he patented was the portable metal heater which is placed under these tables and keeps several courses hot while guests dawdle over the first course. These inventions not only speed up room service and make it possible to deliver hot meals to the rooms, but they make it possible to serve a larger number of rooms with a smaller staff. Room service at the Mayflower, for example, requires only eighteen waiters, two captains and four telephone operators.

The two inventions should have made Dennis wealthy, but the fact is that they didn't. Dennis has no major regrets about this.

"It just didn't turn out that way," he says. "I hadn't enough money to put them over in the necessary way. Let's call them my contribution to a business I love."

It was the Mayflower, also, which was the first to solve a problem that has plagued many a hotel. Kitchens often are at basement level in hotels to keep odors and noise from the dining room. If not in the basement they are on the first floor and the dining room is on the second. Until the Mayflower did it, waiters used to have to walk up and down the connecting stairway, often juggling huge, heavily laden trays. Waiters at the Mayflower's Presidential Dining Room now have it much easier. They take an electric escalator, with consequent speeding of service and less wear and tear on waiters.

"It's a hard job," Hilton says. "Waiters deserve all the help they can get."

His prowls through the hotels, unadvertised and often enough completely unexpected, result in such rooms as the Oak Room at the Palmer House and his discovery that men and women of accomplishment are on his payrolls. He noted that 4,000 persons a day passed through the lower arcade of the Palmer House and that there were no bar facilities to serve them. The Town and Country Room was created, and has been an immediate success. He is candid in his delight over such discoveries and often suggests that his managers do a little prowling on their own.

"If you are packing a box, you get the most in that you

140

can," he says. "There is nothing shameful in operating at a profit."

It had been his hope, when he bought the Palmer House, to increase its profits by, perhaps, $50,000 a month over the preceding year. The actual, certified increase the first year was $1,450,000. One decision was to put all restaurants on a seven-day basis. Theretofore some of them had been inoperative weekends on the basis that business traffic in that area of Chicago was at home on Saturdays and Sundays. He found room for 60 additional guest rooms by eliminating whole rows of lockers that were not essential. The Palmer House had a photographic department eating up space and not producing many pictures. He installed a small, intimate night club which turned up at the end of the first year with a $20,000 profit.

The consolidation of three laundries in New York was but an extension of a similar move in Chicago, when he consolidated the Conrad Hilton and Palmer House laundries and saved $230,000 annually.

When peak rental conditions arise, as during a war, a convention period or similar pressure of people, he is not content to turn the overflow away or disgruntle people waiting for their reservations to be freed by previous guests. He remembers how it was at the Mobley with men standing around the lobby first on one foot and then on another. For the Palmer House, for example, he created the Interim Club, which is comfortable, spacious, has newspapers and magazines and other facilities. Guests who have to wait an hour or so for their reserved space to be vacated do so in a pleasant, relaxing atmosphere. At the Town House, in a city where frantic telephone calls seem to be indigenous, he installed telephones even in the elevators. The Roosevelt, in a city where theatergoing is habitual, has a pleasant service for lovers of drama who are taking midnight trains. The guests check out before going to theater, give their train reservation locations to the bell captain and, during the evening, as the trains are made up, bellmen take the luggage and install it in the proper Pullman compartments or berths. Thus the guests can go direct from theater to their trains without the agonizing anxiety of having to check out and lose precious time when minutes count most.

The Plaza has set up a pool of university students who speak several foreign languages and are available as baby sitters for the children of guests from other countries. These students not only can converse with the parents but know nursery rhymes and bedtime stories in a variety of languages. Thus they can quickly gain the confidence of a shy child who speaks only its native tongue.

One thing that must be on his desk by noon daily is a detailed weather report from each city in which he has a hotel. Study of these reports enables him to estimate each hotel's income for the next twenty-four hours within 10 percent of accuracy. This, again, is one of his prides. He has found, over the years, that he often comes much closer than that in his estimates.

He has further pride in his public speaking. Expansion of his hotels to foreign countries has increased the calls on his speaking time. His favored topics are the United Europe movement, the menace of Communism in a free world and the need for morality and leadership in government. Probably his most quoted address was on "The Battle For Freedom," which earned for him the annual Brotherhood Award from the National Conference of Christians and Jews. And he received the Freedom Foundations Award for another speech, "Blueprint For Freedom." The annual convention of the American Hotel Association asked him to speak on "The America I'd Like to Live In" and the University of Detroit invited him, last June, to make the commencement address at which time the honorary degree of Doctor of Laws was conferred on him.

This last February he arranged for the second annual

142

Prayer Breakfast at the Mayflower. This was attended by President Eisenhower, as it was in 1953; Vice-President Nixon, cabinet officers, the Senate in almost its entirety and most of the House, in addition to dignitaries from foreign governments and ranking ministers from all denominations. This is a breakfast at which the force of prayer is restated and re-dedication to prayer as a means to peace is pledged. Hilton believes implicitly and without the slightest question in the power of prayer. This faith was instilled in him early by his mother and he has had demonstrable proof of its efficacy through the years. President Eisenhower is another man who often publicly states his faith in prayer. Although both men long have been friends, the annual Prayer Breakfast brings them together in common cause.

Hilton believes just as implicitly in the future and destiny of the United States. He believes that the nation's future is strong and shining. He foresees struggle and debate and the necessity of belief that a nation rightly dedicated to peace is a nation possessed of a philosophy which ultimately must triumph. He has found that he is not without government approval of his foreign operations and has said so publicly.

"It is the feeling of the government, and one in which I heartily concur," he says, "that the operation of first-class American hotels in free countries of the world will do a great deal to stimulate the spending of the tourist dollar, and that in this way American business can make a concrete contribution to the economy of friendly nations."

No one can successfully argue that down. From the beginning, when federal aid began going to foreign countries to strengthen them against aggression, it has been a principle of the effort that in time American private industry and enterprise would assume a large portion of the needful burden. Hilton has been in the van of the principle with his hotels wisely compounded of local currency, insuring national pride, and American ingenuity, insuring local profit.

143

Since each hotel in a foreign country represents the spending of several millions of dollars the immediate stimulation is plain to see. Native money, earmarked for the project, goes into materials and wages. Labor is the first direct beneficiary and, in turn, passes this money on down to retail levels. Artists, represented by architects, painters, decorators, upholsterers, weavers, and so on, benefit right from the beginning and they, too, pass their fees on to retail levels. Dealers in materials, steel, concrete, fixtures, ceramics, glass, wool, linens and like commodities similarly benefit, finding sales where none existed before. The electrical trades benefit in exactly the way that other groups do and, when the hotel is a finished product, the several million dollars have been plowed deep into the economic strata of the nation.

With each hotel completed and ready for operation, employment rises. Jobs are created. The staffs, almost totally local employees, give work and income to several hundred persons from the kitchens and storerooms to the lobby and offices. Retail shops spring into being. Native skills and arts go on sale to visiting guests from other lands. The food markets of a city are stimulated by the new outlet for sales at the hotel. Taxicab and car rental agencies flourish. Indeed, it would be difficult to find any corner of, say, Madrid or Istanbul not directly benefitted by the new enterprise and a major virtue is that a hotel is a continuing stimulation to the economy and not a temporary operation. Hotels successfully operated bring constant fresh money into the community. The original investment in time is dwarfed by the steady flow of new money from dozens of other and outside sources. Few visitors to any country confine their expenditures to a hotel. They tour a city, visit other restaurants and entertainments, buy goods and souvenirs, hire guides and transportation.

The American government would, obviously, welcome any enterprise creating this new economy in a friendly nation and the nation itself obviously would choose to participate in it actively. Hilton's problem, once the international hotel dream began to be a reality, never was the originating arrangement but, rather, convincing himself in each case that a real contribution to local economics was being achieved. It is not monumentally difficult to design and build a hotel. But to erect and operate one in a locale certain to support the hotel is another question. It was imperative that continuing success be unavoidable. Problematic was not enough. Possibly was not enough. It had almost to amount to a certified pre-fact. Many foreign cities need new hotel facilities. Many of them seem, superficially, to promise success and rewards. But only seem. Hilton and his international staff have evolved a wise and foolproof set of tests and measurements which supply them with a predictable estimation. At this point in his career the last thing he wants is a hotel opening with a world-wide flourish and closing miserably with a world-wide bang. He is not accustomed to failure and it certainly would not become him at this stage. Or any other from here on in.

It is a fact that several foreign emmissaries have approached him with rosy offers for participation in a hotel venture and have received from him a polite but final decision not to participate. In each case he has done them the courtesy of a careful survey and his decision not to enter into the proposal has been arrived at after the survey has shown small chance for success of the projected hotel.

"It would be doing such people a painful disservice to encourage them," he says. "And it is important that, in the end, our own country, because I am an American, would receive some of the bitter censure for a failure. It is healthier and more honest to state right at the start of such proposals that all indications are against a successful operation. There is disappointment at first, but later comes realization that they received the best possible advice and saved themselves a costly licking."

He favors an old saying from his Texas days, and one still

used in Texas by the fabled men of oil: "I like to see everybody get a little rich." It has happened in his official family, it has happened to those who backed him when things were crashing all around him. His common sense tells him today that if an American can help everybody in a foreign country to get a little rich the credit will in time redound to America itself and, in this way, he will have contributed a little to the world welfare and esteem of the United States. The same common sense tells him that a reckless American prodding foreign capital into investments doomed to failure is not only bringing discredit upon himself but, by the same turn, upon the United States. The man and the nation, in these days and in foreign eyes, are inextricably tied together.

It is in the nature of competition for one side to eye the other side with slight suspicion. There are hotel men in America who eye Hilton's expansion abroad with a jaundiced glance. They do not hesitate to say that he is traveling too fast for his shoes. A percentage of this kind of comment arises out of business jealousies and can be stricken out as emotional caterwauling. The remaining percentage honestly believes that this swift foreign expansion is a dangerous game. It seems only fair to answer them. A careful, unprejudiced, impersonal study of the entire structure of Hilton Hotels International gives no evidence that it is dangerous. It is first of all a business organization. Not one arrangement has been arrived at without long and careful study of every predictable factor. Financing has received scrupulous attention. The relation between cost and foreseeable return has been balanced with care. Nowhere has cost been allowed to stray beyond the rigid fact of compensating revenues. The best financial opinion in America and Europe is that safe ground is being trod upon. Indeed, it comes down to a simple point: if it falls apart it will be because of world conflict, in which case nothing would have value. Hilton had to confront this kind of thinking before when war panic on the West Coast put a decision squarely up to him. He was being offered jewels at the cost of paste, so to speak, because many persons thought the Japanese would arrive any day and take over. Hilton didn't think they would arrive "any day." If they did, he reasoned, no one would have anything anyway. If they didn't, he would have acquired the beautiful Town House at a fraction of its value.

He now believes that there will not be world conflict and his foreign holdings will be eminently successful as well as a direct benefit to this country's prestige abroad. If there is world conflict again and the enemy moves in on Europe, nothing will mean anything by any measurement. All concerned will lose together. But not because of any deed of his.

That is an honest answer to any carping. It an earnest result of long study of all of the tangibles. Hilton thinks big but is not foolhardy and certainly it must be apparent that an unsuccessful operation irks him. He doesn't think in terms of maybe. He thinks in terms of exactness. He would no more enter into a questionable or flighty arrangement than he would donate the Waldorf to a newsboy on the corner. He is not, to use a term from the oil fields, a wildcatter. And no doubt the first to subscribe to that would be his stockholders. He hasn't left any of them holding a yawning and dismaying sack.

This particular aspect of the Hilton foreign operations is gone into here in such detail because American business is at the threshold of opportunity in other countries. Leaders in other lines of business have the same chance to expand their efforts as Hilton has had. Nations scarred by war are crying for mutual endeavors. The oil business has long since moved overseas to the benefit of nationals and governments in participating countries and to stockholders back home. At least one soft drink combine is moving into countries which never before heard of the product. American soldiers abroad helped popularize the drink and, when the war ended, the parent company without hesitation began operations in foreign areas. Hilton is leading the American hotel business overseas and into Latin-America. Manufacturers of heavy equipment of all kinds, notably agricultural machinery, are combing foreign markets for business and setting up participating organizations.

Hilton, however, is a leader in his move into the international hotel market. He is as alone as he was when he had the brains to foresee the end of a depression and a boom in hotels. Hotel men from coast to coast wrung their hands and cried the blues. Not only were their hotels empty but their stocks and bonds were scraping the floor. Instead of seeing that an upswing had to come and that a smart man could make a dollar by buying the securities lying limply on the floor, they kept on moaning while Hilton went to work and acquired prize hotels at rock-bottom prices.

It is impossible to see how any man could be censured for it.

CHAPTER SEVEN

IF anything reported thus far in the Hilton story has aroused a hotel man anywhere to dreaming of selling his house to Hilton, let him, before he writes a letter or picks up the telephone, ask himself if the hotel he wants to sell is by any stretch of the imagination a resort hotel. If it is he can save stamps. Hilton has a built-in resistance to resort operation. He had an early disaffection for the Las Vegas purchase, and sold it as soon as he could. That it brought a $1,000,000 profit is beside the point. He would have sold it for an even break. He had an unhappy experience in Bermuda and another at Palm Beach in Florida.

His name is on the Caribe Hilton in Puerto Rico, true, but that magnificent house was built by the government of Puerto Rico, and Hilton is on a leasing arrangement. It should be remembered that Puerto Rico, much more than is the case with Bermuda, is an island of both pleasure and also business. Hilton doesn't like gambling any more today than he liked it in Las Vegas, but the government requested him to operate a casino in the hotel. The country gets revenues from the casino. When the place was being built and it was obvious that the casino would be a major attraction, he asked a lot of questions about legalized gambling on a strictly controlled and honest basis. He learned about house percentages, wheel percentages and similar folderol and still wasn't satisfied. Asking more questions, he learned that a man named John Scarne was America's foremost professional expert on cards, dice and percentages, and that Scarne did not gamble. Scarne made his living exposing cheats and sharpers and inventing harmless parlor games. He asked Scarne to come to see him, which Scarne forthwith did. The meeting was short and helpful.

"I want you to tell me, Mr. Scarne," said Hilton, "how best to set the casino up so that the public, the men and women who play, have a slightly better edge. I want this hotel to succeed as I want any hotel to succeed. If people go down there to Puerto Rico and lose a lot of money it isn't going to do either the country or the hotel any good. There is enough fleecing elsewhere in the Caribbean as it is. I'm sure you know that."

"I do," said Scarne. "It's my business to know."

"Well, I won't name countries or cities, but this operation is going to be clean. The government wants it clean—I want it clean—it's going to be clean. It's tough enough to win under the best circumstances. I want some idea of better than best circumstances. Is there some way to give the customer a better shake even under rigidly honest conditions?"

"There is in blackjack, Mr. Hilton," said Scarne. "You set a house rule that the dealer must draw to 16 and must stand on 17. I didn't invent the rule. It's in use in the better casinos the world over. But it gives the player a slightly better edge. As to dice, there isn't much you can do to the established odds. They are time-honored. As to roulette, that also is time-honored in its odds. They guarantee the house a percentage but they also give the player a fair shake, else gaming men and women the world over would not play and Monte Carlo would not exist. And anyone, man, mule or boy, who plays birdcage, deserves the trimming he is bound to get. That's really the tiger of the lot. It is thoroughly honest, it is not easy to gimmick, but it gives the player the trimming of his life. It's murderous."

Hilton thanked Scarne for his valuable help and bade him goodbye. As Scarne turned to leave he noticed figures on Hilton's memo pad; They read: "16-17."

It was of a piece with all of his personal investigation of anything having to do with hotels. He is constantly reading technical, furnishing and materials trade publications in order

150

to keep up with the latest developments. He was years ahead of the hotel business when he installed primitive air-conditioning in Waco, and he early became interested in a plastic floor tile that did not require mastic to make it adhere to the floor. Each tile had tiny suction cups on its base and all an installer had to do was place a tile in position, stamp on it and it would adhere. If a tile cracked or wore, it was a simple matter to pry it up and stamp down a new one, avoiding mastic, labor and time. The materials that go into a corridor carpet interest Hilton; machines that mix dough or bake pies or roast ham interest him. Infra-red cooking occupied his attention for weeks.

He believes that modern hotels must strive to remain modern and modern hotel managers must be on their toes in order to keep their houses at a maximum level of modernity with a minimum cost. He doesn't believe in throwing money around like confetti, but when money has to be spent he doesn't pinch it.

"We had some pretty odd rooms in some of the little houses back in Texas," he says. "I remember the Mobley probably had the oddest. It was in the days when a wooden chair, a single bed and a drugstore calendar on the wall made for something pretty fancy in hotel decor. Later on, for example the Dallas Hilton, we went up the ladder a few rungs in the decor department. But great hotels demand taste in room decoration. Your clientele comes from homes of taste. Come to think of it, I don't think I've seen a chair scarred by spurs in twenty years. When I first broke into the business, even the lobby floor was pock-marked by spurs."

It is a relatively easy thing, once equipped with zeal and a slide rule, to assemble a hatful of statistics concerning any large, successful and therefore active hotel. Large hotels are thriving cities in miniature. It is an old hotel story that in such houses as the Waldorf-Astoria or the Conrad Hilton a person literally could hole up for years and never set foot out

151

on the sidewalk. He could shower jewels and furs on his girl, he could assemble a wardrobe for himself, complete with morning and evening wear, visit barbers, baths, doctors, dentists, florists and a dozen other professions and trades. He could be shod and pedicured. He could have surgery up to and including an appendectomy. Meanwhile, thousands of sheets, towels, pounds of butter and layer cakes would be processed, the elevators would make, if all their trips for a year were measured, so-and-so many round trips to the moon. Such figures might be interesting to a statistician with a psychotic bent toward his profession, but to the layman they mean virtually nothing at all except that should he or his wife ever require any of these things the hotel could provide them.

What Hilton has worked for is not the providing of standard and luxury services, since they go with any self-respecting hotel like clean linen and fresh soap. His task has been to preserve tradition and spirit where they existed and to create spirit and house personality where they did not exist. Tradition he leaves to time since that is its only genuine source.

"You can make a hotel glisten from roof to basement, have the best dining room for counties around, have an efficient staff and excellent shops," he says, "but there is an indefinable quality that must be found and supplied else you have the most elegant ice-house in town. There is nothing colder than a hotel without a soul."

He opened the Caribe Hilton in mid-December of 1949 with the warmth already intact. Hilton was one of seven noted American hoteliers who were asked by mail to express themselves in the matter of taking over a hotel in Puerto Rico which would have everything, including a romantic seascape. Everything except a fine hotel man at the helm. It is some sort of commentary that six of them wrote back business-like, unimaginative and therefore slightly forbidding letters in purest front office English. They hedged and asked for more information and behaved for all the world like bankers being asked for a sizable loan by a total stranger. Hilton answered in perfect Spanish, using the graceful, *simpatico* salutation: *"Muy estimado amigo,"* i.e., "Very esteemed friend." The other six were in the doghouse forthwith and Hilton got the hotel.

And what did three considerate, warm words in Spanish get Hilton. A $7,500,000 hotel of smashing beauty. His income from the Caribe, which hovers at around $300,000 a year, is not only Hilton's to keep—but is tax free. If this hasn't driven all other American hoteliers to buying Spanish-English dictionaries and learning something about the Spanish language and—more important—Latin temperament, they are showing even less imagination than they did when they replied stiffly to invitational letters from Puerto Rico. Hilton's associates estimate his charming salutation as being worth about a million dollars a word.

Hilton uses words to mean something. He is a sparing semanticist. A writer for *Time,* assigned to prepare a story on Hilton, became entranced with the millions which boiled and bubbled around the man, and decided to ask Hilton direct by mail what he did with the half a million dollars a year which found their way direct to him, personally. It was an audacious, but important, request. Most business men would have either retreated behind the screen of calling it private information or would have suggested that the reporter consult one of his corporation executives. A detailed, honest answer, for example, necessitated an impeccable tax statement. None of these considerations froze Hilton. He did the simple if unexpected thing. He sat down at a desk and answered the question in detailed fullness and with frankness:

"Dear Sir:
You were asking me about my income for the year 1948. It was as follows:
My total income received was $577,222.53
Here's what became of it:

153

I paid Federal taxes of	316,672.04
I paid state income taxes to the	
State of California of	31,393.89
I paid miscellaneous taxes of	4,038.18

Making a total in taxes of:	$352,104.11
I gave away in charitable contributions	
to hospitals, schools, etc.	$ 80,944.50
I paid out in travel and business expenses	19,659.65
I had insurance premiums of	11,433.53
The maintenance of my residences in	
Bel-Air and Arrowhead cost	32,160.29
I made gifts to members of my family	
and others	36,526.74
My automobile and boat expenses	
amounted to	6,476.85
My clothing expense was	4,171.63
My club dues and entertainment	
amounted to	12,385.27

| All of the above itemized expenses | |
| amounted to | $555,862.57 |

So, out of my total income of $577,222.53, I was able to save approximately $21,000.

> Sincerely yours,
> (signed) C. N. Hilton."

The statement is clear, forthright and succinct, and there is a complete absence of economic jargon and double talk.

Hilton's concern for guests, demonstrated when he sent for Scarne and explored the possibility of more relaxed odds in favor of casino patrons, is habitual. He is no lobby boniface, although he wants to know what is going on in the lobby, for it is the pulse of a hotel. He works from home or office, directing the application of individual touches that will gratify noted guests. He had heard a vague report, for example, that Helen Traubel's husband liked to cook and was somewhat of an expert at his avocation. When the opera singer registered at the Town House she was delighted to find a Baldwin piano tuned and in the living room of her suite, but a mite stunned to find a joint of beef and a portable oven in a library of the suite next to her husband's bedroom. The oven came complete with apron, chef's cap, knives, kitchen forks and the makings of gravy, with a little note inviting the singer's mate to cook to his heart's content.

At a theatrical party Hilton once noticed that Gertrude Lawrence arrived wearing small white roses. During the evening he overheard her say that they were her favorite flower. Three years later Miss Lawrence registered at the Town House. When she walked into her suite she found a living room massed with white roses and fresh cuttings of them were put there daily during her stay. The late star was not herself unobservant. She told her life-long friend Noel Coward a year later: "You're going to Los Angeles? For goodness' sake put up at Connie Hilton's Town House. Being a playwright, you'll probably find a new typewriter, a waiting secretary and for all I know the complete first act of a play in your living room. He has a fantastic sense of anticipating a guest's desires." The British dramatist followed her suggestion. There was no typewriter, there was no secretary, there was not even an outline of a new play. But there was a living plant of the beautiful brown and green orchid that Coward finds interesting as an item of bizarre flora.

Whatever his guests may do while under his many roofs, quitting time for Hilton is 6 P.M. At that hour he showers, puts on fresh clothing and sets out to dine and dance. He'll pay fancy prices for food at any other man's restaurant, but when he encounters Fort Knox price tags on food in his hotel restaurants he makes a mental note to look into it the next day. Hilton loves parties when the day's work is done, but not until then. He is a waltz expert and is most proficient at an odd but graceful dance valled the Varsoviana. Movie-making king David O. Selznick once converted a high speed novel called *Duel In The Sun* into a lusty motion picture, one sequence of which called on Jennifer Jones and Gregory Peck to dance the Varsoviana. Selznick's press agents seized upon this sequence as an opportunity to grab some free newspaper space by foisting it, together with diagrams showing how to dance it, on papers from coast to coast.

Hilton was flying from New York to Los Angeles when he happened to read one of the papers clarioning the new dance sensation.

"Why, I've been doing that dance for years," he told a flying companion. "They've got the second step in it wrong, by the way."

The care with which he outfits his hotels is carried out in his Bel-Air home, a sprawling, magnificently appointed mansion through which he incessantly prowls, seeking ways to improve it. This house in his own words, is "the one I couldn't resist." He acquired it after testing out the Bel-Air development's charm for him in a smaller house. The smaller house had a virtue denied to the mansion. It rested hard by the ninth hole of the community's golf course and Hilton, who is an indefatigable golfer who has played with them all from Ben Hogan to Dwight David Eisenhower, liked to sit on his terrace and watch the form that other men brought to the game. Sometimes the player would be a professional and Hilton made no bones about taking advantage of his terrace to get some free golf pointers. He would sit at his ease, a No. 3 iron across his lap, and soak up every move the professional made. When the pro had moved on to the tenth hole, Hilton would get up and start making practice swings, hopefully trying to match the perfect form exhibited by the pro.

Hilton has always been watchful of his general well being. "There was a time," he says, "when I prided myself on just missing six feet two in height, being sixty-six years old and hitting one hundred and eighty-five pounds on the scales right to the ounce. I'm a little past sixty-six now but I still weigh in at one hundred and eighty-five. It's my happiest weight and any time I stray from it on the plus side I start to golf, dance, walk fast and look for a new hotel. That trims it off." Guests who look forward to even greater Hilton projects can be thankful that he doesn't necessarily wait for an increase in poundage before stalking a new opportunity.

Hilton's mansion, at 10644 Bellagio Road, is a spacious, cool and inviting house with 35,000 square feet of living space in it. If any one is bemused with figures, he can get a head start on a mental picture of the place by remembering that the average city block has 90,000 square feet. If one takes in other buildings on the nine acres of ground, the total comes to more than a full acre of floor space. Even a tall, tall man can't feel fenced in or crowded down under those conditions. He thought about a name for it for a long time and arrived at nothing that seemed exactly right. Walking under its trees one night, with California moonlight breaking the shadows into lacey patterns, he told his companion: "This is an enchanted place." That was it—he had only to convert the thought into his beloved Spanish and it became what it is now—"Casa Encantada." This was no damaging thing when he went to Spain to open the Castellana Hilton in Madrid. All Madrilenos and most other citizens of Spain were themselves enchanted to learn that Hilton's own house—his *casa propria*—had a Spanish name.

Millionaires aren't building these kinds of houses any more and Hilton would himself not set out to build one like it. It would beggar most fortunes to reproduce it. He acquired it for a fraction of its value, however. Should any man commission an architect to develop a house of elegance and charm, the architect could do much worse than ask Hilton's permission to tour the Casa Encantada. The original builder and owner was Mrs. Hilda Boldt Weber and she gave architect J. E. Dolena a free hand. She only wanted one end result: "The intimacy of a small cottage on these proportions." Dolena succeeded. For all of its square footage, the house has astonishing intimacy and the true warmth of a carefully designed and decorated maisonette. Robsjohn-Gibbings did the decoration and did not mar or set askew anything achieved by Dolena.

Inside and out the house is modern Georgian with a faint overlay of Grecian influence. Its floor to ceiling windows look out upon beautiful, curving gardens. Statues dot these curves at points where the major windows of the ground floor frame them. Its draperies, rugs and upholstering were loomed for the house individually. The main dwelling contains four master bedrooms, each complete with sitting room, dressing rooms and a marble bath. Hilton's own bedroom has an Italian marble bathroom with gold fittings on the fixtures. This one suite has an adjoining steam room and a matching suite has a massage and maid's room.

There are twelve rooms for the service staff, each of which has its own bath with marble floor. There are five kitchens, spaced so as to serve whatever area of the house the owner is using at the time. In the main kitchen, warming ovens set in the walls can heat 100 dinner plates simultaneously. For the preparation of exotic, foreign dishes likely to make the atmosphere redolent if not powerful, there is a separate kitchen with oversize blowers in walls and ceiling. The garlic clove hasn't been grown that can dominate the air in this kitchen. Salads and deserts are prepared in a chilled room with cooling coils running behind the marble walls. And adjacent to the pantry there is a silver room, lined with green billiard cloth to discourage tarnish. The room also has electric polishers and a selection of silver cleaning preparations. This silver vault has labeled drawers on ball-bearings and each drawer is cloth-lined. They can hold more than 1,000 pieces of flatware.

The estate's laundry can wash, clean, dry and press the wardrobes of the equivalent of 25 average families. The estate uses enough power to light a thirteen-story building. Music is available anywhere in the house through speakers concealed in the walls.

Hilton can remember, as he uncannily remembers so many other things, not only the identity of every guest who ever entered the grounds but the favorite dish of each. His memory is phenomenal. When he first met a writer planning to do a book on him he took a long look at the author and said: "Why, I know you. A picture producer named Henry Blanke gave a pre-wedding party for you and your bride-to-be on the Saturday night before the wedding the next Thursday, Arthur Rubinstein was among the guests and played the wedding music for you, which was taped, and given to you at the end of the party. I had a wonderful time."

The writer looked at Hilton in utter astonishment. That had been in September, 1943, and he was meeting Hilton for the first time since in October, 1953.

The magazines no longer carry those memory-course ads which used to begin: "Why, I remember you, you are Addison Sims of Seattle." But Hilton would never have had any use for such a course. His own memory would leave the instructions far behind.

There have been many men around Hilton and most of them have remained with him. They have prospered by the association, but it seems fair to say that the prospects of it were not what attracted them to the man. Those closest to him made their first association at a time when the rewards were tiny and the prospects dim. They remained with him, giving loyally of their time and work, during long weeks and months when their only prospect seemed to be that of unemployment. When the Texas structure was collapsing around Hilton in the depression, many could have moved on to what looked like immediate security but they preferred to fight it out alongside him and, if necessary, go to the wall with him. He is incapable of forgetting this kind of loyalty and has seen to it that no man who stuck by him has been injured. When he turned over a profitable Texas hotel to certain associates he did so because he believed they merited this reward not only for having served him but, also, for having served their country.

Hilton has three sons, two of them old enough to be active in his hotel empire. It is plain that in time they will inherit his personal holdings in the corporation, but long-time associates undoubtedly will find themselves substantial heirs to the huge structure which they not only helped so valiantly to create but who, knowing more than any other men about its details and ramifications, will be experienced enough and wise enough to preserve it.

There have been more men than women in Hilton's life, but of all the women who have touched it his mother emerges as the principal force. There was a close and abiding relationship between her oldest son and the pioneer woman. She died at an advanced age, knowing that after seeing her son pass through triumphs and disasters, he had come at last to a point where he had found his life work and made of it a success.

Mary Hilton's son is past sixty-six now, he is a man of vigor with a healthy, stout heart and controlled nerves. He is known as a graceful, expert dancer and as a man of consequence who squires young and attractive women to dinners and dances. What is not known is that in pursuing this life after dark he is faithfully following medical advice.

His New York physician, a man who cannot for ethical reasons be identified, long ago gave Hilton the prescription which keeps him enthusiastic and active at a time and age when most men of his means would either be thinking of retiring or have already done so.

"He had one serious illness in his life," the physician said, "and recovered from it vital and unimpaired. His only peril was his inability to think in any terms save of hotels. We had long, illuminating talks and from these and my examinations of his physical structure I arrived at a firm prescription. I told him he must set up rules for himself. One was to shut off all business calls at 6 P.M. every day. No matter what, 6 P.M. was the business deadline. The other side of the prescription was to get out socially, dance, meet with friends, talk to pretty girls and enjoy himself. There is nothing frivolous about such a regimen. It accounts for his bursting health. He enjoys dancing and it is healthful exercise. It keeps him in perfect trim. Another form of exercise he devised for himself. He carries a golf iron around with him in his office and while walking about the room dictating, planning, listening to reports or evolving new management rules he takes practice swings at nothing at all, but his muscles in legs, arms, shoulders and back are kept elastic and supple. This is a healthy man and he is healthy because he keeps to a regimen that is both helpful and enjoyable. I'm sorry for a man who can't sit in an attractively decorated room within ear-shot of the strains of a good orchestra and enjoy talking to a beautiful woman. He is a man whom life has passed by in the coldest, most dismal way there is. Hilton enjoys it, gets good from it and will live longer because of it. It's better for him than a warehouse full of bottled medicine."

Hilton once put into moving words the way he felt about his mother. He wrote them after her death and, because of their simplicity and power, they were widely reprinted. They deserve one more attention here:

"On that summer day in 1947 when my mother was seized with a heart attack, I was in the midst of some of the most ambitious negotiations of my life. Mother knew I kept a picture of an enormous hotel on my desk. Across it I had scrawled: 'The Greatest of Them All.' That day I had hoped to be able to tell her that at last I had bought the Waldorf-Astoria.

"Once at her bedside I knew she was dying. 'It may be hours,' the doctor said, 'or she may linger. . . .'

"Eighty-five years of vigorous, alert living finally running out. I sat down to wait and watch. My vigil was to last five weeks. They tell me that associates kept phoning that my presence at the office was vital. I can't recall any messages.

"I was living again my years with this stricken lady, whose faith was my guiding star.

"Mother was the most religious person I ever knew; my father was the least. Gus Hilton made and lost fortunes, staking, claiming, working and buying his land.

"When Gus married Mary, he took his bride to New Mexico. It was a land of storms, where snakes, wild animals, Apache Indians, a horse under you and Spanish in your mouth were all a matter of course.

"Here, my mother raised eight children. I was the first son, born on Christmas. Mother rode me eleven miles, a bodyguard riding beside us, to have me baptized. She could do without most things in life, but never without her church. As a young mother, she and her kids rode every Sunday those eleven miles from San Antonio to Socorro, always with an armed escort because Indians had once nearly killed Gus.

"I have heard many people say, 'I just can't get to church,' but I never heard mother say that.

"Her program for us children was religion, food and learning, and in that order, while my father was becoming coal king of the countryside. We were sent away to schools. I planned going to Dartmouth and felt the world was mine. Came the 1907 panic and I couldn't go.

" 'Who says Dartmouth's best for you?' mother demanded. 'Maybe the Lord knows what is for the best.'

"It didn't seem for the best. Because after two years at the New Mexico School of Mines I had to quit. Dad's money was gone. We all came back home. Our house was ten rooms over a general store. Mother stowed us all, the ten of us, in five

162

rooms, so that the others could be rented. She cooked for all.

"That experience started me in the hotel business. I went to bed before sunset, got up at midnight to meet the southbound train and then waited for the northbound at 3 A.M. I toted the bags of traveling salesmen, hustled up eggs and coffee, pumped the strangers for news of the outside world and bedded them down. Then I would catch a few hours' sleep before getting up early again and running the store.

"Father was not a man to stay down long. Within two years he had organized a bank in Hot Springs. Soon he built a home in Socorro and moved the family there, where mother had her church. I was left behind to run the old San Antonio general store and 'hotel' in full partnership and I organized the first bank in San Antonio.

"How often during those hectic years mother would say to me: 'Don't talk to me about the important people you have to see, Connie. You get along over to church first and see God. Prayer is the best investment you'll ever make. Don't you forget it.'

"My father was killed in an auto crash while I was at Army Headquarters in Paris in 1919. I got my discharge to become head of Pop's family, with three of us still in school. His estate had shrunk and even with the remains of my bank, now sold, my share was only $5,000. Since my one idea was to extend my operations, I bought my first hotel in Cisco. I put in my whole $5,000. Mother put in hers.

"For a time things flowered and prospered. I bought more hotels on credit; I married a girl who had been visiting Dallas relatives. I tasted the thrill, too, of building a hotel and incorporating.

"Then the stock market exploded and kept on going down. No salesmen were on the road, nobody taking vacations, every one eating at home. And by this time I had 1,800 rooms. Desperately, I cut off whole floors to save heat. We even had to

163

take out room phones, but we saved fifteen cents rental on each.

"But elevators had to be run, lights must be turned on. Furnaces had to be fed. First, no profits. Then I couldn't meet the interest on notes. Next, I couldn't pay taxes—finally, current bills.

"Imagine trying to pay a $100,000 furniture bill at $10 a week! Men were jumping out of hotel windows . . . some of them my hotel windows. Mother said: 'Some men jump out of windows—some go to church.'

"An insurance company, the mortgagee on my hotels, foreclosed. There went my collateral. I prayed then . . . like a lost child.

"It seemed everything blew up all at once. My brother, Gus Jr., died suddenly that spring. I owed over a half a million dollars in debts. On sufferance, I slept in a room in a hotel I once had owned. All my belongings were in a suitcase. If I wanted to make a phone call I had to talk publicly at the lobby pay phone.

"When I got back from church that dreary day a bellboy named Eddie Fowler called me aside and put his life savings, $300, in my hand.

" 'Just eating money, Mr. Hilton,' is all he said. I couldn't answer.

"There was a message for me from the insurance company president asking if I would operate their hotels and my own. I went to Galveston and signed a contract which stipulated that if ever my contract was broken, I'd get one hotel back for every one that they took.

"I went to work. But I was harassed by a boss who signed every check and watched my slightest move. When I found I had to explain buying twelve towels instead of eight, I decided to keep away from him. At that he entered suit to cancel our contract.

" 'What if he doesn't trust you,' mother said, 'as long as God trusts you? You march yourself to church.'

"I marched to church every morning at five o'clock through that desperate time. Often mother was in the pew beside me. One morning I marched out of church inexplicably full of courage. I filed a counter suit against my boss. Upon that, he decided court fights would do no one any good. So he tore up my contract and gave me back my hotels except the best two.

"These and other memories filled me as I sat beside the woman who had meant more to my life than any other person. Each morning, when conscious, she received Communion, while I knelt beside her. When she grew too weak to speak, she was still praying, her rosary clasped tightly in her hands.

"I buried mother in New Mexico, laying her beside Gus. The stores closed in her honor and almost the whole town turned out, saluting one of the last of the frontier women.

"Beside me stood my boyhood chum, J. B. Herndon, who always had been one of my top hotel associates. I turned with him and left the past.

"Not for another two years could I buy the Waldorf-Astoria.

"When I first took up residence there, some columnists noted my daily church visits. Strangely enough, I had to hit New York and its village-like interest in a Somebody's doing for this habit to rate comment. But as I walk from the Waldorf each day over to the Cathedral I feel like saying to everybody I see: 'Come in with me and visit the Lord. It's the best investment you'll ever make!' "

No more simple and encompassing statement of a life has ever been made. It recites the salient points of his career, its disasters, its triumphs, but more importantly it testifies to his great love for his mother and for the faith in which she brought him up. And it makes plain that this energetic, bounding, successful man found not only courage but guidance in a daily moment of earnest prayer. It is no posture with him when he visits the Cathedral of his religion and wishes, as he enters to pray, that all others visible to him would turn from their ways and go in with him.

Mary Hilton died in Los Angeles on August 26, 1947. On her burial day, with the stores closed and the streets deserted, one figure at her funeral was more to be noticed than all the others. He was a bent, gnarled, mahogany-tanned old man, so old that most people in Socorro had forgotten his true age. Some clue to it may be found in the fact that Constancio Miera, who had come the eleven miles from San Antonio that day to be a pall-bearer for his beloved and revered eighty-five-year-old friend, was a grown man that day, decades past, when Gus Hilton escaped from the Apaches. Miera walked in the funeral procession proudly, striving to straighten his old back in a stride of erectness, but he could not. Those about him did not dare to help him along. He might have been, and probably was, about a hundred years old and the August sun of New Mexico beat on his old frame. But he walked behind the coffin to the grave, stood there unassisted, and walked back to Socorro, a mile or so from the graveyard.

When an editorial in the El Paso *Herald-Post* was read to him that night, he asked that it be clipped out for him and he tucked it away in a wrinkled old fold of leather in his pocket.

"She was a true pioneer matriarch," the editorial said in part, "one of the kind that did so much to make America. Here in the Southwest they found their last frontier."

Eight children had Mary Hilton borne, each in his or her way a good citizen, and some of them going beyond the average of life. There was daughter Rosemary, who became a popular ingénue on Broadway; and son Carl, who became a graduate of Annapolis and rose to captain in the United States Navy. And, of course, son Conrad, whom she lived to see become the world's most active and astounding hotelier. She once had backed him with the last $5,000 she claimed in the world.

Other times she came to his help with the last dollar of her resources, but each time she got it back many fold.

One of Hilton's early backers in Texas, a man who gave Hilton money when no one else would and when there was no discernible hope of getting it back, has described his motivation:

"You have to throw away the rules of credit sometimes. A man can be dead broke, wallowing in debt and fighting the touch of the wall at his back and be, in all truth, a better risk than a man with extensive bank credit and liquid assets. I twice saw Connie Hilton perform miracles of courage and determination. Once he almost literally moved mountains to give back to Mary Hilton the money she had entrusted to him. He missed meals and humbled himself before men to fulfill his obligation to his mother. The other time was when he rushed from Galveston to Fort Worth to give back to Eddie Fowler the $300 that loyal bellboy had put into Hilton's hand when he needed that puny sum most. I saw that happen. I would trust Connie with my life. Banks were screaming, contractors were on his neck, notes were piled up like snow. But Mary Hilton and Eddie Fowler got their money back first and that was good enough for me. It's always been good enough for me. No man whose behavior comes to that mark can ever be recreant to his backers and friends."

Mary Hilton's death touched Hilton for life. But, as he says, he turned from her grave and "left the past."

She would ever be the most important and influential woman who had come into his life. But there were others. He courted the breadth of New Mexico when he was a young man just back from the war and seeking both a career and a wife. The ill and dying old man in Albuquerque who advised him to go to Texas was the father of a girl Hilton was courting seriously. It didn't work out. Once he ranged as far as Indiana, but that didn't work out, either. As in every young man's life, there were perhaps half a dozen romances before he met Mary

Barron, visiting friends in Dallas. The second Mary touched his life and he was married to her in a few months and she, too, thus became Mary Hilton. They had three sons, Nicky, Barron and Eric Michael, in that order and the latter born in 1933.

The birth of Eric came at a horrendous time in Hilton's life. He literally waked each day not knowing what he would be by sunset. Each day, actually each hour, offered a new peril to his existence. The depression was deep and lacerating at this point. Each day was a new punishment for Hilton. It was no easier for Mary. Her anxieties for him and their children were profound. Many families were torn apart in that corroding era. No city or town but had its domestic tragedies arising out of the poignant strains of the times. At last, Mary could not bear her burdens any longer. Hilton was rarely home, when he did come home he was exhausted and badgered. She recognized that the tumult and wrack of the times had broken them apart. They had nothing left for each other or to say to each other. She could understand the agonizing strain he was under, but could not reconcile it with her own lot. They ended their marriage on this piteous note, one more couple sundered by their times. Nick and Barron remained with Hilton and Mary took the infant Eric with her. It was a clean break but a devastating experience. The boys were taught from the first day to revere and adore their mother. Hilton would not countenance anything else from them. His mother-in-law, Mayme Barron, came to Dallas and helped rear the eldest sons. That, too, is testament to the nature of the end of the marriage. Mary's own mother had only sympathy and great compassion for Hilton. Mary later remarried and her sons still adore her, which is what Hilton wanted most.

Later, much later, Zsa Zsa Gabor moved swiftly into his life and almost as swiftly out of it. It was a bizarre interlude and touched neither of them deeply. Nor did it endanger Hilton's relationship to his faith, because it was a civil marriage. No other woman has figured importantly in his life since.

His life is now divided between active leadership of his hotel family, the recreation which keeps him alert and vigorous, and prayer. He has created a series of prayer meetings across the country. Washington has its prayer breakfast, always with the President of the United States as honored guest. In Chicago it is prayer luncheon, drawing the top business and civic leaders of the area to its solemn purpose. In California the prayer meetings come either at breakfast or lunch.

He has taken up for dissemination to his fellow man three phrases of English speech which motivate his life:

"A visit with God in prayer is the best investment man can make," which is his own credo.

"We are not prisoners of history, we are free men," which is President Eisenhower's credo.

"*We* are the Early Americans," a Hilton concept in five words which is his way of saying that this relatively young republic has centuries of opportunity and freedom lying ahead of it. He believes that the three hundred odd years of activity in the United States and the less than two hundred years of liberty are but a bare start. We are still an infant nation, he says, scarcely learning to walk at this point. We have in our grasp spiritual leadership of the world. By the age standards of other countries we are just beginning. Paris, he points out, has celebrated its 2,000th anniversary. London is an aged man compared to us. He sincerely believes that we are still pioneers on a broader frontier of spiritual and economic leadership and that it will be centuries hence before we arrive at our true destiny.

His passion for America is profound. He abhors ideologies which do not first take into account spiritual forces and the inherent dignity of the individual man. His Christian leadership is militant and constant, but takes into account a respect for a basic concept of the founding fathers which promised

169

freedom of religion in this country. He is a member of the board of directors of the National Conference of Christians and Jews and, at the annual meeting last November 11 at the Mayflower in Washington, was the principal speaker. Three years ago he received the major annual award of the conference for his work in inter-faith relations. Binns, the general manager at the Waldorf, is another Hilton associate who works within the conference, and is currently on a scholarship committee which manages $10,000 a year in educational projects for teachers, policemen and others in civic work who wish to broaden their activities.

The National Conference of Christians and Jews is not an organization created by men of good will who seek to fight against only anti-Semitism. Actually, it was founded in 1928 because of the horrifying bigotry which grew out of the presidential nomination of Alfred E. Smith, a Catholic. For the first time in the history of the United States a religious concept became part of a political campaign and its peril to America so disturbed men that a few met together to create the conference. Moving forces in its creation were Charles Evans Hughes and Newton D. Baker, neither of whom was either a Catholic or a Democrat. They were Republicans and Protestants, but their horror over the ignorance and bigotry loosed by Smith's candidacy was so great that they strove to set up an agency designed to bring Americans back to recognition of the rights of all faiths to dwell and grow in the United States and, hopefully, the world. It has since grown to astonishing proportions, thanks to active participation of such men as Hilton and Binns, and it is accounted one of the major social forces in our country. Hilton has for years been a constant and tireless participant in the work of the conference.

"We are a nation in its youth," he said at the University of Detroit. "*We* are the early Americans. What do I mean? I mean this. From 1776 to 1953 is one hundred seventy-seven years. When France was one hundred seventy-seven years old,

Charlemagne was not yet born. When Poland was one hundred seventy-seven years old, King Casimir was just putting together a primitive government. When England was one hundred seventy-seven years old, Julius Caesar had not yet crossed the Channel to swallow them into his empire. At one hundred seventy-seven years, the Germans were just coming out of northern forests, Horatius was still at the bridge in Italy, St. Patrick was just driving the last snake out of Ireland.

"That is what I mean when I say we are still the early Americans. We are still one with Washington, Jefferson, Madison and Adams. We are still one with their permanent revolution. Leon Trotzky was the first to use that term, permanent revolution, and he used it in reference to Communism, a cheap, second-rate kind of revolution, built and building on the ignorance of uninformed peoples across the world. A revolution which could not possibly be permanent because it is without a spiritual dynamic.

"It is because of our youth that we are so close to the spiritual dynamic of our amazing American revolution, fount of so many of the fine things in our nation's history. We should never forget that these United States were molded by a Christian people, firmly convinced of the reality of the spiritual. There are those who tell us that this was merely a superstitious hangover from an earlier, unscientific age, but it still remains an historical fact that the architects of our government took it for granted. And the closer we stay to these great men, the closer we are to victory and happiness as a nation of free men. Why? Because these founding fathers of ours are one with the great Christian tradition of freedom under God. . . . And we might say right here that human dignity and its appreciation did not start with Christianity. There were thinking men always who were aware of the meaning of personality and the eternal law which safeguards it. The two great giants of antiquity were, of course, Plato and Aristotle, standing at the philosophic

171

beginnings of this permanent revolution, the fruit of which we are enjoying in 1953 America.

"Despite the antiquity of our political philosophy, we are still a young nation and a young people. And we possess the virtues and vices of youth. As a young nation we have vigor, stamina, imagination; we have pride, alert thinking, volatile emotion. Like adolescents, we neither love very deeply, nor hate very deeply. With one hand we can drop an atom bomb; with the other deluge the same nation with Marshall Plan wealth. And, like youngsters too, we are somewhat indifferent to spiritual values. It has not seemed of particular importance to us that we be, and demonstrate to the world that we are a people of some philosophical and moral depth.

"But the last few years have matured us and matured our national thinking considerably. President Eisenhower's address, a few weeks ago, to the American Society of Newspaper Editors was exhilarating proof of how far we have come down the road to maturity. Splendid proof that we are aware of our destiny. This simple re-definition of America was like something out of the writings of our founding fathers and illustrated for me again how close we are to them, how very much we are still early Americans. It illustrated the administration's awareness of the challenge to counter-revolution. If Communism is a system of revolutionary ideas we must match it with another system of ideas. That we are doing. In fact, our system begins where theirs ends. The Communist revolutionary says he wants enough world power to set all men free. The American revolutionary sets men free to build their own power. There is a splendid logic about these two revolutionists confronting each other at last. It is just as it should be. With Stalin dead and Eisenhower alive, history is at the crossroads."

This long, direct quotation and the one concerning Hilton's mother and her influence on his life have been made deliberately. There is a growing tendency in the biographies of men of our times to hasten through their business accomplishments,

172

cap this with a froth of superficial detail concerning what they eat, what they wear and how many showers they take in a day and winding up the glossy recitation with a few kind words. Any human life which deserves to be written about deserves more than this cavalier prose. Fully to know a man worth reading about is fully to explore him, not only in terms of his economic accomplishments and habits of personal life, however colorful and fascinating they may be, but also in terms of his philosophic and spiritual stature as a man. Until one explores into and finds evidence of a personal philosophy, a spiritual conviction and a devotion to God and nation, colored by a sense of responsibility to one's fellow men, there is no truly rounded life. It is the difference between saying: "This is Conrad Hilton" and "This, too, is Conrad Hilton." The first is bare bones and a few connecting sinews of fact. The latter is the whole man, intact and complete. His own words, at length and in detail, must be cited fully to see the complex which is any mature, active and intelligent being.

CHAPTER EIGHT

Richard Connell, in a frequently reprinted classic of a short story called "The Most Dangerous Game," wrote: "God makes some men poets. Some He makes kings, some beggars."

Providence, together with some help from Conrad Hilton, has made the men immediately surrounding the king of the hotel realm exceedingly fortunate. They are not kings, but they are a long way from being beggars. They have been rewarded for loyalty, hard work and brisk mentalities. Some of them started with him in the hotel business in Texas. All have been trained from the beginning in Hilton methods and Hilton philosophies and have been graduated from small, expertly operated hotels to management of hotels so large that four of them, indeed, comprise the four largest of all hotels in the world.

One of them, Robert P. Williford, is a typical Texan and he is now the executive vice-president of Hilton Hotels Corporation. He started as a key clerk in the Dallas Hilton.

An interviewer once impetuously asked Williford what could have made Hilton abruptly move him from management of a Texas hotel to management of the huge Roosevelt Hotel in New York.

"What did he think you would do?" he was asked harshly.

Williford gave the interviewer a long, cool Texas look without a trace of annoyance or perplexity in it.

"I don't know what he thought I would do," Williford replied at last, "but I expect he knew what I wouldn't do."

It was a perfect answer to an imperfect question.

Many key executives of Hilton Hotels Corporation are men who gave what they had to Hilton before and during his monumental struggle to keep his head above water during the depression. They were loyal to him then and he has not forgotten it. Any man can command friends when his wallet is full. But when the wrinkles in his belly match the wrinkles in his pants, the test of truest friendship and loyalty gets a rugged going over.

The officers of the corporation are:

Conrad N. Hilton, president.
Robert P. Williford, executive vice president.
Joseph P. Binns, vice president.
Henry Crown, vice president.
Spearl Ellison, vice president.
Charles L. Fletcher, vice president.
John W. Houser, vice president.
Lynn H. Montjoy, vice president.
William J. Friedman, secretary.
Herbert E. Holt, treasurer and comptroller.

The members of the Board of Directors are:

Joseph P. Binns, vice president
Henry Crown, chairman, Material Service Corp.,
    Chicago.
Spearl Ellison, vice president.
Horace C. Flanigan, president, Manufacturers Trust Co.,
    New York.
Y. Frank Freeman, executive vice president, Paramount
    Pictures, Inc.
Conrad N. Hilton.
Willard W. Keith, president, Cosgrove & Co.,
    Los Angeles.
Lawrence Stern, president, American National Bank
    & Trust Co. of Chicago.
Robert P. Williford, executive vice president.

175

Charles Deere Wiman, president, Deere & Co.,
Moline, Ill.
Sam D. Young, president, El Paso National Bank,
El Paso, Tex.

The relationship of each of these men to Hilton is a personal one and its roots go back deep into Hilton's earliest years as a modest Texas hotel man, with the exception of the few men who came into the Hilton orbit when he moved into Chicago.

Each has a story of considerable fascination and it will be told here. But before getting to these, it would be well to complete the listing the corporate structure's details by naming the banks which act as transfer agents and registrars for the common and preferred stocks of the corporation. For a man who once chased $30,000 they form an impressive testament to Hilton's current business stature.

For the common stock, the transfer agents are the First National Bank of Chicago, the Manufacturers Trust Company of New York and the Bank of America N T & S A, Los Angeles. The registrars are the American National Bank and Trust Company of Chicago, the Chemical Bank and Trust Company of New York and the California Trust Company of Los Angeles.

For the preferred stock, the transfer agents are the Manufacturers Trust Company of New York and the First National Bank of Chicago. The registrars are the Marine Midland Trust Company of New York and the American National Bank and Trust Company of Chicago.

In all, fulfilling all functions, there are six large banking institutions concerned with the Hilton fiscal operation.

To get back to Robert Williford, he has a Texan's slow, deliberate way of thinking out a problem, has not allowed a big-city executive position to turn him into a slicker in striped pants. If he had he would not be with Hilton today. He is a canny, shrewd, wise, smart and completely aware hotel man who never has been frightened by size or position. He could, almost, paraphrase the late Gertrude Stein and say "A hotel is a hotel is a hotel." It might be the huge Conrad Hilton in Chicago or the gleaming Town House in Los Angeles, the Roosevelt in New York or the Dallas Hilton, where he got his first job. Basically, the operation is the same: you have X number of rooms to keep track of, rent out, keep clean and make available. You please a guest to the utmost of your managerial ability but being a guest doesn't give a person any privilege to abuse the help or skip the bill. Williford's first job at the Dallas Hilton paid him $30 a month—which did not include free board or free room. He worked hard, learned the business from the working end of a vacuum cleaner to the chair side of an executive desk. He still remembers the cold, blustery, winter afternoon when his telephone rang in the manager's office of the El Paso Hilton. It was 1943 and Williford had done well. He had advanced to a respected, secure job in the Hilton organization and was working eighteen hours a day to justify the promotions which had come his way. He picked up the receiver and heard Hilton say:

"You didn't answer my postcard inviting you to come up here to New York and look around."

"Haven't had time," said Williford. "I'm just winding up one full-house convention and another moves in two days from now. But thanks, anyway. Some other time."

"I hoped you could come," said Hilton. "I need your hand with a job I've got going up here."

"Why, sure, Connie, sure," said Williford. "Only thing is . . . these conventions. They mean a lot to the house and need watching to see that everything goes right. Maybe right after. What was the job?"

"Running a hotel," said Hilton.

"In New York?" cried Williford, astounded.

"What's wrong with it being in New York?" asked Hilton quietly. "Give you a case of shake leg?"

Williford wouldn't take that. He was a Texan first, a hotel manager second.

"Nothing gives me shake leg!" he said stoutly. "What's the name of the place?"

"Roosevelt."

"It's a long way up there . . ." began Williford.

"Sure is," said Hilton, "but the last I heard the trains were making it all right every day, right on the nose. They find it without any trouble."

"I'll be seeing you . . ." Williford began again.

"Not for awhile," said Hilton. "I'm off on a deal. But you just walk over from the Grand Central depot and take over. I left your name at the desk. Run it real good for me, you hear, Bob?"

Which is exactly how Bob Williford was graduated from a Texas operation to the first step of his growth to executive vice president of the corporation. Hilton knew how to talk to a Texan and he knew what a Texan could do for him.

"Funny thing," Williford says. "He dropped the bait right there in those few words on a penny postcard and I was so busy I didn't really read it straight. It crossed my mind he just thought I ought to go up to New York and play for a little while, and I was too busy at the time to get underway. I certainly never dreamed he meant running the Roosevelt, though."

Joseph A. Harper, manager of the Jefferson in St. Louis, had a more than modest beginning with Hilton. He started as a pot-walloper at about five dollars a month, as did, for the same salary, Spearl Ellison. Ellison was a boy in his teens when he got his kitchen job. Vernon Herndon gave up dreams of being a college professor and got his first Hilton job as assistant in the storeroom at Albuquerque. Many have risen from equally humble jobs as sweepers, elevator operators and

178

silver polishers. One of the top executives, who does not wish to be identified has a sense of humor about his elevator operator beginning.

"It never occurred to me until now, but you know Dorothy Lamour and I have something in common. We chauffeured elevators. Come to think about it, looking at her and then at me, it's about the only thing we do have in common."

Later, Williford was moved from the Roosevelt to the Conrad Hilton in Chicago and Dean Carpenter, a brother-in-law of Hilton, upon which relationship neither man has ever traded or imposed, was moved from managing the Albuquerque hotel to the Roosevelt. Williford was at the Town House temporarily when Hilton bought the Waldorf and was not too surprised by news of the purchase. Right in front of him, as he answered the long distance call from New York, was the old, worn picture of the Waldorf which we have mentioned previously. Williford found the news of the Waldorf purchase unexpected—but not amazing. He was amazement-proof by that time.

Vernon Herndon, manager of the Palmer House, is a brother of J. B. Herndon Jr., associated with Hilton since the frantic days in Texas, a man who once carefully had built up a bank credit of $300 and, when the chips were down and the Hilton structure in Texas was threatened by depression, arranged a loan for the entire sum of his credit and turned it over to Hilton. J. B. Herndon Jr., died in 1952 and to this day Hilton not only feels personally but corporately the loss of a staunch, resolute friend who never for a moment wavered in his loyalty to or faith in Hilton. Herndon scoured Texas trying to sell Hilton securities early in the building of the Hilton hotels in that state, came back smiling for dear life when he met rebuffs on every hand and lived not only to become a ranking Hilton executive but to see the man he believed in become the foremost hotel operator in the world.

Joseph P. Binns, vice president of the hotel corporation and general manager of the Waldorf-Astoria, is still a young man for an executive of his stature. A Quaker born in the very heartland of Quakerism, Philadelphia, he got into the hotel business early and made his first mark in hotels in Atlantic City. Just before the outbreak of the war he was, at thirty-two years of age, manager of the Stevens in Chicago. He was known as the Boy Wonder of the Hotel Business, having proved during the bleakest days of the depression in Atlantic City, a resort which purse-thin people found they could avoid without serious effect on their lives, that a manager with gumption and imagination could make a hotel so desirable that people would say: "We can't afford it, but let's get to Atlantic City for a week or so and forget our troubles." Since most persons had troubles during the depression, the books of his seaside hotel were a revelation to owners of other hotels in which the only human beings in sight were employees, and not too many of them.

The owners of the Stevens heard of Binns and besought him to come to that mammoth and see what he could do about keeping it at least partially filled. He was in the midst of a bang-up job in this cause when the Army took the Stevens over as a barracks for Air Force trainees. It may be said for the Army that it assigned smart men to the task of turning the huge hotel into a barracks. Not only, when it was all over, did the Army emerge as having turned a fancy penny for itself, operating the Stevens at much less per capita cost than most training camps could boast, but the original commission which came to survey the Stevens had joint brains enough to see that Binns was essential. He was young enough and healthy enough to be drafted and probably would have been sooner or later. They saw this facet at once, and deduced just as quickly that it would be an appalling waste of manpower. They, therefore, transformed Binns from a civilian manager into a second lieutenant assigned to management of the Stevens as a military installation. All he had to do was change his clothes. He swapped civilian blue serge for Air Force uniforms and continued his same duties. If one wonders how a second lieutenant could cope with majors and colonels, let the wonderer remember that the manager of any hotel often has to cope with recalcitrant guests, some of whom have enormous power and considerable means. Coping with a colonel stuffed with authority and spleen is no more difficult than coping with a billious millionaire. It requires tact in either case.

Binns emerged from the war as a full colonel, a demonstration that the lowly lieutenant must have done a superb job right from the start. Flying lieutenants often became colonels at about the time they were learning to shave, but promotion was slower for non-flyers and Binns moved right up the line in steady progression. The task at what the trainees called, jokingly, Camp Stevens, was neither easy nor lacking in complexities. Binns declines comment of any kind, being a man whose mind is on today's job and not on the past.

He was in the service when Hilton finally pried it loose from Healy, the contractor, and has been a valuable executive for Hilton ever since joining him. Hilton sent him to New York and the Plaza when the Hilton guns began to train on the Waldorf. It was Binns' assignment to keep watch for a crack in the Waldorf door and put a foot in it when the crack became evident. It took better than two years, indeed, almost three years, before there was the faintest sign of any yielding at the Waldorf. When the sign came Binns was not only there to move swiftly for Hilton but had prepared the secret groundwork so thoroughly that the entire completion of the purchase agreement took only a week. It was a quick resolution of a long-term stalk.

One of the youngest of the Hilton executives is John W. Houser, a Marine veteran and a lawyer by education. After some thought and investigation of the prospects for his future, Houser accepted the Hilton invitation when it came and became executive vice-president of Hilton Hotels International,

Inc., a job with a built-in hazard. Houser has had to conduct delicate and protracted negotiations with a succession of nationals from many countries. He has had to arm himself with economic and governmental facts about many countries. He has had to learn the spirit of each country involved, the prospects for its health in a troubled post-war world. Often, he has had to vote against a project on the basis of what he has learned about a country which desired a Hilton hotel. His responsibilities are enormous and tangible to any one who thinks out the essential nature of his duties. It would be easy to make errors, either of omission or commission. None, thus far, has been made.

Associated with Houser in the international arm of the Hilton operations is William Irwin, a World War I friend of Hilton and long a business associate. Irwin is now a vice president of HHI. Dean Carpenter is another vice-president. Robert Caverly, of the Caribe Hilton and an associate of Binns during the war period at the Stevens, and Walter Schneyder, manager of the Castellana Hilton and, before that manager of the Caribe Hilton, also are on the roster of HHI. Binns, Fletcher, Wangeman, Rudy Basler and Curt Strand finish the group.

The loss of Herndon, who sometimes acted as a balance wheel to the enthusiasm which has led Hilton to his present leadership in world hotel operation, is not discernible in the corporate structure because it was Herndon himself with whom Hilton conferred in choosing executive manpower. Herndon and Hilton both were, as religious men, aware of the mortality of man. Herndon had risen to the presidency of the American Hotel Association when death claimed him, but his impress on the Hilton organization was deep and lasting. And although essentially a serious, hard-working man he had a lively sense of humor.

Once Hilton was talking in a lively fashion about the days in Texas and how stimulating they had been, even when despair rode at his right elbow.

"It was wonderful," he said nostalgically. "Just wonderful."

"Was it wonderful, Connie, the day we had exactly three guests in the Wortham?" Herndon asked wryly.

Hilton treasures an estimation which Herndon once made of him in a public statement:

"He's the damndest man I ever saw!"

Henry Crown, a Chicago business executive, financier, Hilton confidante is a man who rests little. He has an enthusiasm for life, for business, for Chicago and for Hilton. He deeply respects the courage which Hilton has brought to hotel operation. As vice president of the executive committee of the organization and as a member of the Hilton board of directors, he is in close contact with Hilton and, probably, knows him as well as any man alive today. He is both an associate and a friend.

William Friedman was a major architect of the Hilton Hotels Corporation, is a noted lawyer and represents both Hilton and the corporation. He wore himself to a frazzle in setting it up. He also wore out Harry L. Ludwig, Hilton's accountant, in the process. Hilton's contribution in the wear-and-tear department was a broken knee, acquired in his hurrying about tying all the loose ends together.

Elmiger, incidentally, will move from Madrid to Beverly Hills when the Beverly Hilton opens this coming Spring.

Hilton's creative deeds have been spectacular and denote a valuable combination of courage and enterprise. It is in his impingement on life itself that perspective begins. It is more significant that his life is lived on a foundation of prayer and good will to his fellow man than that the Town House is a jewel box of a hotel operated to the hilt of its capacities. It is significant that a man can be vital and active and restless at sixty-six and yet have a life motivated by a humble approach to his faith. It is significant that such a man, with twenty-five hotels of record as his anxiety and obligation, can not only find but take time to do personal work in the fields of inter-faith and the good of his country.

These are the larger deeds and the stronger accomplishments and loom much more fully than the idle discovery that Hilton likes to dance and enjoy himself. It is in the nature of our times, perhaps, that more people say: "Hilton is a terrific man on a dance floor," than say: "Hilton is a phenomenon of the hotel business and a devout man." This may be because we tend to find more color in the former. Yet, the fact is that his social entertainment is but one facet, whereas devoutness and patriotism, both absolute and implemented, are whole factors in his makeup.

There is an extension which merits close study in arriving at an estimation of the Hilton character. Once his participation was sought in the management of a hotel in another country. That was the hotel in Chihuahua, Mexico. He had not lifted a finger to invite this partnership. The Mexican family which controlled the property came to him. At that time there were more important American hotel men and, certainly, better publicized men. But they did seek him out and he did arrive at a partnership agreement and it exists to this day.

When the Puerto Rican government sent out letters to American hotel men soliciting their interest in joint operation of a new, de luxe hotel to be built in San Juan it either received no reply at all or else chilly, guarded replies in English. Only Hilton had the courtesy, and good sense if you will, to reply in Spanish. The Caribe Hilton is his now to operate and it is a rich member of the Hilton organization.

His scrupulous management of these two Latin-American hotels did not go unnoticed and when other nations came to the conclusion that they needed new, tourist-luring hotels they turned without question to Hilton. It is no secret that he at one time had engulfing business troubles. Nations, and the governments of nations, do not negotiate with an individual without knowing all there is to know about him. His liquidation of his

184

troubles must have been both impressive and confidence making. It is the best kind of evidence, in formulating the definitive life of a man, to know his stature in world terms. The growing roster of foreign hotels under Hilton management is the firm base of the evidence.

Hilton introduced new ideas in hotel operation in Europe. One was the time-honored old institution of free soap in every bathroom. What is taken as a matter of course in even the smallest hotels in the United States was considered a startling innovation in Madrid. It is the custom in Europe to take one's soap around from place to place in one's luggage. The Castellana Hilton has done away with that damp, slippery item of packing. As in American hotels small cakes, wrapped in the identifying design of the hotel, are above every bathtub and hand basin. They have been a collector's item since the hotel was opened, but as other Hilton European operations get under way they probably will lose their value in the collecting field. Or, collectors being what they are, the time will come when an original Castellana Hilton bar of soap, in mint condition, will fetch three Istanbul Hilton's or four Nile Hilton's.

His other innovation was fresh bed linen and bath towels daily for every room, a custom common to American hotels but not to European hotels. More frugal customs have obtained in Europe, where linen was changed whenever a new guest registered for a room or at the mid-week for permanent guests. Madrilenos still haven't recovered from that innovation and look upon it as the truest demonstration of American know-how since Coca-Cola and jet planes.

People who keep an eye on such things say that these are further contributions by Hilton to the economics of a country. Lest this declaration seem easily arrived at, even absurd, a quick look at the total figures involved as of the writing of this book will dispel any doubts.

It is manifestly impossible for a man to control 16,000-odd hotel rooms in the United States, requiring 14,455 employees, without making a visible impression on every commodity market from soap and linens to food, liquors, carpets, furniture and electric power.

Already accounted for in foreign countries are 1,780 rooms employing the paid services of 1,840 men and women, with consequent impression on the local economies. Still to come, but contracted for, are 2,100 more rooms in foreign countries utilizing the services of 1,700 employees and, again, with consequent impression on local economies.

The total of rooms, when all of these hotels will have opened, will be 19,908 across the face of the earth with approximately 17,995 employees on the payrolls of Hilton. The latter figure would be the population figure of a reasonably large city with all its economies of food, clothing, salaries, entertainment, taxes, furnishings, rentals or home purchases, cars, education and so on.

There is nothing cozy in such an authenticated tabulation.

The business heart of Hilton's organization is in the Conrad Hilton in Chicago. Under Williford's watchful eye, the complex is reduced to a relatively simple operation in which each hotel, looked upon as an individual problem, makes daily reports. These reports are matched against filed reports covering the same day, week and month of previous years. Thus, a quick, comprehensive and accurate graph of each hotel's business status is available at all times. If a hotel begins to show a sag that is lasting, an examination is made to trace the reasons for the sag. This does not mean that the manager is automatically looked upon as at fault. There are dozens of reasons for a hotel to turn pale and begin running an economic temperature, and not all of them are the result of managerial laxity. A gradual movement of business, for example, from the area in which a hotel is located might be reflected in a drop in its receipts. The opening of a rival hotel, or the refurbishing of a rival hotel, might draw business away from the Hilton house. Temporary recessions in a city's own economics could account for a drop in a hotel's business. Whatever the cause, it is first watched to see if it seems to be lasting, then the hotel is surveyed from top to bottom and, finally, the reason is analyzed. Once the answer is in hand, it is corrected.

There was a period a year or so ago when one of the Hilton houses began to show a perceptible drop in revenues. The management was popular, the books of the hotel were in perfect order and there seemed to exist no immediate explanation. When the answer was found, it was simple: a rival hotel had re-decorated its banquet rooms and, to pay off the cost, was putting on an intensive campaign to capture the banquet and convention business of the city. Convention groups were being offered benefits in room prices, for one thing. The Hilton management turned to and put on a campaign of its own. Result: revenues began to climb back up again and have remained level ever since.

Simplification of the comparison system of controls has reduced headquarters operation to a small staff. Less than eighteen persons have the entire picture of the Hilton empire under their constant watch. This reduction and simplification brings about a consequent diminution of headquarters costs and, thus, adds to the Hilton profit statement and results in increasing dividends passed on to stockholders. It seems almost impossible to conceive of less than eighteen persons being able to keep the vast, intricate structure on such a simple basis, but it works. It can also be said with a nod to Hilton accompanied by the grind of gnashing teeth from rival hotel executives that in general every Hilton hotel is a more profitable operation, room for room and dollar for dollar, than any other hotel in a comparable class in size and location. For example, in 1953, the Hilton corporate net profit after taxes was about $6,414,000, whereas his nearest rival in a group operation was about $4,000,000. Nor is size and huge structure Hilton's motivation in creating his empire. Prestige emerges as the major force.

In the management of convention business, always essential

as running about 15 percent of a hotel's gross, Hilton has long since discovered that this healthy chunk of revenue actually means more than the book value of 15 percent. It can be booked well in advance, every detail can be blueprinted long before the active date and every dollar can be cost-controlled. There is nothing maverick about his convention department. They can pinpoint it to the last cent and that included the twin cyclones that came to Chicago in 1952 when both the Republican and Democratic National conventions nested in that city. He has a fantastically trim system of cost control. And not one angle of it is left neglected. There was a time in Texas when the fifteen cents a month instrument rental for one telephone in one room was important. That same fifteen cents is still important, no matter what direction it may come from or to what department it is allocated. No businessman worth his salt could quarrel with that kind of sentry duty.

The heart of Hilton's close-watched operation is a profit and loss forecast prepared each month in advance for each hotel predicated on such tangibles as weather averages, guest flow, convention bookings and the reports of several previous years for a matching time of the year. This forecast, which says in effect to each hotel manager: "This is what your house ought to do in the next month," goes out to the managers about ten days before the end of the current month and covers the whole of the next month. Thus, around November 20, each manager receives his December forecast. Then, each day in December, he sends in to the Chicago headquarters his revenues and disbursements statements for the preceding day. A copy goes to Hilton wherever he may be, as does the day's weather forecast for the next day after that in every Hilton city. At no time is any manager, and most certainly headquarters, more than twenty-four hours behind the economic picture. Few corporations so large are that close in time to an accurate estimation of the whole corporation's position. In that vast an operation twenty-four hours of information amounts to a control operating as of that minute. It is rightly called an instantaneous picture.

One factor in such control is payroll monitoring. It is always possible, with figures coming in less than twenty-four hours behind the fact, to keep an elastic payroll position. Extra waiters and floor maids can be called in, for example, when the press of room rentals is going to make a predictable rise. By the same measurement, extra help can be dispensed with when the forecast shows a drop in business can be expected. Any hotel counts between 36 and 38 percent of its costs in payroll. It averages, at today's wages, 37 percent almost on the button. If this percentage can be stabilized by the forecasting system, it means a healthy costs condition in that area of money outgo. Actually, except during national conventions or a multiplicity of business conventions and banquets, the payroll factor in Hilton hotels is amazingly stable. Naturally, extra help comes and goes as business in the hotels waxes and wanes, but Hilton long ago learned the necessity of creating a stable staff for each hotel and passing on to them the now widely accepted benefits of group insurance and hospitalization plans. He also learned that a loyal, securely employed staff, intimate in its knowledge of the character and personality of the hotel and the character of the guests it attracts, is valuable beyond definition. Dislocations of service occur in hotels with green help. They are not used to the tone of the hotel, the tenor of the management or the physical layout of the premises. The Waldorf, the Palmer House, the Town House and the Plaza, for example, are outstanding models of veteran staff operation. The employees know the guests, cater to whims, can determine in advance what a known guest will want in attentions and, thus, can provide them. There is no "I'm new here, but I'll see what I can do for you" shock for a veteran guest in any of these houses. The staffs know what a certain railroad tycoon or steel king or visiting contessa from Rome expect and they

189

supply the expectancy immediately and without a ruffle of emotions or nerves.

Over and over in such hotels occur demonstrations of the value of this kind of operation. Not long ago a famed motion picture executive flew in from Hollywood and took a suite at the Waldorf. He had not been in New York for three years, yet when he picked up the telephone for room service and announced himself as hungry but undecided as to what he wanted, the captain at the other end said:

"How nice to hear your voice again. You flew? That means you had steak and vegetable and a small salad for dinner. We suggested Eggs Benedict under similar circumstances for you when you were here last. You will want to sleep for some hours and rest from your trip and it is a light dish that will not disturb your rest. If you are really hungry perhaps also an ice and warm milk, not coffee."

No guest can expect, or hope to get, that kind of personalized attention from a constantly changing staff. Nor is it possible for management to buy this kind of service from its staff in return for payroll wages. It arises out of pride, loyalty and willingness.

Any one who knows anything about economics knows that hotels do not sell out their rooms today as they did during the war. Hotels have balanced the rental decline with a consequent increase in room fees. This has been necessary also to keep pace with rising labor costs and food costs. The average room, which in 1945 and 1946 was, say, $7 is now somewhere between $10 and $12. The rental average in first-class hotels is now at about 76 percent of capacity, which is enough. Any hotel man knows he can make some money at 75 percent of capacity. Hilton foresaw the decline that would come when the war ended and strove, in a series of meetings with his management executives, to arrive at an operation system where there was no plaguing danger even at 50 percent of capacity. This had to be done without impairing service, letting hotels

190

run down in their physical plant or creating a morale problem among the employees.

"There was a time when I had to open up every faucet labeled salesmanship that I had at hand," Hilton told them. "Let's open them up again. There is nothing shameful about salesmanship conducted on a high plane. I don't want people pulled in by their coat lapels, but I want such an attractive operation set up that they will be pulled in by their own wishes. I want them to think of Hilton as a synonym for hotel." This was some time before Spain accommodated him by doing exactly that.

That was all he needed to say. The autonomy he gives his general managers allowed each one to set to work on his own house and bring about public hunger for his house in his locality.

This autonomy is much more than an expression of Hilton's personal confidence in each executive. It is a safeguard of his empire. With his kind of health and his kind of enthusiasm there is nothing to indicate that he will retire soon from active leadership of his hotels. But, when he does, it will cause virtually no disturbance in the corporation. He wants it that way. He is strongly aware of man's mortality and just as strongly aware that a rigid one-man operation is an operation headed for trouble when that one man isn't there any more. He has chosen his top executives and officers with infinite care and after long consideration. His mind is at ease. His conscientious attitude toward his stockholders is at ease. Hilton, the man, could conceivably and demonstrably move out tonight and the empire would continue on a safe, even course.

This carefully devised safeguard has more than emotion or loyalty or personal zeal at its base, however laudable they may be as human attributes. The strongest stone in the base is the conviction of obligation to stockholders. The corporation is now on the boards of stock exchanges, a recognized investment. Not one executive but is as aware of that as a banker is of the sanctity of his bank's honor.

"I know a motion picture producer, president of a large company with its own studio in California," Hilton said recently. "This man was criticized during the war for something he did. An organization of ladies doing canteen and social work with service men in the Los Angeles area had devised a way of raising money to finance their work. They prevailed on several major studios to give them the receipts from the opening night of big pictures in Los Angeles. They came, at last, to this man and asked him to give them the opening night receipts from a picture soon to be released and with one of his major, moneymaking stars in it. He received the ladies in his office, heard them out to the last word, even though he knew what they wanted in advance, and when they finished their plea he said: 'Ladies, I deeply regret I cannot do this for you. I am not responsible for what other studios have done to help you. That is their concern, not mine. But I am responsible to another group. I don't own this picture. I didn't pay for it. Thousands of stockholders own it and I am responsible to each of them. I have no right to give away my stockholders' money.' The ladies went away fuming. They felt rebuffed. He was exactly right in every department, legally, ethically and as a responsible executive. He could not give away his stockholders' money. Later, that same afternoon, he found out what the ladies had averaged in revenues from other pictures turned over to them and sent his personal check to cover, a matter of some $9,000. They stopped fuming, but by then they had already expressed their indignation. To this day some people in Hollywood believe he acted churlishly. He acted, in my opinion, as a good, honest executive and as a gentleman."

One of the ideas burgeoning from Hilton's order to install supersalesmanship was the creation of a group of salesmen for each big hotel. They are constantly on the go selling Hilton hotels to clubs, unions, wedding parties, corporations and political associations. They cite location, service, food and price and booking the banquet and convention business. This has resulted in an upsurge of this kind of business for each of the Hilton houses. Travel counsellors are not overlooked, either, and the probabilities are that some of the larger gas station operators also have been made aware of Hilton hotels and asked to direct inquiring motorists to them. Some cities have specialized groups which are solicited by the salesmen. Thus, in Washington, embassy and consulate social secretaries know all about the Mayflower and what it can do for a country planning a state dinner. In New York, the handsome glass house holding the United Nations secretariat is hunting ground for Hilton salesmen, each acquainting the proper officials with the virtues of the Waldorf, the Plaza, the Roosevelt and the New Yorker. Publicity is not overlooked. Notices of forthcoming banquets, weddings, conventions and testimonial dinners are sent to the press well in advance of each event, plus some newsworthy note concerning what the principal speaker will say.

Hilton has made a survey of conventions and has sought to alter them for the benefit of all hotels and, of course, for Hilton hotels. He soon discovered in his hotel operation that weekends were the constant lows in hotel room rentals. He has spearheaded a campaign to induce convening organizations to bring their representatives in on Saturdays and Sundays, with the twin benefit of filling houses on these days and preventing frantic log jams on Mondays. He also is working with the American Trade Association in a hopeful plan to spread conventions out over a full year instead of lumping most of them into the months of August and October. This would result in better accommodations, less pressure for every one and even and predictable revenue schedule for hotels. He sees benefits passed on to railroads and airplane companies, to souvenir and printing trades and all other groups having directly to do with convention business.

"It is the public in the end that receives the conveniences," he says. "Travel reservations, entertainment tickets, available taxies, all become easier, or would if conventions were spread out across twelve months instead of being lumped into two months.

The cost schedules over which each general manager mounts guard are the concern of each department in each hotel. The laundry, the restaurants, the desk, the payrolls, the furnace room, the pantry, the kitchens, all are aware of the wish to operate at the highest peak of efficiency with the least possible cost. In one thing Hilton will not yield an inch and would have a firm talk with any general manager who did yield an inch. He will not allow his hotels to become run down. He cannot abide a shabby hotel. Not only is shabbiness immediately seen by the public, with loss of house prestige, but actually records show that it is less costly to keep a house up day by day than to do a major job of restoration after a period of carelessness. He often surveys all of the houses and orders rehabilitation for those he finds in need of it. The millions he spent for restyling and smartening up in Columbus and St. Louis are proof of his credo that the only good hotel is a shining, sparkling hotel. He looks upon the money spent as a necessary investment. There are no torn drapes or ragged carpet edges in Hilton hotels. Nor chipped china and scarred furniture. They either gleam or Hilton finds out why.

He looks upon all these things, forecasts, cost controls, autonomy operation, immaculate hotels and trained staffs as cushions against trouble when and if there is an economic decline.

"A man in this business cannot provide too many cushions," he says.

He is, of course, right. The hotel business is one of the first to detect and suffer from declines. One of a hotel's principal duties is to provide entertainment. Nothing shuts off faster when a public pinch is felt. Another duty is to provide lodging.

194

Travel withers at the first sign of decline. First, pleasure travel and then business travel.

"A constant twenty-four hour check on the entire operation," one of his executives said recently, "is not any too close. You have to keep on top of things from one sunset to the next sunrise or you soon won't have a business."

His executives and general managers are young men. He brought most of them into his hotel family when they were very young. Binns is only forty-eight, Williford, with Hilton all these many years, is fifty-four. Spearl Ellison is but forty-one and has been with Hilton since he was fourteen years old, a total of twenty-seven years. Charles L. Fletcher is young for his responsibilities as financial vice president and John Houser served in combat with the Marine Corps at Iwo Jima. Vernon Herndon is young, his face unlined. He now operates the Palmer House. Frank Wangeman of the New Yorker is young by any standards and so is Robert Quain, general manager of the Conrad Hilton, one of the most important men. Before this book reaches print Wangeman will go to the New Yorker and Wallace Lee will manage the Roosevelt. Joe Harper of the Jefferson, Mort Odell of the Albuquerque Hilton, Art Griffith of the Fort Worth Hilton, Carl Prather in El Paso, all of these have been Hilton men for twenty years and more and they all started as very young men. Porter Parris, at the Plaza, is another Texas graduate of the Hilton hotel business in the days when it was rugged. C. J. Mack has been with the Mayflower for twenty-five years and when Hilton bought the house was glad to become part of the Hilton family. Fletcher Brummit at the Dayton Hilton and Truett Gore at the Deshler Hilton also are graduates of the Texas days.

Hilton's personal holdings are not totally committed to the hotel empire. He has, for example, 400,000 shares of the 1,621,000 outstanding shares of the common stock of the American Crystal Sugar Company. It is only one American corporation in which he has extensive holdings. There was a time when he could not have financed the purchase of a newspaper at the corner stand. There are degrees of being broke, but he can claim membership in 33 Degree Brokeness. He not only did not have five cents in liquid assets, he owed half a million dollars. Which means that he was $500,000 from point zero. Some men consider themselves broke when they are at point zero. That's for amateurs. It's easy not to have any money at all. What takes doing is not to have any money at all and owe half a million dollars more than that. What also takes doing is to get up off the floor, straighten your necktie and wade in with both hands until every creditor is paid and happy, your backers have their money back and you have begun to walk into banks to deposit money instead of borrowing it.

As Hilton moved up into the sunshine of being in a liquid position he received encouragement from a rich, cautious and imaginative source. Floyd Odlum and his Atlas Corporation made it known that they liked the way Hilton did things and would not shut the door in his face if he came calling. The Atlas Corporation was not created as an eleemosynary institution designed to stuff money down impoverished men's throats. It does listen to men and business organizations who have something attractive to offer and which promises a profit for both sides. Atlas has stepped in with blood transfusions for department stores, air lines, hotels, motion picture companies and other momentarily ailing enterprises. Like Odlum, its chief, it expects something to happen after the transfusion. Health, for one thing.

Hilton was no disappointment to Odlum and when the time came for settlement and Hilton's right to proceed on his way without Atlas help both sides were satisfied. One detail of their association is sufficient to establish what Atlas did for Hilton and, more spectacularly, what Hilton did for Atlas.

Atlas invested $1,424,074 in Hilton's operations. When Hilton Hotels Corporation was created and became a fact, with consequent exchanges of previous common and preferred stocks in individual Hilton hotels, Atlas emerged with $4,203,794 in the stock of the Hilton Hotels Corporation. This is known as pumping blood into the right veins.

Another source of Hilton money when he needed it to swing the Chicago deals was Colonel Henry Crown, acknowledged as one of the foremost financiers in Chicago. Chicago has had many financiers, most of them excellent men and grimly scrupulous. Some have not been. Crown was of a school of the finest and when Hilton came to him he was welcomed warmly. Crown went over the entire Hilton history, the current position and the future hopes. They looked, and were, solid and substantial. Crown became a finance participant in the Hilton operations.

He has never regretted his investments in Hilton and is today a member of the board of directors, a vice president and member of the executive committee of Hilton Hotels Incorporated. Hilton and Crown are not only business associates but warm, good friends.

Another director whose name stands for wealth and prestige in Chicago and in the finance world anywhere is Charles Deere Wiman of the Deere agricultural machinery family. Willard Keith is an insurance executive and represents Los Angeles money. Lawrence Stern is another symbol of financial indestructibility on the board.

There is an abundance of proof that Crown has almost limitless faith in Hilton. It came when the final negotiations for the Palmer House had reached the stage of signing documents and passing certified checks across the table. Quick tabulation leading to execution of these checks showed that Hilton was still exactly one million dollars short of the essential cash. Most men would have folded in the middle like a hinge. Instead, and with his associates and advisors looking on in some consternation, Hilton picked up a telephone, doodling on a nearby sheet of paper as he waited for the connection to be completed. When it came it resulted in probably the shortest million dollar conversation on record.

"Henry," said Hilton, addressing Crown on the other end of the line, "we've put our figures on the Palmer House together in one piece and we come out short a million dollars. We are in that stage . . ."

"That's all right, Connie," said Crown, interrupting. "I'll let you have it."

Hilton put his telephone back in its cradle and bent in silence over the table. He has never revealed what solemn thoughts went through his mind in that short moment of silence, but when he looked up again there were tears in his eyes. It may have been a prayer of thanks, a pledge of undying friendship for Crown, a flash of bitter memory from the days when he was not only flat broke but cruelly hounded, or simply overwhelmed relief. In any case, he has never discussed it even with intimates.

"All right," he said quietly, looking at his associates. "We can proceed."

There are other evidences of this kind of integrity. Once, in error, a secretary drew a check for $100,000 on a bank in which Hilton did not have one cent on deposit or a dime in its safety deposit vaults. He had no connection whatsoever with the bank except that he knew its president. Since he had never had any reason to study batches of checks drawn for his signature, Hilton signed the mistakenly drawn check along with several others without scrutinizing them. The check was drawn on the First National Bank of Albuquerque.

Several days later, Hilton's telephone in Chicago rang and he picked it up.

"Connie," said C. W. Carson, the bank's president, "we've got your check here and I'm pleased to pay it at once. When you get time, make out a note for it and mail it on to me. No special hurry."

Hilton checked quickly with his secretary and discovered

the mistake. He thanked Carson for his courtesy and asked that the check be mailed back to him, explaining what had happened.

"You don't have to go into all that nonsense about a new check, Connie," Carson protested. "We're glad to pay it. Your paper is good all the way up the line."

Hilton, then, is a man who leads a happy life and an honored one. He has built his personal prestige and credit to a high place. He has opened up avenues for America across the world with the mutually dependent concepts of commerce and good will. Commerce between nations without good will is useless, and good will without implementing commerce is almost equally fragile. A man of thought once said: "If goods do not cross frontiers, armies will." Hilton's extension of his operations to other countries, with consequent growth and stabilization of the economies of those countries, has the blessing of his government.

All of these things are the good things, yet if one pries long enough and persuasively enough one discovers that the men around him still have one reservation concerning Hilton: Hilton is unable under any circumstances to be other than fully and dismayingly frank. He will tell anyone who will listen astonishingly candid details about his operations. It has happened with total strangers on airplanes and in trains and on city streets.

If any newspaper man had, during the long and secret negotiations for either the Palmer House or the Waldorf-Astoria, gone to Hilton and said: "Are you negotiating for this hotel?" he would have received a direct, open answer: "Yes, I am." He is apparently incapable of the usual and time-honored evasions which accompany such deals. Most men of his business stature have long ago learned to say at least "No comment," or, if pressed by a resolute reporter, to take the reporter into confidence with an "If this is off the record I'll tell you" reply. Hilton goes in for none of these conveniences. He believes that if a man asks you a question you are bound to answer it.

This is one reason why, when the negotiations for the Waldorf reached a live stage, his lawyers joined in the warning cited earlier in this book. They told him bluntly to keep away from the Waldorf, not to be seen anywhere near it and not even to think about it too much lest he blurt it to some one and spill the beans. He found a way around the warning by studying the towering hotel from another side of Park Avenue early in the morning, but even this understandable enthusiasm caused his lawyers to turn pale.

"Connie," they cried, "you keep away from that place. Your picture has made you easy to identify. Your height makes you an unmistakable identity. Suppose some assistant manager with insomnia decided to go walking at that time and saw you across the street hoping almost out loud to get your hands on the place? Why, he'd have it all over the hotel in fifteen minutes!"

"You're right, you're absolutely right," said Hilton.

But the next morning, at 6 o'clock, he was on Park Avenue again sneaking looks at the prize he wanted so much and had wanted so long.

In the end, lawyers and associates abandoned all hope of curbing him and set earnestly to praying that nothing he did would complicate the negotiations and cause what happened in Chicago when Hilton, wearing the Stevens on his sleeve so to speak, made it possible for Healy to keep raising the ante, secure in the knowledge that Hilton wanted that hotel the way he wanted life.

"We never knew," an associate says, "what was going to happen. It was like Connie to fall in talk with a passing stranger at that hour on Park Avenue and say: 'See that hotel over there. I'm going to buy it.' We almost had fits of fear that that might happen. He is a product of his times and the frank, direct and undevious spirit of the Southwest. He learned to speak out candidly as a boy in New Mexico, sharpened that virtue, if it is a virtue in business, in Texas, where people go around telling other people their business. I never saw such a place for having men stop you in the street and tell you the darndest things about themselves. They seem eager to give away precious, business secrets out of the sheer joy both of sharing and of being part of these secrets."

They all crossed their fingers and hoped for the best the day a press conference was called to announce his purchase of the Palmer House. Not less than sixty-two news men and women in all categories showed up with pads, pencils and cameras. Some were city room reporters, some Sunday feature writers, some had important magazine connections and some had cameras pointed right in Hilton's face. Some wanted the financial story, some the personal story, some the historical background and all of them were curious to see this tall man from Texas who was moving into the very fabric of Chicago life. They also were impatient to see what kind of man he was and what mettle he had. No man could hope to buy the Palmer House away from the family and not undergo trial by press.

He was the New Boy in town and he could expect a thorough going over. He got it. But not for long.

Hilton strode into the room with a smile and an outstretched hand. Hands shook his in return, but the faces above the hands were a little mocking, a little doubtful, a little suspicious.

"What can you tell us about the consideration involved?" a reporter shot at him, to get things started.

"Why, the whole story," said Hilton. "There is nothing to conceal and nothing that isn't on public record in the tax and real estate transfer offices. What did you want to know exactly?"

The reporters looked at each other.

"What was the price, who got what and how was it whacked up?" the first speaker countered.

Hilton answered in complete detail, revealing the transaction in its entirety. He held back nothing, including direct quotes from the negotiators. The reporters looked their consternation. Was this big, tall individual kidding them in a new way? He wasn't. They had asked a specific question, they got a detailed reply.

"Is it true that you signed and paid over a check for $7,500,000?" another reporter demanded.

"Yes, I did," said Hilton quietly.

"May we see this check?"

"It is no longer in my possession," he said. "It is held by the trustees of the Palmer estate."

"Well, was there a photograph made of you signing it?"

"Yes, there was," said Hilton without hesitation.

"May we have the picture?"

"I'm sorry, but I am in honor bound neither to show it nor to use it," said Hilton with quiet dignity.

"What kind of an answer is that?" another reporter said fiercely.

"It's the only answer I know," said Hilton simply. "I was allowed to have a photographic record made of the incident in return for my promise not to use the picture in any way except for my personal files. I don't break promises."

That closed off that trend of questioning, but they went on and on, with Hilton answering every question with unreserved frankness. When the press conference was over, his associates mopped their brows. Hilton hadn't balked once, had added details that hadn't been asked for, had laid the entire transaction and his own principles right out in the open. Those around Hilton hoped he had been right to be so candid. Only the next editions would tell them. Except for one advance clue.

Some friends, out in the lobby, overheard reporters talking to each other as they left the hotel.

"Sometimes," one had said cynically, "you can cover up a lot by being apparently open. I don't fall for these earnest, candid boys who never conceal anything. Or seem not to."

"I do," said his companion. "In this case I do. I have the belief that this Hilton is absolutely on the level. I think, if we would have asked him, he would have told us how much he pays for haircuts and what brand of toothpaste he uses. You can't splatter a man around for levelling with you. I could use a few more like him in my job."

"You really think he was spilling his soul in there?" the cynic asked, doubtfully.

"Look, Ed," came the reply, "you and I are trained like bloodhounds to spot phonies. That is no phoney. That's considerable of a gent."

This information was hastened to Hilton and his colleagues, the latter of whom could not conceal their relief.

"It figured," said Hilton to them. "If you tell the truth you always get a square deal. What was worrying you?"

This blind spot, if it can be called a blind spot, is about the only one he has. He doesn't understand evasion and subterfuge. Truth to him is truth. Having never been nipped by telling the truth he is unable to fathom why those nearest him worry about his candor. They have tried to tell him that they do not recommend untruth, they only recommend ordinary discretion.

"Well, if a man asks me a question and I know the answer," he argues, "I'm bound to answer him the best I can."

"But you don't have to start the conversation," they tell him.

"How are you going to sit next to some one for ten hours on a plane," he replies, "and not talk? If you talk you are bound to talk about what you know something about. I know about hotels, so I talk about hotels. I know about mine best, so I talk about mine. We're running an open, honest, legal business, boys. What is there to hide?"

At this point they all give up in despair.

Hilton isn't always coddled by the press, however. As a man who loves a party, he is often taken over the jumps by columnists who think his parties are a little on the opulent side. When the twenty-fifth anniversary of the Mayflower was celebrated in 1950, Hilton decided to make it a big party. He invited official Washington and a considerable number appeared at the party, among them the now late Chief Justice Vinson. Less than two days later, Hilton was amazed when several columnists questioned the taste of Mr. Vinson in (a) attending the function and (b) allowing himself to be photographed at it. The opinion seemed to be that in a business the size of Hilton's there would be, sooner or later, court action of some kind concerning some aspect of the operation. It was possible that some of these suits would reach the Supreme Court for final decision and, therefore, it was improper for Vinson to be a guest of a man over whom he, at some time, might have to render a grave decision. Justice Clark also was a guest and he was ordered to the showers for the same reason. Although neither justice ever commented in reply, they probably were as stunned as Hilton. It would never occur to Hilton that a bang-up celebration could be construed as a means of influence peddling. He doesn't do business that way.

Hilton's parties seldom cause this kind of tumult and even the party he gave when the Castellana Hilton was opened brewed only minor storms. Some guest columnists, flown from the United States to the event, were careful to note that the electric current went off once, that the elevators balked twice, that certain statuary and mural art was unfinished and that, perhaps, Hilton was a little hasty, in his formal address, in citing Spain as a state that had defeated Communism. They cited some of the help that Franco had.

204

Hilton has little or no comment to make on these occasions and others like them.

"Reporters call the facts and the news as they see them," he says. "That is what they are trained to do and engaged to do. It is their duty. If an elevator doesn't run or a window falls in or a faucet is dry in a new hotel I expect those items to become news. I wouldn't respect a man who concealed them. Of perhaps one hundred reporters at the Mayflower party fewer than five made an incident of Chief Justice Vinson's presence. I was amazed at the line of reasoning but I didn't lift a hand to beg off. I don't invite the press to parties to lock up their typewriters. The last I heard, we still were ready to fight for a free press in this country."

On only two incidents in his life is Hilton unwilling to talk at length and, since both were domestic incidents, that seems reasonable. It would be in doubtful taste for him to comment on his two marriages and he doesn't do so. Both women are still alive and even if they were not it would be a questionable line of discussion. The end of his first marriage was brought about by stresses to which the partners were unequal and he lets it go at that. His second marriage was scarcely a marriage at all and since it began and ended outside the jurisdiction of his church, no harm has been done to either party.

In the matter of his business attitude, no man could build the business he has built in a constant atmosphere of sweetness and light. That he is a prayerful man does not prevent him from being an aggressive man. That he has operated in an atmosphere of honesty has not prevented him, when the occasion dictated, to fight like a wildcat to hold on to what he had. That he has gained the respect of the community, the blessings of his government and the attention of foreign governments is to his credit but does not by any means establish him as an infallible, self-effacing and flawless human being. It would be the silliest kind of reporting to limn him as a mid-century knight in speckless armor and probably no one would be as embarrassed by it as Hilton. He knows his own faults and acknowledges them.

He has had struggles with labor, yet when it seemed to him right to do so he has stoutly defended labor. When the overseas operations began, it was the culinary workers union of Cuba which offered to take $10,000,000 from its own funds and build the de luxe Havana hotel if he would agree to manage it.

He does, indeed, have a love for parties and the giving of parties, complete with favors for the ladies and two bands going strong, and if this is an odd quirk there are oddities of other kinds to be found among most men of action. Some much less acceptable and more difficult to condone.

A biographer of integrity should not approach his job with stars in his eyes. He must report the valleys as well as the peaks. Therefore, let it be recorded now that Hilton has failings. He also has strengths. He has quirks, he also has demonstrated vision. He is demanding in the extreme, but rewards zeal and loyalty. He allows no nonsense in the operation of his business. He hires more music and entertainment for the floor shows in the public rooms of his hotels than any other individual in the United States and has a frank delight in getting to know these men and women of show business. The records abound with news pictures of Hilton with Mary Martin, Hilton with Hildegard, Hilton with this pretty star and that pretty star. Not since Puritan New England has it been scandalous for a man to sit and talk with or dance with a pretty woman. Most men rush at the chance.

He also likes to invest pretty women with gifts. When he surprised a pretty New York girl with a French poodle he was carrying out a habit of such deeds. When he attached a string that she must call the little dog Waldorf he was insuring one more fragment of publicity for the hotel. He likes to dash in and out of town wearing a milk-white Stetson reputedly worth $100. Some men like hand-painted neckties or sweaters with designs knitted into them. It comes to the same thing. The only possible difference is that the necktie addicts usually buy their own whereas Hilton's cocky Stetson was a gift from Amon Carter of Fort Worth.

The point of all of this is that Hilton has made as many mistakes as the next man and undoubtedly will make more mistakes. But his mistakes have not altered his devotion to faith, his love for his country or his operation of a large business. These are the three major factors in his life. The late Fiorello H. LaGuardia, when Mayor of the City of New York, made himself vastly popular with the frank confession that "When I make a mistake it's a beaut." Hilton without stealing the words or using them seems to have much the same feeling about himself. He has made many, both in his personal way of life and in his business, as attested by the several wringers he went through in Texas.

He still laughs about a session he had with a Texas sheriff who came to either serve papers or collect money and didn't care much which.

"No money," said Hilton. "Haven't a cent."

"Well, now, that puts me in a fix," said the sheriff. "I don't like to serve such papers on a man."

"I won't accept service," said Hilton. "What good would it do? It won't get money where there isn't any."

"The law says you either accept them or I tack them up in a prominent place," said the sheriff. "On the premises. A prominent place would be the lobby."

"Go ahead," shrugged Hilton. "The lobby is right down the stairs."

"I know where it is," the sheriff said truculently. "I just came through it. I got my own hammer and tacks, too."

"Fine," said Hilton. "Help yourself."

In ten minutes the sheriff was back, red in the face and hot under the collar.

"Ain't no place to tack these papers up," he said. "The whole dern lobby is marble!"

"The ceiling is plaster," said Hilton. "I could rent you a ladder for fifty cents."

The papers went away folded in the pocket of the sheriff. Thirty days later Hilton made good on that particular debt. Twenty years or so later he laughs out loud at the memory.

CHAPTER NINE

W<small>HAT</small> does it all add up to?

He is gregarious after dark, and loves a good time among sparkling people. He works hard when he must, makes errors in judgment, is sometimes soft at the wrong time, has to be protected from chisellers. He exacts attention to business from subordinates, shares with literally millions of other men a faith in God, shares with other and some of the same millions a love for his country and conducts his business with personal and corporate honesty. There have been rogues in Hilton's employ. You can't hire men and women by thousands and not have a rascal turn up here and there in the bunch. His devoutness is no greater than that of many, many others, yet it is real and undeviating. If he plumps for prayer in public speeches he makes it is because he believes there isn't enough of it and that people are passing up a direct approach to Deity. If he makes a public statement of his love for country it is because he genuinely feels that we are at a crossroads of history and the United States needs every patriot it can find. If he guards his business zealously and seeks new ways to buttress it, only the bankrupt and wastrels in business have done otherwise.

The result of all this is an average man who has by some force of circumstance and some personal application to work performed an unaverage feat of business.

He likewise shares with hordes a hunger for companionship, a fallibility of judgment, the reputation of being, if you can get at him, a soft touch and a sense of decent regard for truth and simple honesty. These are not individual virtues. They belong to most people.

Those are the basic facts dug out in an effort to clear away a forest of legend and fancy. He is not even unique in his concern for the security of his stockholders. Any corporation executive who does not have the same concern soon will have no stockholders. Men and women invest their money, often their very savings, in corporations in which they believe and which have demonstrated a regular earning capacity. People do not invest in Hilton Hotels Corporation because he wears Amon Carter's sleek Stetson or dances a slick version of the Varsoviana or owns a house with a swimming pool or calls Mary Martin by her first name. All of the business and character attributes detailed here must exist else the corporation would not exist.

Most of the evidence in Hilton's life tends toward the average. Its only departure from the average is in the field of hotel operation. That is so obvious as to make the comment unnecessary. There he was smart beyond the norm.

One of the most tattered words in the American business lexicon is "vision." Some fairly short-sighted men have been described as having "vision," as the debacle of 1929 so shatteringly proved. Men of vision, celebrated for their so-called ability to see far into a rosy and economically storm-proof future, wound up peddling apples on street corners and wondering which side of the head was best for shooting purposes. Some men have it and it is a talent bred up of several dozen attributes in which acute mysticism can be dispensed with as nice to have but not exactly the tool for the purpose.

When he sat down and came upon the twin visions of overseas operations as both good business and a tangible help to American prestige abroad, a concept which soon after took in his conviction that in projecting American hotel methods in foreign countries he was contributing to world peace, he ran into trouble. There is no other way of putting it: he ran into trouble where he least expected it—right at home with his own board of directors.

The board, to make it plain, thought he was crazy, and some individuals on the board said so.

They fought him tooth and nail and he fought back with the same weapons.

"I hate to use those old, tired clichés," a Hilton executive said recently, "but he had vision which few of us shared, and he had courage. I'd call it guts. No man is the whole boss. When he has a corporation he is a divided boss, sliced up into pieces called directors. The directors can yell the loudest 'NO' you ever heard. They yelled it at Hilton. They made it eloquently clear that they thought he was nuts. And every time they rebuffed him, he sailed in and fought twice as hard. I say he had the vision to see the overseas operations and he had the guts to battle for them right on his home grounds. It doesn't matter much what any one says about Hilton, but I'll club the guy who doesn't give him vision and courage."

In time they came around to accepting the Caribe Hilton as partial proof that Hilton hadn't taken leave of his senses. They couldn't very well overlook the rivers of money which poured from it. He thought he had the boys tied down and eating from his hand until, at a board meeting, he revealed the opportunities offered by the Castellana Hilton in Madrid.

"Oh, no you don't!" they shouted all over again. And again he had to wade in and fight for it and argue for it. They gave in at last but weren't entirely mollified, or even in possession of complete understanding of it, until at the inauguration three of them heard Ambassador Dunn say to Hilton:

"How much personal money have you got in this to date?"

"My company's money in it is about $100,000, call it $100,000 even," said Hilton with his usual and dismaying candor.

"Brother, here we go again," muttered one of his executives.

"That's not a drop in the bucket to what we, the government, are going to spend here," said Dunn. "But I have a funny feeling that in personal application to the Spanish people and their regard for America your drop is going to mean more than our bucket."

That did it, with the foreign program for Hilton as already described running into no new major outcries from his directors.

Hilton Hotels International was organized in 1948 and there were transferred to it the Caribe lease, the investment in Bermuda and certain cash. Since then the problem of whether or not to go into a foreign deal has been the problem of the Board of Directors of Hilton Hotels International. This board now consists of the following persons: David G. Baird, Joseph P. Binns, Dean Carpenter, Henry Crown, Robert Dowling, Clifford Folger, Conrad N. Hilton, John Houser, Frank G. Wangeman and Sam D. Young. It has been necessary for Hilton Hotels International to obtain funds from time to time. Hilton Hotels Corporation agreed to make available to it up to $500,000 for five different projects. So far, this money has not been called for.

It takes some months for a book to reach publication. Athens has been mentioned as a possibility in previous pages, but it is now nearer to being a settled fact. Rome is a fact to this extent: that if the group which first arranged a contract with Hilton cannot proceed with him, a second group is waiting to take over from them. He has defined negotiations in Jakarta, Indonesia, and New Delhi, India. Never before made known until this moment are advanced negotiations for a hotel in Manila and one in Tokyo. Settled facts are three hotels for Canada, one each in Toronto, Montreal and Vancouver. He would like a second hotel in Mexico City and has looked at suitable land.

One city for which he himself had no enthusiasm was Paris, never revealed until now. But a plan for Paris has been put before him by Hilton International executives and he is beginning to like it. It involves buying and tearing down a certain old hotel for the land that it is on.

"Nothing doing!" he said bluntly when they first mentioned this hotel. "Why, I remember it when I was in Paris in World War I and it was a doddering antique then!"

"But we don't want the house," they argued. "We want the land."

"I'm still not happy," Hilton owned. "That town's full of hotels it can't fill."

"Because," they retorted, "they aren't proper hotels."

"Go on talking," Hilton conceded.

When they finished he relented to the extent of giving them permission further to explore the Paris opportunity. But he is not inflamed with it as he is with Mexico City, Havana, London, Cairo, Istanbul, Athens, Madrid, San Juan, Acapulco, New Delhi, Tokyo, Madrid and two other locations which, because of the delicacy of the negotiations, cannot be revealed.

His board did not jump with enthusiasm when he told the members that in the Havana operation the $10,000,000 kitty was being put up by the culinary workers' union.

"Did it ever occur to you," said Hilton, firming his jaw, "that both management and labor might benefit sometimes by sitting down in a joint venture? It is not exactly a concept like bombing Mount Vernon, you know. A lot of good could come of management and labor working together and the time will come when it will. It's happening more and more. Well?"

They gave in.

He entered into the Cairo project at a time when the newspapers of Egypt were boiling with anti-American feeling.

"It turned out to be a sort of mass operation," said Hilton, "but not an individual one. They were perfectly willing to deal with any one American businessman on an above-board business-like deal. It's what we find in a lot of places. There is supposed to be a tidal wave of hate America in this place and that and the funny thing is when we sit down to talk there isn't any. They want a deal that means good for them and the national economy. We want a deal that is good for us, for their economy and, we hope, peace and better feeling all around. I think fifty honest American businessmen could swing a lot of peace feeling if they'd get off their duffs and go do it. They might make a buck in the process."

The cause of peace is a strong conviction with Hilton. The cynical may take the point of view that he is working for peace to protect his foreign investments. He does want protection for his investments, since he is not a fool. Others may say that his anxieties for two elder sons once in service and for his youngest now in service motivate him. He was, and is, anxious about sons in service.

But his hunger for world peace and his willingness to work for it are genuine.

And, as for fearing for his investments, the Istanbul Hilton lies exactly 10.3 miles from the Iron Curtain. If his fear was that acute he would not have built so close to that barrier.

In November, 1953, as principal speaker at a dinner of the National Conference of Christians and Jews, he said:

"Peace is neither new nor old. It is the contemporary of every age. It is as old as man. It is constant in the aspiration of man. . . . Isaias spoke of it when he called peace the work of justice. Aristotle insisted that normal human activity as well as the violence of war aim at one thing only . . . peace. I should like to discuss with you a diagnosis of the world situation which has been taking shape in my mind for some time. With your indulgence I will pose the problem as I see it and offer to you, quite humbly, part of a solution as one American businessman sees it.

"Certainly we are in trouble. We as Americans and the whole world are in trouble because we are up against the greatest evil in human history. Sometimes it seems that we

214

are confronted by evil itself, evil personified by the strange, godless men in Moscow. But the situation is not as hopeless as the papers and the commentators would have us believe. In fact, I think what the nation needs most at the moment is the virtue of hope. But what are the foundations of our hope? What is our response to this evil crawling over the world? I can see two attitudes here in America. One is to meet Communist materialism with our own materialism. Match her bomb for bomb, plane for plane, propaganda for propaganda. Beat their own standard of living with our own standard of living. I am all for that. I think the Lord has given us fists to defend ourselves and we have the right, even the obligation, to use them. I think our security lies in bases everywhere, a vast crescent of them, sweeping from the Mediterranean to the Black Sea, so widely dispersed elsewhere across the Western world that even if one section is annihilated there is immediate reprisal from another and no victory for the attacker. A great many of our people think this is enough. They might put a spiritual frosting on this totally materialistic cake, introduce or conclude their speeches and conversations with token notes of the spiritual . . . but their real faith is in that H-bomb.

"This is an attitude . . . which is very steadily being outmoded. Why? One reason is because it has not worked. Because holding this attitude, repudiating the spiritual and putting all our trust and hope in material might, and attempting to live by it, we have jeopardized and are continuing to jeopardize our American heritage which is at center spiritual. . . . I do a great deal of traveling about the country and about the world. More and more frequently, in the last few years, I find the materialist solution under suspicion, even totally repudiated by men and women at every level of society, some of absolutely no religion. But even these realize that insofar as Communism is a false doctrine it must be challenged and destroyed by religious men and women. Democracy by itself is not enough. Do not misunderstand me. I do not disparage

215

democracy. To me it is the highest and purest form of human government. But it is not an absolute. It is not the ultimate concept. More than a century ago a shrewd observer of the American scene wrote in his new classic *Democracy in America,* that religion is much more necessary in a republic than in a monarchy. 'What can be done with a people who are their own masters,' he asks, 'if they are not submissive to the Deity?' I say as a fairly competent American businessman that this is nothing more nor less than common sense.

". . . Destiny is knocking on our door as she has never done before. History is offering us the greatest challenge that ever confronted a nation. I humbly and sincerely believe that Almighty God has seen on our brow the mark of our national origins: the religious spirit of ancient Greece, the religious spirit of ancient Jewry, the religious spirit of Christendom. He has seen the stamp and spirit of our founding fathers and asks us the most amazing thing ever asked any nation—to conquer the world not by war, but by prayer."

His approach and the approach of his associates to negotiations in foreign countries has been a combined effort, made partly in a spirit of peace and partly in the spirit of business. Even in countries which are not essentially Christian he has found that men of government, of finance and of the people understand and respect such an approach.

"Let's look at Indonesia," he says. "They had a long, bitter fight to rid themselves of the white man's domination. The domination was long and often cruelly unjust. Resentment at last reached a point where strength was found to oust the white man and they wanted never to see him again. It was incredibly stupid of the whites to bring about such a condition. They destroyed a bastion of Asia. An important and critical bastion. When we came along, seeing a mutual opportunity, we were received with grave courtesy but back of it we could feel, unspoken, the thought: 'Oh, not all over again, not white men again!' The only way to meet it was openly.

216

Open in our desires for mutual dealing, open in our faith, open in our hopes that this commerce and intercourse between us was one tiny foot of the way back to the goal of mutual respect and interdependence. In making the white man welcome once more we strengthened that corner of the East for all of us both East and West. Some day we may again, with more of the same peaceful intention, remake the bastion. In any case, we shall have arrived at the making of one more patch of peace."

These are serious considerations with Hilton.

He has no confidence in a business arrangement abroad which does not contain the seeds of mutual benefits beyond those of business. Most strongly he felt this in Turkey where the Turks themselves joined the community of peaceful, well-intentioned nations on a double pronged ideal: they wanted to join NATO as an example to that entire area but, also, they wanted to demonstrate that Turkey was worthy of inclusion in the roster of nations committed to peace. Turkey, more than any other nation in which Hilton has interests, nudges the Iron Curtain on its European end. It is literally true that on a clear day you can stand on the roof of his hotel and see into Communist territory. Yet he and the Turks so well understood each other that negotiations were easily arrived at on a basis of mutual understanding that they were all men of peace.

John W. Houser, the man who initiates most of the deals overseas and in Latin American countries like Mexico, is constantly on the move. He may be in Havana on Monday, Rome on Thursday and Istanbul on Saturday. He knows that when stripped of nationalistic symbols, people are rather much the same anywhere. He has found misconceptions about the United States, he has found antagonisms toward the United States among peoples definitely anti-Communist, yet when he came to sitting down and negotiating with individuals in a room he found immediate willingness to listen to him, to put credence in what he had to say about the United States and the assumption that he was there for honest and peaceful reasons.

"The Turks are a direct people," he says. "They say what they have to say. Sometimes bluntly. There is no nonsense. They know quickly what kind of person you are. They don't need your words or even your deeds. They are for you if your intention is good. They know that you are there to make money for all concerned. They would think you foolish if you came for only an altruistic reason. But underneath the exchange of business talk and the discussion of terms they must sense and believe in a kind of integrity or they will refuse the most dazzling project. It is not really different anywhere. Americans aren't hated in the inflamed areas just because they are Americans, but because some of them so patently are the wrong kind of Americans."

Hilton's secretary for eleven years has been Olive Wakeman, a beautiful and hard-working woman who probably knows Hilton better than anyone in association with him.

"It's difficult for most people to believe," she says, "that all of these seeming contradictions exist in the one man. Here is a man who is enormously and sincerely devout, yet has a wonderful time playing when the day is finished. He is capable of working out the most intricate operations, yet is genuinely naive about a great many things. He is incapable of being alone for long. He simply can't stand to be alone. He thinks best under pressure and with action around him. It would seem reasonable for such a man to get away by himself when the action was over. Most men need and want periods of solitude. They drive him crazy. He is forgiving almost to a fault except to a liar. He cannot, he actually cannot condone a lie.

"Once, when things were tough for him long ago one of his associates left him for a better and more secure job. Or what seemed more secure. A few years ago he came back and said: 'I'm sorry I left you and didn't believe in you. I was wrong.

218

I haven't been happy a day since we parted.' Mr. Hilton forgave him and gave him a good job in the organization. His other associates, men who had stuck by him when literally the world was falling to pieces around all of them and had no promise of any kind in it, were aghast. They were quick to say so. They told him: 'How can you take this traitor back, a man who quit the moment things got rough?' 'What could I do?' Mr. Hilton replied. 'He said he was sorry.'

He hates laziness, he hates indecision. The decision can be against him, but so long as it is positive he will go along with it. One of his closest friends, the man who gave him a million dollars on a brief telephone call, is Henry Crown, the Chicago financier. He and Mr. Crown often differ widely and volubly on a variety of things, some of them extremely important. But it never affects their friendship. Mr. Crown is a decisive man. That's enough for him to be a Hilton friend.

"His preoccupation is fantastic. I know a man who greeted him casually one morning at the street entrance of the Conrad Hilton and the man said idly: "Hello, Connie, how do you feel?' Mr. Hilton linked arms with him, walked all the way through that enormous lobby, all the way to the other end, up two flights of stairs to a little office, put up his hat and coat and said: 'Feel? Why, I feel fine, why?'

"He likes to tell things against himself. Did he tell you that he once gave a girl in New York a toy poodle on the promise that she would name it 'Waldorf' because he had just bought it? He usually tells that one. It is exactly reverse, because I was the one who went out and got the little dog and I know. What happened was that the girl told him she would call it 'Waldorf' in celebration of the purchase and he said, no, he didn't think that was the thing to do because people would think he had asked her to do it as publicity for the hotel and himself. He tells it the way he feared people would evaluate it. Now you know the true story.

"He gets restless early in the morning and is at his desk

at 9 o'clock or earlier, although our office doesn't receive mail until 10 o'clock. He will sit there for an hour thinking, but with nothing tangible to do and look up about 9:30 and say: 'Well, we're here, anyway.' He told me once that it wasn't entirely early training and having to meet those trains in San Antonio. He said that, actually, he once slept until 9 o'clock in the morning and he overheard his father, who used to get up at 5 A.M., say to Mrs. Hilton: 'Mary, what are we going to do with that boy Conrad?' He's been getting up early ever since.

"Another thing that still amazes me is that he will be up at 7:30 in the morning, work until 6 P.M., rush through a shower and dressing for the evening, hustle to a speaking dinner engagement, make his speech, remain for the dancing afterward, perhaps go on to see some other friends even later, drop me off at my house, since I go to these dinners and take notes, and when next morning at 9 o'clock I say: 'I'm a little sleepy,' he replies: 'Why? You didn't go home any later than I did.'

"He has two major vanities: his golf and his business, or his business and his golf. I imagine business comes first. He is proud of them both."

When construction of the Beverly Hilton became a settled fact, he had already stopped using the Town House as a Los Angeles office. He built a small office building on a piece of land he owned on nearby Santa Monica Boulevard. His sons Nicky and Barron also have their offices in this building and the three often have long discussions there relating to their mutual enterprises.

Neither of these sons is in the hotel business. The third son, Eric, completed two years in the School of Hotel Administration at Cornell University and then was called into service, where he is now. When he is discharged a year or so hence, he will return to Cornell and complete the course and begin to learn the hotel business at the source in Hilton Hotels. Nicky went to hotel training school, even to the famed Swiss academy in which students do everything from the bottom up. They start cleaning dishes in the kitchens, progress to cleaning rooms, thence to the front desks, then back to the kitchens for a course in food preparation and then a period in purchasing. Nicky did the work but did not believe that hotel management was his forte. Barron never started. He enlisted in the Navy when Nicky went to it and he was under age. When the boys were discharged from the Navy, Barron went to see his father.

"I'd like to talk about my future," he said.

"Fine," said Hilton. "I hoped you would. Let's talk. Tell me what you think."

"I'm in love with a beautiful girl," said Barron. "We intend to marry. We also intend to have children. Children means a nurse. Inside of a year or less than two years after I marry, I'm going to have to have $1,000 a month to meet my domestic expenses of all kinds. I don't think the hotel business pays that kind of money.

"You are exactly right . . . it doesn't," said Hilton. "I wouldn't pay anybody $1,000 a month to learn this business and it takes longer to learn this business than it does to have a baby. Good luck to you. When you get your figuring closer to earth and you think you want to come in at the bottom and learn the whole thing I'll be here."

Barron went out and closeted himself with a friend he had met in the service. They pooled their money and started an orange juice business. They processed oranges and delivered juice from house to house like milk. They concentrated it for the trade. They froze it for the trade. They began to attract wholesale customers. Barron today earns considerably more than $1,000 a month and it is just as well. He and Mrs. Hilton have not one or two but five children and have a goal of six. They started their married life in a small house in Los Angeles, then moved to a house once owned by Hume Cronyn and his wife, Jessica Tandy, the actress. The Cronyns had children and this house could accommodate them. But when more and more small Hiltons came along, Barron needed something larger. He was prospering beyond his hopes in the juice business and was able to buy the former Norma Shearer house at Santa Monica, a dwelling so vast it could hold twenty-six children instead of six. The younger Hiltons no longer feel haunted that their personal contributions to the population will engulf them.

Nicky had made several investments, one of which was in his brother's orange juice canning and marketing business. He also bought into a ballpoint pen company and announced that he intended to sell one to every hotel room in America.

"People will take them," his father argued. "Not because people inherently steal but because ball-point pens are small and people will stick them in their pockets without thinking. Hotels couldn't afford to keep restocking them."

"They won't stick these in their pockets," said Nicky. "These are as long as the old-fashioned desk pens, shaped like them, are too long to fit in coat pockets and won't have caps on them. They can't be put in a pocket on a size basis or a capless basis. They are strictly writing-desk pens. I think guests in hotels will appreciate finding a decent, ball-point pen in the drawers of the desks in their rooms instead of those old nib jobs that are corroded and useless half the time."

He was right. People don't take the pens either absent-mindedly or deliberately. The pens are too long, would stain the pockets with ink, since they have no caps, and most guests are so pleased to find a pen that they take time out to compliment the management. Hilton's hotels and many others have put in these new pens.

"You have to let sons find their best path in life," Hilton says. "I would have liked to have them in with me, but if they have found something they like better that is their right. I am too much of an individualist myself to force my sons into my pattern. Every human being must find his own lot. The woods are full of unhappy, tense and unsuccessful men who became lawyers, doctors, grocers or bookbinders or anything else because their fathers happened to have those jobs before them. They were unsuited to follow their fathers. In my own case, it was never my intention to run a general store in San Antonio or anywhere else just because my father ran one. Nor was my reluctance the result of ineptness on my part. I was a darned good storekeeper. But I knew before I began to shave that in the end it was not going to be my lot in life."

What Hilton has not put into words is that enthusiasm is a twin to talent. Enthusiasm without talent, is a pinwheel operation, all scurry and noise and glitter without true accomplishment. Talent without enthusiasm sums up to drudgery. He would not wish either circumstance for his sons. If Barron has the talent and enthusiasm to create a profitable orange concentrates business, which apparently he has, Hilton is father enough to lay aside his own hopes for succession in the hotel business. If Nicky's talents and enthusiasms are directed into orange concentrates, pens, supplies and similar ventures, then Hilton feels it would be wrong to persuade him into the hotel business. Eric, however, has enthusiasm for his father's work and when his military service is ended will return to advanced study of it. Hilton, on this score, stands between two generations of thinking. In his own life he learned the hotel business by severe trial and often bitter error. It was the old sink or swim formula. In Eric's generation it is learned in schools of two kinds. Schools of hotel administration which teach without lacerations and scars what his father learned in lobbies, behind front desks, poring over the often discouraging books and haggling with salesmen of silver, linens, chinaware, furniture, paint, carpets and the hundred other items which go to make a hotel an operating mechanism. Also, Eric will have his time directed toward the service schools here, in Switzerland and in France in which he will learn kitchen data, linen room data, dietary truths and similar facts of hotel life. These schools exist now in this country. When the elder Hilton got into the business he scuffled his way to the top by daily experience.

One thing he learned early was that the best hotels have a function beyond that of providing rest and restaurant. Certain hotels are not only social assets to the community but social parade grounds. The Oak Room at the Plaza, Peacock Alley at the Waldorf, the Town House in its beautiful entirety, the Palmer House in its Chicago social traditions, all of these are something which Ovid once put into six pertinent words of Latin: *"Spectatum veniunt, veniunt spectentur ut ipsae."*

They come to see, mused sagacious Ovid, they come to be seen.

Peacock Alley has been a promenade since it was created in the 90's, a corridor as fashionable and essential as any walk ever consciously marched in England's great pearl of fashion, Bath. Distinguished women and men of vast and substantial value to the community and the world used it to see and be seen. Its name came from a shaft of early and faintly malicious wit. An aphorist of the period proclaimed that the corridor "seemed like an alley of peacocks." The shaft fell on empty ground. It neither pierced nor gashed. Society continued to trail lovely gowns and flashing jewels through Peacock Alley and made it America's most popular and accepted parade. As many as 35,000 persons passed through it in a day.

When Hilton bought the Waldorf one of his first thoughts was directed toward Peacock Alley. He inspected and surveyed it himself and decided that the Alley was due for a job of refurbishing. This decision, as pointed out earlier, coincided with a determination to oust politely and without incident a shoal of men and women who used the Waldorf lobby as a private roost.

In time, Hilton closed off the Alley, plugged its entrance with a small but beautiful bar, put tables and chairs in the lobby as a luncheon and dining place and sent his men to work.

He assigned James Amster, famed New York decorator, to the task of overseeing the transformation and creating the design motif, a garden vista. Amster also chose the discreet statuary and selected the guiding colors. Marcel Vertes was commissioned to paint 135 yards of wall space in these colors which Amster had the wit and the taste to select as Vertes' favorite colors: green, lavender, pale blue. Vertes was left alone. He could do anything he wished with the walls. He decided to fill them with pert and saucy and decidedly pretty ballet girls frolicking in a verdant wood. He thus not only preserved the charm but the tradition of Peacock Alley. In the opinion of decorators and hotel men the result is the most attractive hotel space to be seen in the world.

Three years ago Hilton made another change at the Waldorf. From the beginning of his ownership of the hotel, he took a liking to the Norse Grill on the Lexington Avenue end of the hotel. Its Scandinavian decor, touching perhaps his Norwegian ancestry, appealed to him. He liked the vast room, 75 feet by 45 feet, with its huge wooden beams and massive arches of stone. He also liked the west wall mural, a large and detailed painting by Aldo Lazzarini which depicts the folklore and mythology of Scandinavia. But he noticed a triangle of waste space, lying mockingly and profitless between the platform from which a guest turns left into the grill and the Lexington Avenue wall. Every time Hilton passed that empty corner he was provided with food for thought while obtaining food for sustenance.

"I don't know how many meals I devoted to thinking about that waste space," he says. "It irked me."

Finally, the problem was solved for him. A brokerage house sought Waldorf space to accommodate its Park Avenue stock and bond customers.

"We need room for a stock quotations board," they said,

225

"some comfortable chairs, a stock ticker and a manager's desk."

"We have exactly the space for you on the lobby level," said Hilton.

This was more than they expected. They remembered, perhaps timorously, that Hilton had scatted one brokerage office off the lobby floor of the Plaza to create more profitable operation. When Hilton mentioned lobby level space, which would obviate their customers having to go to the trouble of using elevators, they were more than pleased.

They looked at the space, measured it, noted with delight that it was impossible to enter or leave the Norse Grill without passing their office and signed up forthwith.

Now Hilton became fascinated by the quotation board. His hotel corporation stock was listed on the big board and he developed the habit of glancing in every time he passed the brokerage office seeking the latest quotation on his stocks.

His habit was noticed by a girl who for twenty years had checked hats and coats at the grill.

"Esther had been with the hotel since practically the beginning," says Binns, its general manager. "Her hat check location was such that she could see Mr. Hilton coming and, soon, she developed the habit of glancing at the board and getting the information for him before he arrived at the door. Daily, she would greet him with " 'It's 18 today, Mr. Hilton,' or 'It's 20 today, Mr. Hilton.' Once or twice, as is the nature of stocks, she had to tell him that it was lower that day. But whenever it was at 18 or better, she met him with a smiling face.

"Mr. Hilton commonly is reputed to be a man with so much on his mind that he cannot notice small things," continued Binns. "I think Esther's story proves the repute to be wrong. He used to come back from lunch and say: 'Amazing girl checking hats in the grill. She notices everything.' Last Christmas he came to me and handed me an envelope addressed to

Esther. 'A little Christmas present for her,' he said. 'See that she gets it right at Christmas. It's my thanks for a consistent job of going out of her way to be helpful to me. I appreciate it.' The envelope contained a note of thanks from Mr. Hilton and ten shares of Hilton Hotels Corporation stock in her name. I never saw any one so overwhelmed in my life. But, when you analyze it, the really overwhelmed person was Mr. Hilton. A person in his employ had daily performed a little, personal service and he could neither overlook it nor leave it unrewarded. I think also he got a personal pleasure out of feeling that now both of them had a reason to look at the board."

Mrs. Olive Wakeman, his secretary, has many such anecdotes to tell about Hilton's ability to notice small things while seemingly preoccupied with larger questions. He can walk the length of a city with an associate and never say a word. Most often he does. He once walked from the Waldorf at 50th Street and Park Avenue to the Empire State Building at 34th Street and Fifth Avenue without uttering a sound. The two men walking with him wondered what was on his mind but did not break into his reverie.

When the three reached the titanic building, Hilton stopped and let his eyes rise slowly from street level to as high as he could see. Then he walked back up Fifth Avenue a block or two and studied the building all the way to the top. Abruptly he turned and walked briskly back to the Waldorf, entering it on the Park Avenue side, went up the stairs to the lobby, through the lobby to the Norse Grill, sat down, ordered lunch, took a drink of water and spoke for the first time in more than an hour.

"It's all right," he said.

"You . . . you aren't going to buy it?" one associate asked as though fearing the answer.

"Friend of mine mentioned an interest in it," said Hilton. "Owed it to him to at least look at it."

As he passes through the Waldorf lobby, he often stops

and looks at the pieces winking and glittering in the crystal vitrines adorning the columns and walls, exhibiting the wares of the jewelers who rent space in the hotel. He also looks at the vitrines exhibiting perfumes, furs and other luxuries. He looks at the sand urns beside each elevator door, placed there for gentlemen to discard cigarettes before entering the elevators. The vitrines bemuse him but the sand urns are business. He has never mentioned the contents of the vitrines one way or another. But if more than three cigarette stubs lie dead in a sand urn, he will start pushing buttons and asking why. He wants them policed regularly, often and carefully. And with determination.

As of a sunny, clear and winter afternoon in New York in early 1954 this is the story, complete and in detail, of Conrad Nicholson Hilton, American. By spring some of it may change. He may buy or sell a hotel, he may announce the fact of a new hotel project abroad.

It is the story of a man who has been both buffeted and blessed by fate. It is the story of a man with strong religious convictions arrived at in boyhood. Of powerful ambitions in many ways arrived at and realized. Of a man with strong virtues and some weaknesses, which is the lot of most of human kind. No man exists but who has fallible points and vulnerable avenues of approach. Most men are fortunate. They balance their mortal weaknesses with sometimes almost divine nobilities. They combine much good with some less admirable qualities. It is the good which makes an impression on a man's times and his fellow men for most of us. Few men have passed through as much tormenting ill luck as Hilton and, by equally fair estimation, few men ever arrive at such success.

He is not alone in any of this. Many men have conquered adversity, many men are weak, many are strong. Many men worship God with personal joy and devotion. Hilton has tried, as much as any layman can, to pass his religious convictions on in the hope that other men will turn to prayer and derive from it the divine help that has been his. He likes the company of men and women, has a profound dislike for being alone. Yet, in the midst of large, merry gatherings, he is often lonely. It has never been easy for him to lose himself in social gatherings. He is not a man of easy humors and immediate wit. Perhaps he has had to work too hard too long ever to become a man totally relaxed and at ease.

But in the final summation of all the faults and all the virtues he emerges as a man who militantly protected his honor and credit when it would have been easy and legal not to do so. He was beaten to the floor and got up from it and started fighting anew. He has never, so far as any friend or foe can detect, wilfully harmed any man or woman.

He is candid to a fault. He is exacting in the operation of his business. He cannot understand people who shun religion or do not passionately love the United States and believe in its destiny. He has never at any time in any place in the wide world found any faith as consoling to him as his own, yet is firm in his belief that all faiths bring strength and divinity to those who seriously and sincerely follow them. He has found no political concept as precious to him as that of the United States. He has found no way of life comparable to what life in the United States means to him.

And, in spite of all guidance leading toward the learning of forgiveness, he cannot learn to forgive a liar. It is, to him, the consummate sin.

If he is no great and easy hand at wit, some of his associates are. They are loyal to him, devoted to him, most of them stuck by him hard and fast when only ruin and disaster were apparent as their reward for this loyalty. They have been richly rewarded since. But they still can find time for a harmless joke.

When the United States created the air base at Thule, not far from the North Pole, they joked among themselves say-

229

ing: "Which one of us will be assigned to open and manage the North Pole Hilton?"

It could be no joke at all. We are learning how to live under Arctic conditions and the vista is beautiful. Also, definable travel to the Pole is growing.

Maybe, one day, it will need a hotel.